WOVEN BEAUTY

Bernhard Gardi (Ed.)

WOVEN BEAUTY
THE ART OF WEST AFRICAN TEXTILES

With articles by Kerstin Bauer, Duncan Clarke,
Bernhard Gardi, Malika Kraamer, John Picton,
and shorter contributions by Rogier M. A. Bedaux,
Jean Borgatti, Kolado Cissé and Annette Schmidt

Museum der Kulturen Basel
Christoph Merian Verlag

1 – A Fulani woman spinning cotton (Niafounké, Mali)

Photo B. Gardi 2.11.1974 – (F)III 9532

FOREWORD

"...the cloth must flow well to wear it, it cannot be stiff ... they want it to feel smooth and soft ... good cloth moves with the person, it catches the sunlight ... it makes people feel proud of our past. They remember their forefathers, their ancestors, where they came from." These words by a Ghanaian weaver, quoted in John Picton's contribution (p. 17), address some of the important issues in the field of textiles; not the production mode as such but the way the finished product captures the eye is what really occupies the weaver. Textiles not only fulfil pragmatic clothing functions, they also evoke associations with deep-felt sentiments and create significant links to key social contexts.

The exhibition *Woven Beauty – The Art of West African Textiles* shown at the Museum der Kulturen Basel and the accompanying publication offer insights into a selection of the museum's textile collection which was assembled to a large part during an extensive research and collecting expedition through various West African countries – from Nigeria to Senegal – by the former curator Renée Boser-Sarivaxévanis and her assistant at the time and present curator of the Africa Department, Bernhard Gardi. Reviewing, publishing and now exhibiting some of the collection highlights stands in a long tradition of research and documentation at the museum and has helped to create the renown of the Basel textile collection. At the same time the show provides an opportunity to approach and inspect the rich collection from a new perspective and with new questions in mind, for example, with regard to the specific skills required by weavers and dyers, to the aesthetics of the designs and the meaning systems embedded in the textiles. Applying a time frame that reaches from present global economic enmeshment to the days when the term globalization was not yet the buzzword, issues dealt with range from developments in the field of textiles generated by the blending of traditional cultural knowledge and practices with innovatory forces and strategies, to the adaptation and incorporation of traditional elements in the modern world of fashion and design.

As in every exhibition project many people were involved in the realization of the show *Woven Beauty – The Art of West African Textiles*. Deep gratitude goes to the curator of the exhibition, Bernhard Gardi, for whom the present show is not only an account of the research expedition back in the 1970s but also his parting gift to the museum and the general audience before he retires from his post as curator of the Africa Department. With calm, a keen eye for the important matters and great dedication he brought the project to fruition.

Over the years Bernhard Gardi received support in his research from a large number of people and institutions, namely Dr. Hartmann P. Koechlin, former Honorary Consul of the Republic of Mali in Basel; the Karl Mayer-Stiftung; Dr. Harald Widmer, Bern; the Freiwillige Akademische Gesellschaft (FAG); and Claude N. Passavant, Basel. The Werenfels-Fonds helped to fund the original research expedition from 1973–1975, and following from this, the present members of the commission of the Werenfels-Fonds were kind enough to generously support the present project. For their commitment I would like to express my profound gratitude. Their contribution not only laid the foundation for the exhibition project but also enabled the publication of the exhibition catalogue in German and English.

Anna Schmid
Director Museum der Kulturen Basel

INTRODUCTION
Bernhard Gardi

The present book is the accompanying publication to the exhibition of the same title. The volume also renders account of the research expedition undertaken by Dr. Renée Boser-Sarivaxévanis (1921–2004) for the Museum der Kulturen Basel from October 1973 to February 1975. The 16-month journey began in Lagos and ended in Dakar. For 14 months I, as a young man, was her companion and assistant. This gives the book also a personal, biographic touch. The aim of the venture was to
  – establish an inventory of the local textile industry
  – provide a comparative terminology of weaving and indigo-dyeing
  – assemble a systematic collection of textiles

The project was funded by the Swiss National Science Foundation, the Canton Basel-Stadt and the Werenfels Foundation. [1] The epic journey is described in detail in a separate chapter. Boser-Sarivaxévanis only wrote a provisional report on the expedition (Boser 1975). Unfortunately her deteriorating health prevented her from ever publishing a comprehensive study. [2]

The volume focuses on weaving. It deals neither with the great traditions of indigo resist-dyeing – with the exception of 'ikat' since this technique is encountered in conjunction with other weaving techniques – nor with the various decorative techniques such as embroidery or appliqué. We rely completely on pieces from our own museum holdings, with emphasis on the collection assembled between 1973 and 1975. It comprises masterpieces as well as simple, everyday cloths found at local markets everywhere. Due to the scope and quality of documentation, the Basel collection could be described as *the* benchmark collection.

The textile collection at the Museum der Kulturen Basel is legendary, just as are its research and publications on the subject. The Basel tradition of collecting, documenting and researching textile techniques in their cultural-historical context goes back to the textile manufacturer and collector Fritz Iklé-Huber (1877–1946) who compiled a collection according to technical criteria. In 1935 he donated his collection to the Basel museum, thus creating new research and exhibition perspectives for the house. [3] On the basis of Iklé's spadework, Kristin Oppenheim wrote a PhD thesis which she submitted to the University of Basel and which today is regarded as the first systematic study of basic textile techniques. Her husband Alfred Bühler, curator at the museum from 1938 on, recognized the potential that lay in collecting and analyzing textiles, and in 1948 they together published a more comprehensive systematic study of textile techniques. [4] Later, when Bühler became director of the museum and professor of anthropology at the university, he systematically developed the textile collection and encouraged his pupils to work on the subject. [5] In 1972, Boser-Sarivaxévanis published her PhD thesis on West African textiles under Bühler. Actually, it was the first dissertation on this subject ever. It was based on the study of museum collections. [6]

While Boser-Sarivaxévanis was doing her research – in the latter half of the 1960s – Brigitte Menzel was working on a three-volume catalogue of the Berlin collection, which was published in 1972 and 1973. As against Boser-Sarivaxévanis' book, Menzel's work was based on fieldwork in Africa, with a focus on accurate descriptions and ascriptions. [7] Boser-Sarivaxévanis, on the other hand, was busy developing diffusionist hypotheses in an attempt to explain how weaving came to Africa. This aspect will be dealt with in the chapter

2 — Very finely spun cotton yarn. To be
used for the warp. Weft yarn is usually thicker
(Katsina, Nigeria), 29 cm

Collected by Boser/Gardi 1974 – III 21003

3 — Spun woollen yarn on a spindle
(Niafounké, Mali), 27 cm

Collected by Boser/Gardi 1974 – III 21017

4 — Cluster of wild silkworm cocoons
(Bankass, Mali), 19 cm

Collected by B.Gardi 1979 – III 22038

5 — Wild silk, not yet spun, magenta-coloured
(Zaria, Nigeria), 14 cm

Collected by Boser/Gardi 1974 – III 21690

on the history of looms. The two scholars, who highly appreciated each other's work, were the first to publish substantial studies on the textile culture of West Africa, providing convincing evidence that weaving and indigo-dyeing were highly developed technologies in the local civilizations. From 1975 on, Venice Lamb published a number of books containing numerous field photographs.

What is our interest in West African textiles today? How should we speak and write about them? On which aspects should the focus be? Should we concentrate on the symbolism of the patterns which so fascinate viewers in Europe and the United States? Should we foreground aesthetics, or production methods? Or should we concentrate on innovations and adaptations to modern life styles? Does the dynamic of change in recent decades hold interest for us? And what have African weavers and dyers to say to their own creations? The body of literature on these and similar issues keeps growing, and the days when Clouzot (1930) was able to write in the introduction to his book the strange sentence "Les tissues nègres ont fait une entrée tardive dans la curiosité," are definitely over.

Textiles reflect everyday life and address all spheres of existence. This is what makes work on textiles so fascinating. How many metres of yarn was a woman able to spin in one day? How many cloths per year could she order from a weaver? How many metres can a weaver produce in a day? As world economic history goes to show these are not trivial issues: after all, the industrial revolution had its roots in the field of spinning and weaving in the 18th century, and at the beginning of the 20th century whole villages in the Sahel still were obliged to supply their masters with yarn and cloths (Meillassoux 1973). The issue of pattern symbolism, omnipresent and often so overruling in Europe, does not really seem to interest the weavers as much as one might believe. Their focus is more on the weaving techniques as such. Many of the patterns – triangles, diamonds, squares – are the result of basic weaving techniques and can be combined in almost endless variations. The names of patterns are usually descriptive and prosaic. Olivier de Sardan (1978: 406) even goes as far as to say that one often gets the impression that the richer and more complex the patterns become, the less the people know about them.

Nevertheless, different aesthetic canons did develop in the various regions of West Africa. One is able recognize where a specific cloth is from just by looking at it, and, similar to works of art, clear-cut styles are distinguishable, just as there have always been craftsmen who ranked as master weavers, both men and women.

To this date more than ten PhD studies have been published on the subject of African textiles, next to numerous 'coffee-table books' and uncountable research articles. The strength of the present publication lies in the fact that all the authors have themselves conducted field research. They all feel committed to passing on their findings, delivering well-grounded facts, disclosing interrelationships, explaining matters of interest and telling stories – stories that, in the end, should lead to a better understanding of significant issues – and textiles are significant issues! – in West Africa's cultural history.

The volume focuses on four countries, each one significant in its own way for the understanding of West African textile art. The four countries are dealt with in separate chapters, with each author focusing on a specific dual aspect in his or her contribution: for Nigeria, Duncan Clarke compares women's weaving with men's weaving; for Ghana (and neighbouring Togo), Malika Kraamer discusses the kente cloth tradition as practiced by both

Ewe and Asante; Kerstin Bauer investigates the interrelationship between Baule and Dyula weaving practices in Côte d'Ivoire; I myself highlight the relationship between wool and cotton weaving traditions in Mali.

John Picton, co-author of the standard work *African Textiles* published by the British Museum (1979, 1989) follows up the question why African textiles hold such fascination for people in Europe and the United States. It is a subject that he has broached in earlier works before, at the same time addressing the exciting perspectives that textiles hold in store for art historians. He also describes the different usages and practices of textiles.

In a way his contribution brings matters round full circle, at least for me, because before Renée Boser-Sarivaxévanis and I set out for West Africa we visited the British Museum to see Charles Beving's beautiful textile collection held there. At the time, John Picton was a curator at the museum; he opened the gates to his world for us.

Two contributions were written by former students of John Picton – Duncan Clarke and Malika Kraamer. Kerstin Bauer who recently (2007) published her research on the history and transformation of clothes and clothing practices in Côte d'Ivoire is familiar with the Basel collection. At present she is a lecturer at the University of Basel. Jean Borgatti I got to know on the university campus in Ibadan in 1974. Recently she has renewed her old contacts in Nigeria. I met Rogier Bedaux for the first time in 1971 in Mopti. Boser-Sarivaxévanis was a friend of his for many years and stood in close contact with him especially with regard to the archaeological Tellem textile finds. I myself spent close on 20 months in Mali, mainly in Mopti, between 1978 and 1982, during which I became friends with Kolado Cissé, an embroiderer and now textile merchant in Bamako, whom I often quote.

Textiles are, and always have been, constructions that not only rely on the necessary technical equipment but also demand special knowledge and abilities – and taste! These forms of knowledge and ability, which include growing cotton, rearing sheep, spinning or mastering the chemical processes for making dyes are embedded in the economic and cultural fabric of a society in manifold ways. It is this interlocking of diverse factors beyond the mere analysis of technical issues that makes the study of textiles so rewarding. Is it not fascinating, for example, that the Bwa (Mali) as well as the neighbouring Bobo (Burkina Faso) only began weaving in the course of the 1930s under the influence of the missions and because they believed that 'nakedness' was preventing the spread of the word of God, while, at the same time, neighbouring groups such as the Fulani of the Inland Niger Delta or the Dyula of Burkina Faso and northern Côte d'Ivoire ranked among West Africa's great master weavers? The Bwa and Bobo were well aware of the fact that their Muslim neighbours wore clothes, but they – like many other West African peoples – preferred to dress and adorn themselves differently.

And what does the fact tell us that the Dowayo and Koma of northern Cameroon practiced weaving but did not use textiles for clothing, but for funerary purposes and as bride valuables instead?

The two examples underline how important historical conditions and the cultural environment are in trying to better understand the sphere of textiles in West Africa. Not all of the hundreds of cultural, or ethnic, groups in West Africa were acquainted with weaving, and not all the groups that practiced weaving actually produced patterned cloths. Roughly 150 years ago, the great majority of woven cloths were either white, or blue and white striped, others were indigo-blue throughout, or dyed brown or yellow. Weft float patterns were not common and only found in a few restricted areas, but through the import of European yarn, they experienced a tremendous innovatory boost.

It is also important to specify which part of West Africa we are speaking of: the Niger delta area, for example, looks back on a five hundred year-old history of trade with Europe. In the middle of the 19th century steamships were regularly being loaded there with palm oil kernels while, during the same period, there were only very few Europeans living in Mali. Consequently, all along the Guinea coast contact with Europeans resulted in a stream of innovations.

The process from raw material to finished cloth is complex and long. Handling thousands of metres of yarn without it becoming entangled is a task that has to be learnt. In the present volume the technical details and the various steps in the production process are not dealt with in detail.

When speaking of Africa one often tends to think in terms of ethnic groups or tribes. Occasionally this makes sense, for example, when trying to explain to someone which people one is talking about. But even back in the 1970s, urban settings very often did not conform to clear ethnic categories. In the rural setting one used to come – and still comes – across textiles that could only be produced in 'inter-ethnic' cooperation, for example, where one group produced the indigo dyes and the other was responsible for the weaving. Occasionally we find a similar division of labour by social stratification, for example, when the members of one social class do the weaving while the other group does the sewing and embroidery work.

With regard to technology, West African textile craftsmanship may appear simple and easy to grasp, but in aesthetic terms the products are magnificent and can occasionally, through a leaning towards a minimalist style, even look highly modern. At the same time, textiles are intertwined with the social and economic fabric in highly elaborated and complex ways. It is these interrelationships that the present volume attempts to unravel, with each author providing fascinating stories about the forms of this enmeshment.

West Africa with its 16 constituent countries in no way forms a uniform cultural, linguistic or economic entity. In the context of textile technology we find the following social divisions of labour:

- Spinning yarn is women's work. The only exception is the mountain region of northern Cameroon where this task is performed by men.
- Men use the double-heddle loom for weaving (other terms used include shaft or treadle loom).
- In Nigeria and neighbouring Benin and Togo women use a vertical loom that functions on a different principle than the men's double-heddle loom.
- In all parts of West Africa men are responsible for the sewing and embroidery work.
- Indigo-dyeing is practiced by men in northern Nigeria, Burkina Faso and Côte d'Ivoire; in southern Nigeria and the western regions of West Africa the dyeing is done by women.

This division of labour is no longer strictly upheld. Today, economic concerns override old traditions. Spelling and pronunciation of African terms follow conventional usage. The letter 'c' is pronounced 'ch' as in 'church'.

6 — Handling thousands of metres of yarn has to be learnt:
preparing the warp (Ilorin, Nigeria)

Photo B. Gardi 20.3.1974 – (F)III 7970

7 – ROLL OF CLOTH, SIDE-VIEW. MALI.
Two rolled strips of cloth, 225 m long, 12 cm wide, weight 11 kg. The cotton is hand-spun, the cloth hand-woven. A hundred years ago, rolls of cloth like this still served as currency, suitable for buying horses, millet, salt or gold. Cloth was money. Purchased on the market 'Medina Kura' in Bamako

Collected by B. Gardi 2002 – III 27549

The following story shows how extensive weaving still was in the middle of the 20th century:

On 29 January 1945 the Governor General in Dakar ordered from the Governor in Bamako (Mali) two million metres of cloth strips, in other words, a length of two thousand kilometres! The project was regarded as the contribution of the West African farmers to the general war effort. The produce was to be distributed according to the following key: 750,000 metres for the civilian population in Senegal in general, the same amount for the population in and around Dakar and 500,000 metres for the troops. The entrepreneur Maurice Khalifat accepted the assignment, purchased 40,000 tons of ginned cotton and then put the people to work spinning, spooling, weaving, and rolling up the finished strips. Four months later he was able to deliver the first 500,000 metres.

I cannot imagine how Maurice Khalifat organized the production, considering that, first of all, the women had to spin an incredibly large amount of yarn; then the spun yarn had to be transferred to spindles, and, in a next step, transferred to the smaller spools in the shuttles. A Gargantuan manufacturing machinery had to be set in motion (Archives Nationales du Mali à Kolouba. 1 Q 241).

Rolls of cloth in the shape of Swiss cheese in bulk-form are still found at markets in the towns and villages of the Sahel today, but they are becoming increasingly rare. Most of these cloth rolls are produced in the Dogon area in Mali or in the Yatenga region around Ouahigouya in Burkina Faso.

Incidentally, a roll of cloth measures approximately two hundred metres; this means Maurice Khalifat had placed an order for something like ten thousand rolls.

TWO MILLION METRES OF CLOTH

Bernhard Gardi

Cloth was money. Next to cowries, cloth served as a currency in nearly all parts of West Africa. Folded by the cubit or in the form of rolls of cloth, weave strips could be easily transported over long distances. Fabrics usually came as white, undecorated strips which were then cut to length and sewn together. Many ruling Soninke families in Goumbou (Mali) became rich in the 18th and 19th centuries because their slaves 'produced' money, in other words, they were made to weave cloth (Meillassoux 1971, 1973). The economic history of the Sahel and the West African savannah is closely linked to weaving. In hundreds if not thousands of villages between the southern fringe of the Sahara and the tropical region to the south men were engaged in weaving during the dry season to supplement their income.

BOTTOM TELLS THE STORY OF CLOTH

John Picton

Ừm'ọ́kụ́kụ́ ụ̀m'ọ́bọ̀bà; ìrùvo pịt'ácị̀
Olden time, present time: bottom tells the story of cloth

This essay begins in three places. The first is the many experiences of working with textiles in West Africa, and the people who make, sell and use textiles, from the first time I entered Jankara market soon after I arrived in Lagos in 1961. The continuing profusion of technologies, colours, textures and forms is both well known and well published (Barbican Art Gallery 1995; Gardi, 2000; Picton & Mack 1989; Picton 2004b, 2008; Ross 1998). The second subsists in my experience of working with Ebira people in the Niger-Benue confluence region of Nigeria during the late 1960s. My specific interests were in the institutions and implications of masquerade. In its context performance entailed, among many other things, a reiteration of proverbial wisdom, an example of which is given above. This points towards the recognition that textiles provide a context of ideas about things other than themselves, as in that proverb, where 'cloth' stands as a metaphor for tradition, still a central aspect of West African social practice and process. The third point of departure for this essay is a pair of exhibitions in New York that I saw in November 2008: *The Essential Art of African Textiles: Design Without End*, curated by Alisa LaGamma and Christine Giuntini at the Metropolitan Museum of Art, and *The Poetics of Cloth: African Textiles/Recent Art*, curated by Lynn Gumpert at the Grey Art Gallery of New York University. They nurtured my continuing reflection upon the relationships between past and present, between novelty and the inheritance of tradition. These exhibitions remind us of the simple fact that textiles are not simply a set of art practices contemporary with our own times. They also provide subject matter for artists working in other media, and they give definition to local West African modernities more overtly than any other form of visual practice; this might seem, to some perhaps, an extravagant claim. The work of this essay, therefore, is to summarize its justification.

Most people in Europe have little or no experience of making or designing textiles, and although we all wear cloth in one form or another we remain ignorant of the processes of design and manufacture. We buy most of our clothes ready made, and the provision of counterpanes, carpets and curtains is usually achieved via the retail outlets particular to each form. In West Africa it is not quite like this. Although much of the cloth on sale in the market is factory made, hand-woven and hand-dyed cloths remain commonplace, sometimes available in local markets, and sometimes directly from the makers. Most people will know where to go to find textiles, weavers and dyers; and the cloth they acquire is a more-or-less direct response to local demand amongst people such as themselves, rather than something cooked up by a remote fashion industry catering for an elite or celebrity clientele. The demand in northern Nigeria, or in the Asante nation of central Ghana, for woollen blankets woven in the Niger Inland Delta region of Mali might seem to stretch this paradigm close to its breaking point; yet weaving, and dyeing, in all three areas is or was commonplace. Even when cloth is traded over several hundred miles it is traded among people for whom weaving or dyeing are easy-to-witness occupations, and the textures, colours and forms particular to a given region or place, do not subvert the desirability of things from further away.

Perhaps the most striking thing about a textile woven in West Africa is the narrow-strip format[8] which means that it is only when a sufficient length has been woven, and it is cut into pieces and sewn together edge-to-edge, that the visual effects intended by the weaver can be seen. It will have been realized by means of an arithmetic in the necessarily precise counting of warps and wefts, and a geometry in the layout of pattern. Weavers must keep in mind a corpus of imagery and mathematical formulae on the basis of which they can reproduce the textiles in popular demand, as well as figure out how to develop a given tradition. And, in keeping ahead of their customers' interests, they ensure the continued florescence of that tradition.

Yet, in spite of the attention given to pattern in its making, once a cloth is wrapped or draped around the body, the full effects of its design are necessarily obscured, perhaps even denied; for the cloth as it emerges from its maker is not the end of the process: it is not where the art ceases!

Employed as backdrops, spatial dividers, or voluminous garments that are draped, layered, or wrapped around the body, textiles are not rigidly two-dimensional but rather shaped by light and shadow, movement, wind and the human form (La Gamma 2008: 10). This quotation echoes another, which I have used before (cited in Geurts 2002: 151–152), from a discussion with a Ghanaian weaver: "... the cloth must flow well to wear it, it cannot be stiff ... they want it to feel smooth and soft ... good cloth moves with the person, it catches the sunlight ... it makes people feel proud of our past. They remember their forefathers, their ancestors, where they came from. It's not really easy to wear this cloth ... you have to stand upright, you have to assume a dignity to keep it from falling off ... this cloth makes you feel that you belong to Anlo. It's very different than wearing a suit and tie ... A suit is tight and makes you feel stiff. But this cloth, well, it flows around me as I walk."

Clearly pattern does matter, for the repertoires of weavers, dyers and factory-based designers continue to evolve within particular traditions of textile and dress design, distinctively from one centre to another, especially with the use of new fibres, textures and colours. Moreover, that distinctiveness does not rely upon isolation but, perhaps paradoxically, upon a West African distribution of particular forms, whether of cloth, pattern or garment, that is complex in the interrelationships of its regions and centres. There are many histories in which the traditions of a given locality have become engaged with forms and fabrics introduced from elsewhere, whether from within West Africa or from North Africa, especially since the advent of Islam, or from Europe or India since the late 15th century as a result of the direct mercantile engagements opened up by the Portuguese and then taken up by other nations. These engagements have proved fundamental to the formation of a succession of local modernities, [9] each taken for granted within its own place and time.

This discussion leads us to the possibilities of a West African aesthetic revealed in textiles, an aesthetic comprised of at least three elements. The first is all about the evident delight in breaking up an otherwise plain surface. This is not just about clearly articulated motifs: it is also about the contrast between plain and variegated ground colouration. Of course, there are cloths made of just one colour and without pattern, but in my experience this often indicates a specific ritual context set apart from both the everyday and the ceremonial uses of cloth (see, for example, Renne 1995). The second element of this aesthetic is revealed in the ways in which cloth is used to enhance movement; while the third is revealed in the elaboration of a tradition through a reworking of received forms, drawing upon an eclectic mix of things from here and there. At this point we must be careful: the West African character of this aesthetic cannot be located in, or reduced to, the field of universals or general principle. There is, after all, nothing specifically African about an eclectic mix of things, nor about the relationship between cloth and movement, nor about a delight in pattern. You can find all of it anywhere, a fact that proves nothing in particular. What makes it West African is the corpus of specificities, the practical manifestation in this or that place, region, tradition, artist. This aesthetic is seen in the ways in which traditions of social practice have evolved historically to provide specifically local responses to these common human concerns, via the technologies of weaving and dyeing, of embroidery and appliqué, and the forms of dress, whether elite or commonplace, that are distinctive of West Africa.

Moreover, cloth serves its social purposes not just in its domestic, ceremonial and ritual uses, or as an aesthetic that reveals particular kinds of technological and formal histories, but as a context of ideas. The word 'context', derived from the Latin *texere*, to weave, is a case in point, even though most of us have forgotten the allusion. It draws a likeness between the interrelationships of signs and/or practices on the one hand, and the interlacing of warps and wefts on the other. The proverb at the head of this essay sets before us a pair of contrasts, the first between past and present, the second between cloth and the backside that sits upon it. The dress tradition drawn upon in this proverb is one in which women wore lengths of cloth as wraparound skirts, and men wore cloth thrown over the left shoulder. Even if a man owned a wide-sleeved gown, until the advent of a colonial material culture there were no tight-fitting sleeves and trousers in which one's knees and elbows could wear holes. The word *iruvo* in the second phrase of the proverb refers to the root of a tree, the reason for something, and the base of a thing, as well as the human backside; and just as a person's bottom tests the strength and durability of the cloth worn around it, so the past allows us to examine the present. The past is the root of the present. The proverb thereby reiterates the place of tradition in determining current social practice, and it does so by way of the relative impermanence of cloth, standing here as a metaphor of the shifting circumstances and fashions of the present wherein we find ourselves.

This is but one example of the reiteration of the necessity of tradition; but tradition is not the mere repetition of past practice, for in the process of 'handing over' (from the Latin *tradere*) we have the possibilities and mechanisms of change and development. Tradition enables change, and particular traditions define the possibilities of, and thereby shape, its development. Of course, the period since the mid-19th century has been a time of often radical change in which new practices and forms were introduced that were without obvious precedent: photography is the most obvious example. Yet new forms of practice, and especially of clothing, pattern and yarn, did not spell the complete demise of an inheritance from the past. It is true that the advent of cheap factory-made cotton, and African-print fabrics, meant that weaving for purely domestic uses was not always necessary. But in most other aspects of local textile manufacture, the new yarns and colours provided new opportunities for creativity on the part of textile makers, while certain forms retained their cultural relevance in any case. However, just imagine for a moment, what would happen if I were to walk down through the streets where I live dressed in the manner of a British Islander of the 18th or early 19th century. Most people would think it very strange: perhaps I was on my way to a fancy dress party; perhaps I was mad. Yet when a Nigerian wears a wide-sleeved gown in the streets of the town or city where he lives, it is entirely normal; and this is a garment with its origin in Saharan camel-riding dress, that depends on the advent and history of Islam for its distribution through West Africa, that is worn by men of all religions and none, and that has recently been adapted for use in the vestments of the Christian priesthood. Yet we can be sure from early museum collections in Europe that these are not garments of recent inception (see for example LaGamma & Giuntini 2008: 59, 61; also Gardi 2000: 74, 106, 107; and Kriger 2006 who collates much of the available evidence). The textile fragments of the Tellem caves (Bolland 1991; Gardi 2000: 45) indicate that some aspects of this tradition were well established from five hundred to perhaps a thousand years ago. Of course, that gown might now be tailored of plain machine-woven cotton; it might be machine embroidered, and so on. But it might also be woven of hand-spun, indigo-dyed cotton, and hand-embroidered in the wild silk that is native to West Africa (again, see Gardi 2000). The clothes people choose to wear permit an identity with a sense of tradition that is continually being brought up-to-date. Tradition and modernity subsist in the same garments, and that modernity is entirely local; it is not contingent upon either a colonial or some kind of post-colonial international material culture. Part of the reason for the persistence of tradition might reside in the aesthetic discussed above; but attachment to it was reinforced, often overtly, in the use of dress and textiles in the politics of resistance to colonial rule. [10]

The idea of local modernity brings us to the third point of departure for this essay: the two New York exhibitions. The Metropolitan Museum show placed greater emphasis on an inheritance from the past by means of some of the finest examples of textiles from the 19th century, including many on loan from the British Museum, whereas the Grey Art Gallery was much more of a recent art show. Taken together, the two exhibitions showed us many of the breaks and continuities between past and present, in whichever medium; and in so doing they emphasized the largely vacuous distinction sometimes made between the 'traditional' and the 'modern'. The latter word is, after all, derived from the Latin *modo*, 'just now'. To be modern is nothing more than to be where a community is at; and hand-woven and -dyed cloth is part of it. Moreover, given that much of what happens in all aspects of social practice contemporary with the present time is governed by the traditions of any given place or community, those traditions are in effect the conditions of local modernity. Yet tradition does not mean stasis, and in West Africa the period since about 1850 is one in which, unlike much of the past, it is relatively easy to document contrasting forms of change and development. While this cannot be taken as a precise date, it marks a period in which transatlantic slavery was replaced by (a relatively brief period of) colonial rule. However, through the 19th century, and especially in the coastal cities of West Africa, an elite intellectual class of West African people emerged, professionally trained in British and other European universities. They provided leadership to the resistance to colonial rule as it then began to develop; they initiated the documentation of local traditions; and they saw the necessity of defining both national and ethnic identities for the modern world they were helping to create; and this provided the context for developments in visual practice. Some traditions (e.g. wood sculpture) slowly descended into obsolescence. Many others (e.g. dress, textiles, masquerade) did not merely survive, they flourished and developed, while new traditions came into being (factory-printed cloth, photography, easel painting, printmaking and public sculpture). They all continue to be among the elements of evolving local modernities.

The attachment to tradition, with all its formal, technological and aesthetic dimensions, is confirmed by three of the more obvious developments since the late 19th century: photography, African-print cloth, and 'modernist' developments mostly since the 1950s. As photography developed as a West African visual practice, and people chose to have themselves photographed, as often as not, they wore the dress traditions of their place or region (Magnin 1997; Revue Noire 1998; Wendl & Behrend 1998). African-print fabrics emerged in a late 19th-century Dutch attempt to mechanize the production of batik textiles. Because of the failure to eradicated the variegated background to the motifs intended to appeal to Indonesian taste the Dutch project was unsuccessful, but the cloths sold well on the colonial Gold Coast and as that market developed it led to new forms of imagery based upon the visualization of proverbs, local political emblems, and so forth, and the Dutch designers were inadvertently drawn into that West African aesthetic already discussed.[11] Textiles are inevitably entailed in all kinds of memories and identities, gendered, ethnic, political, and so forth; they can embody the history of a household or lineage, whether by means of the commissioning of a specific design or simply through the acquisition and continued presence of particular cloths within the group; people can be remembered, commemorated, among other things, through their ownership of textiles, perhaps now inherited and worn by their descendants; there are textiles that commemorate particular events, textiles that provide for the visualization of proverbial wisdom, these things constituting a body of local knowledge shared, as it were, between people and cloth, and recognized even when that cloth is folded or draped and thus not fully visible; and textiles have aesthetic value. Whether as part of the subject matter in a photograph, or in the capacity to signify or, indeed, question a sense of identity with an inherited tradition, or because of the range of concerns addressed via textiles, or simply because of all the colours and shapes, it was inevitable that textiles would inform other forms of visual practice, including those of relatively recent inception, such as the works of artists on show in New York in 2008, artists of the calibre of El Anatsui, Yinka Shonibare MBE, Atta Kwami, and others (see Gumpert 2008; also Picton 2004a) whose works confirm the enduring relevance of West African textiles in the world of today.

8 – In the 'traditional' view of African art, sculpture has been the subject of interest in Europe and America; in reality,
this was a tradition already obsolescent before the 1960s while textiles and local dress forms, represented here
by the woman in the background warping her loom, have continued to flourish. The veranda post is the work of Olowe
of Ise-Ekiti who died around 1939. This post is now in the Staatliches Museum für Völkerkunde, Munich.

Photo John Picton 1965; reproduced by permission of the National Commission for Museums and Monuments, Nigeria

INDIGO

Bernhard Gardi

All across West Africa, countless women in innumerable villages cultivated *Indigofera* – the plant from which the chemical agent indigo is extracted – or at least attended to the shrubs growing in the nearby bush. The plant comes in a large variety of kinds. After picking, being pounded in a mortar, formed into balls and left to dry, indigo can be stored for years. Indigo balls were traded to the north via the old trans-Saharan trade routes. Berber carpets from the Atlas Mountains often contained indigo from Mali or Senegal; at the same time, valuable indigo from the old Kanem-Bornu Empire in Chad was exported to Egypt.

There are two large plant species that have leaves which are suitable for manufacturing blue dyes: in tropical and sub-tropical areas these refer to the *Indigofera* plants which belong to the *Faboideae* sub-family. Of the five hundred known species only a few are really suitable for dyeing. In the temperate zones mainly woad (*Isatis tinctoria*) was used, but the tropical *Indigofera* provided pigments that were clearly superior to woad which is said to produce a rather 'dull' blue. [12]

The saying goes that even the worst African indigo was miles better than the best European indigo. The truth is, there was no good blue in Europe, which is why high-quality vibrant pigments from India were in such high demand. But transportation overland from India to Europe made the products exorbitantly expensive.

During the age of discovery, tropical blue began to be imported to Europe in large quantities. It was called ultramarine – the blue that came from 'across the sea'. This thirst for a high-quality blue pigment had economic repercussions on both Europe and Africa: the Portuguese shipped slaves from the African continent to the, until then, unpopulated Cape Verde Islands to grow cotton and indigo, some of which was sold on the European market, while the rest was used locally to produce richly patterned textiles, which were traded in for goods and slaves on the African continent (Carreira 1968). This goes to show that West Africa was already then part of the globalized world, with all its implications.

In West Africa the main sources of indigo were *Indigofera arrecta*, a shrub that grows mainly in the savannah, and the indigo vine *Lonchocarpus cyanescens* which grows in the rainforest. [13]

In Nigeria, Yoruba women used large pots for dyeing, preferably mixing indigo from the savannah with the rainforest kind. In northern Nigeria it was the men who did (and occasionally still do) the dyeing in deep dye pits. The Hausa dye pit tradition is found all across the savannah region, from the area east of Lake Chad to Côte d'Ivoire.

In Mali and Senegal, women prepare the dyes in large pots. Especially Soninke and Wolof women rank as great dye specialists.

In West African languages there is no term for blue. As a rule, indigo blue is described as black. [14]

Let us remain in the field of linguistics for a moment and check out a few semantic tracks: from Mauritania in the north to the Rio Nunez on the Atlantic coast to Burkina Faso in the east we find in more than 12 languages always the same term for indigo: *gara* or *gala*. This suggests that there must have been historical connections. The women dyers are usually Mande speakers, which we can take as a clue that, in the course of the decline of the old Ghana empire and the move of Soninke families – Mande speakers – to the south, knowledge about indigo-dyeing spread with them.

Correspondent with the two traditions of indigo-dyeing found in Nigeria – Hausa and Yoruba respectively – we find two different terms for indigo: *baba* (Hausa) and *elu* (Yoruba). [15]

Last but not least: nowadays we tend to ignore the natural features and qualities of many cultivated plants. The Badische Anilin- und Soda-Fabrik Ludwigshafen, better known as BASF, was the first company to introduce synthetic indigo. But before this new pigment could be marketed, costumers had to be convinced in a campaign that the new product was up to the quality of the old vegetable indigo. This was achieved by adding a synthetic smell to the pigment, emulating natural indigo that discharges a special odour.

23

9 — Up to 40 dye pits are to be seen, or at least guessed, on this photograph.
The Dyula living in Baule country were the great indigo-dyers. They built their dye pits
in the same fashion as the Hausa of northern Nigeria (Béoumi, Côte d'Ivoire)

Photo Urs Rahm, January 1957 – EIII-7

**10 – THE VINE *LONCHOCARPUS CYANESCENS* CON-
TAINS INDIGO. SOMORIKA, NIGERIA**

Photo B. Gardi 6.1.1974 – (F)III 100577

**11 – LEAVES OF AN *INDIGOFERA* PLANT, PROBABLY
INDIGOFERA ARECTA. SAWANA, BURKINA FASO**

Photo B. Gardi 21.7.1974 – (F)III 101199

**12 – THREE DRIED INDIGO BALLS. REPUBLIC OF BENIN.
The largest one measures 7.5 cm in diameter**

Collected by René Gardi 1963 – III 17626

13 – FILTER POTS. SOMORIKA. NIGERIA.
Alkaline water drips into the pot below

Photo B. Gardi 31.12.1973 – (F)III 7470

14 – IN A QUARTER OF AKURE, NIGERIA.
Several women indigo-dyers have their workshop here

Photo B. Gardi 10.3.1974 – (F)III 7912

IYA ALARU, THE MOTHER OF ASH
Bernhard Gardi

Among the Yoruba of Nigeria there were women specialists called *iya alaru*, 'mother of ash', who produced *laru*, 'potent ash', from normal kitchen ash, which was used by the women dyers for their indigo baths.

Various ingredients go into an indigo bath: water, indigo balls, potash and ash. Mixed in the right ratio, at a certain outside temperature and observing a certain rhythm of stirring ... and your indigo bath is ready.

The details of each work step are a professional secret and, of course, the ratio of ingredients must be strictly observed. All good dyers, both men and women, rely on their own individual recipe which they guard closely. Uncontrollable factors such as the weather and temperature also play an important role, and the quality of the indigo balls and the ash is likely to vary too, so a lot of experience is required. [16]

Apart from the water and the indigo, the quality of the ash is decisive for triggering off the desired chemical process. Good, suitable ash leaves behind a tingling, sour taste on the tip of the tongue as against old, exhausted ash.

In my fieldnotes of 5 May 1974 from Kano, the main city in northern Nigeria, I wrote: "The composition of the indigo bath varies according to the size of the dye pit. A possible mixture is as follows:

1.) 20 buckets of water, each containing 18 litres; [17]
2.) 1 to 1.5 bags of dried indigo balls;
3.) 20 buckets of *toka*, i.e. kitchen ash
4.) 5 buckets of *katsi*, i.e. fired ash."

This recipe applies to male dyers using dye pits.

One dye pit I examined in Kano measured 2.3 metres in depth and had a diameter of 70 centimetres, with a capacity of 1,600 litres. When the bath is exhausted it is replenished by adding new indigo, fired ash or water, whichever it needs; ideally, this process can be kept up for months.

Women dyers start by soaking the indigo balls in water. A good dye pot takes roughly 50 balls. After fermentation sets in, the balls are removed, placed in a large dye pot and covered with water from an old indigo bath. Then a next pot with an inbuilt filter is filled with ash and placed on the pot containing the indigo. Water is filled in from the top, causing the minerals salts to be washed out and drip into the dye pot below, thereby increasing the pH-value. From time to time, the concoction needs a gentle stir. After three to five days, greenish foam develops and the surface of the indigo bath turns almost purple. Now dyeing can commence.

Let us return to the *iya alaru*. The kiln she owns is built by her husband. It is made of clay and has an intermediate floor with holes. [18] In her workshop the 'mother of ash' keeps many pots, buckets and metal bowls where she stores the kitchen ash which women from the neighbourhood bring to her. Other containers are filled with straw or millet stems needed for firing the kiln, and gourds for ladling ash, for storing ash ready for sale, and for collecting water.

The *iya alaru* adds water to the kitchen ash and kneads the mass, forming dozens of ash balls, or cakes, which she lays out on the floor to dry. As soon as they are dry they are placed in the kiln, often covered with pottery shards, while a strong fire is lit from below. The ash from the crumbling cakes falls through the openings of the intermediate floor and is removed, leaving behind alkaline ash which is then sold to the dyers.

15 – MRS HUN MANI AKANKE, A *IYA ALARU*. EDE. NIGERIA.
The kiln has been fired. Ash cakes are drying on the ground

Photo B. Gardi 4.3.1974 – (F)III 7787

THE RESEARCH EXPEDITION 1973–1975
Bernhard Gardi

When Renée Boser-Sarivaxévanis and I left Basel for Africa on 17 October 1973 the personal computer had not yet been invented. Fieldnotes still had to be written by hand. Before departure I spent a few days in a workshop learning about the technicalities of the Landrover we had purchased from a dealer at a 10 percent discount. All our material was packed in Swiss army crates, and the technical crew at the museum had built us a robust roof rack for our fuel cans.

We had no idea what the future held in store for us. We took along with us what we believed we would need on our journey: water filters, pots and pans, knives and forks, a few cups and plates, a mechanical typewriter and a kerosene lamp – the usual items on an expedition. We also had three cameras and a film supply for 16 months.

Renée – as I shall call her in this more personal chapter – had planned our itinerary in detail. We had long lists of African vocabularies taken from various sources which we wanted to check up on, and for the purpose of which she had developed a 15-page questionnaire. [19] We embarked with our Landrover on a ship in Marseille which took us via Valencia, Dakar, Freetown, Lomé and Cotonou to Lagos.

The real journey began on 10 November 1973 in Apapa, the port of Lagos. A great time lay ahead of us. For the next six months in Nigeria we were under the auspices of the Federal Department of Antiquities. [20]

For me the journey ended a year later in November 1974 in Mopti (Mali). I had to return to continue my studies at university. Renée travelled on with a Malian driver and finally returned to Basel from Dakar in February 1975.

We were rather an unusual team. I was 27 years old, Renée was 52. Before our departure we had spent long evenings together during which Renée initiated me into her world of ideas and theories. Apart from explaining the secrets of textile technology – which were not too difficult to understand but which did not really interest me – she kept returning to the topic of the invention and diffusion of the loom. Some of her main tenets included the idea that at differing times different types of loom had been invented, functioning on diverse working principles. Once a certain type of loom had been invented it represented an almost perfected device which, in substance, could not be altered after that. Thus, the first loom ever to be invented was the horizontal loom with a fixed heddle, usually called a ground loom, as used by the Ancient Egyptians; followed by the warp-weighted loom of the Ancient Greeks and Neolithic lake dwellers in Europe, but not found in Africa; the vertical loom with a fixed heddle and a continuous warp as used by women in Nigeria; and, finally, the double-heddle loom, the most elaborate pre-industrial type of loom, commonly worked by men in all parts of West Africa.

These technical issues were more up my street; but at the same time they raised questions that begged an answer: how could one possibly prove that a mechanical device, invented at some point in time in the Near East or somewhere in Asia, had found its way across the Sahara? For Renée the answer lay hidden in the textile techniques and, concomitantly, in the textile terminology. I internalized much of what she said, complementing this fund of knowledge with own observations made in the course of our journey. Many of her

16 – A woman from a well-to-do family in an *ebase*
wrap cloth (Somorika, Nigeria)

Photo B. Gardi 30.12.1973 – (F)III 100607

ideas and views about the history of West African textiles certainly proved more convincing than much of what I found on the subject in the literature later on. Renée was a diffusionist. She did not believe that the different looms had been invented repeatedly in separate places and at different times. Such a complex device could only have spread from a single source. And in order to prove this she developed various, stimulating approaches.

NIGERIA

With regard to Nigeria one of her arguments runs as follows: the upright loom used by Yoruba women is, in terms of mechanical working order, a more simple construction – less automated and thus less efficient – than the men's double-heddle loom. Therefore, the argument runs, it must have been invented and brought to Nigeria at an earlier point in time than the more complex double-heddle loom. But what did the people centuries ago in southern Nigeria use for weaving material? Cotton was unknown at the time, yet one knew that textiles produced in the 9th and 10th century in Igbo-Ukwu had been made of plant fibres – but not of cotton (Shaw 1977).

Thus, for Renée one of the first questions that needed answering was: what other vegetable fibres are suitable for spinning and weaving? It was only a matter of weeks before we had found such a fibre. East of Benin, in the Igbo territory, this fibre was generally known as *ufa*, in Igara and Somorika it was called *ebase*, and in Okene *orupa*. The yarn was produced and prepared from the inner bark fibres of a certain tree. From this material beautiful and heavy cloths were woven; they served as insignia of rank but were also used as shrouds. These cloths ranked among the most expensive pieces that we collected. [21]

This kind of research was exciting and there was a lot to discover. But we also experienced setbacks, for instance in Benin City, where, in spite of two audiences with the Oba, we were not allowed to enter the palace grounds. This meant that we did not get a chance to speak to the weavers who were said to work inside the palace area, specialized on weaving the insignia of high-ranking dignitaries. Nevertheless, we had the opportunity to investigate two examples of these special cloths, namely sashes called *iterhuan* and pendants termed *ègbèle*. They are woven differently from ordinary cloths, in the sense that the warp threads are tied into thick bundles. These adornments are worn by chiefs over their wrap cloths as insignia of rank on the occasion of palace ceremonies (Ben-Amos Girshik 2007).

In Benin City we searched in vain for local women weavers. There were none to be found! We received nothing but vague answers to our questions in this direction, from which we were forced to conclude that there was no such thing as specific Edo-weaving in Benin City. The weavers we encountered were in-married women, some of them from the northern Akoko Edo division, most of them from Igara. So we drove to Igara.

Igara and the neighbouring town of Somorika turned out to be one of the most rewarding and intensive stops on the entire journey. The landscape was overwhelming and the people were marvellous; during our visits to weavers and dyers, but also at the local markets, we discovered the most beautiful and, to us, many unknown fabrics made of hand-spun yarn and dyed with fragrant, vegetable indigo.

Of special interest to us was the ikat technique we happened to come across here, namely because this tie-and-dye technique is one of the specialities of the Basel collection. [22] A little later, in Owo, we got to know probably one of the last Yoruba women who was able to show us how tie off the warp. Her name was Mrs Janet Adedeke [23] Her hands

17 — Leaves and fruit of the *ufa* tree (*Tabernaemontana pachysinphon*, Stapf) [21] as it is called in Igbo. From the inside of the bark a fibre is produced, called *ebase* in Somorika (Ubulu Uku, Nigeria)

Photo B. Gardi 27.1.1974 – (F)III 7633

18 — An indigo-dyer at her workplace (Somorika, Nigeria)

Photo B. Gardi 6.1.1974 – (F)III 100579

are shown on the last photograph of this book (see fig. 145). Renée believed that the great ikat cloths produced by the weavers of Somorika and Igara represented a survival from an older Yoruba tradition. We stayed in the area for two weeks – longer than anywhere else on our journey.

Our next, equally impressive stop was Ilorin. While in Somorika and Igara weaving was women's work, we encountered in Ilorin hundreds of male weavers with their warps stretched out on large open squares. The picture in Iseyin was similar. Here too we purchased many cloths. I especially remember an extraordinary night market in Ilorin – with hundreds of little oil-lamps lighting up the scene – where we were nearly overrun by women wishing to sell us baby-ties and used 'wrappers', as the wrap cloths are called in English in Nigeria. Some of the most beautiful textiles we saw here were made of pure wild silk in shades of gentle brown and beige.

In the course of the journey, Renée and I developed our own form of division of labour. I was responsible for the Landrover, the bookkeeping and the collecting, while Renée mainly busied herself with linguistic matters, meticulously compiling word lists of African textile terms. Especially in the early stage of our journey in Nigeria, it was important to identify terms that were specific and had reference character, because these designations were useful for comparative purposes. We suspected that it was rather like other cases of cultural adoption: just as the term 'radio' came together with the object 'radio', the same was to be expected in the case of a device like the loom. It soon showed that the different terms used for 'heddle' in different Nigerian languages are comparable; the term used for the women's upright loom was *asa* (or some very similar term), and the men's double-heddle loom was *niiri* (or, again, a very similar term).

These linguistic inquiries needed explaining and editing by language experts, [24] so, where- and whenever possible, we contacted linguistics – but also archaeologists [25] – at the local universities. I especially remember working with Thurstan Shaw, a famous professor in Ibadan. In 1960 he had been in charge of the excavations at Igbo-Ukwu where the oldest textile fragments ever found in West Africa had been discovered, next to the works in bronze which today form a significant part of West African art history. We made an appointment to visit Thurstan Shaw. Renée, I remember, was very nervous. In the early stages of the conversation he let Renée do the talking before suddenly throwing his hands up in the air and exclaiming: "But I have been waiting for someone like you for years!" The consequence of the meeting was that we spent the next three days cleaning ten textile fragments from the 9th/10th century in distilled water, after which we were able to measure them precisely. [26]

Next to being vast and densely populated, Nigeria was exciting. Weaving was ubiquitous! The markets in Okene, Ibadan, Ilorin and Lagos were literally overflowing with hand-woven textiles. The dominating cloth was *aso oke* which is woven by men using industrial yarn. Clearly, men practiced weaving as a profession; their output was huge, their produce to be found in all markets. Male weavers were much easier to locate than women weavers, not least because the men worked in public areas; to be precise, they were compelled to work in spacious locations because the length of the warp was too long for a home compound. In contrast, most of the women worked at home, which meant we had to go in search of them. They were less productive, and it soon became apparent that, for women, weaving was a supplementary occupation to household work, usually performed by elder women who no

19 – On the market in Bida, Nigeria

Photo B. Gardi 31.3.1974 – (F)III 8051

20 – Blue-and-white striped 'pagnes' for sale on the market. 'Pagnes' like these used to be the everyday dress of rural women (Bénéna, Mali)

Photo B. Gardi 12.1.1979 – 16/20

longer had children to take care of. We were too immersed in our historical theories as to really notice what Nigerian men and women wore in everyday life; usually Western-style clothes or industrially printed cloths, it seemed. Hand-woven textiles appeared to be worn more frequently in the villages – and, of course, as special dress on festive occasions to which we, as travellers, usually had no access. We had little interest in modern fibres such as lurex (see Picton 1995).

On the entire journey we rarely spent more than three or four days in the same place. We slept in cheap 'resthouses', in expensive hotels and in villages, depending on the circumstances. In Idah, an armed soldier in uniform was stationed in front of our house. In Mankono, Côte d'Ivoire, an American missionary couple turned us down because we were not married; instead, the wife of the district commander, a mother of six children, had pity on us and took us in.

We soon realized that we were running behind schedule, so we dropped the idea of visiting the upper Benue area. Instead, we drove northwards via Bida, the main Nupe town.

NIGER

We travelled through many very arid regions. The area was suffering from a severe drought that had set in a year before, causing serious famine. We were relieved that we were able to restrict our research to the environs around Niamey and along the Niger River where the effects of the drought and famine were less evident than further inland where weaving was less common anyhow. All in all we spent approximately five weeks in Niger.

The language situation had also changed, from English to French. Cloths were no longer called 'wrappers', but 'pagnes' instead.

Because of the drought, Renée had decided to change the original itinerary: instead of setting off from Dakar we had started our journey in Lagos, which caused certain disadvantages as we found out later – for example with regard to Zarma weaving. The large Zarma cloths were sold in large numbers at the markets in Niamey, Dosso, Bonkoukou or Filingué, and we spent long hours with the weavers who had set up their work sheds in the park of the National Museum in Niamey. Had we arrived from the west – via Mali – we would have quickly realized that Zarma weaving was an offshoot of Fulani wool weaving. The motif blocks on the Zarma blankets were actually very similar to the weft-float patterns on the *arkilla kerka* marriage blankets. After the abolishment of slavery 1905/1908, it took at least a generation until the people really were, and felt, free. Many Fulani from northern Mali, that is, from the Songhay-speaking area along the Niger River bend, began to move south, finally reaching Niamey and Dosso – or at least the western part of this enormous country – where they developed the famous Zarma blankets. According to the information we received there were no such cloths before the Second World War; woven textiles were produced (if at all) in the Hausa fashion, or consisting of plain white strips. In the course of the 1960s, the Zarma blankets changed their look: they were now richly decorated with patterns and it became fashionable to embellish them with Niger's national colours, i.e. red, white and green. [27]

Important for research was our first contact with wool weaving. Outside Tillabéry we visited the village of Sawani located on a small island in the Niger River. It was inhabited by Wogo people, a Songhay-speaking minority, originally Fulani, who had arrived there more than a hundred years ago from the Niger Inland Delta in Mali. They used to harvest sheep's wool; until recently it still had been custom that the bride brought a *kunta arkilla* (or *arkilla*

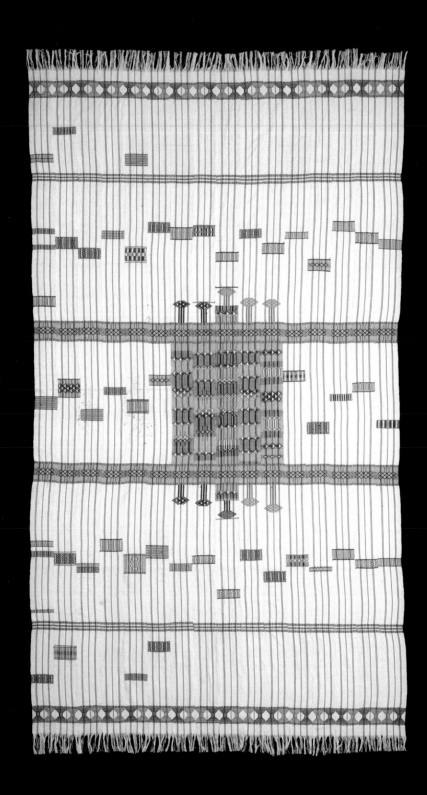

21 – COTTON BLANKET. ZARMA. NIGER.
The motif blocks are like the patterns on the *arkilla kerka* marriage blankets (fig. 67).
Industrial cotton yarn. Purchased in Malanville, Republic of Benin

263 × 150 cm. 16 strips, each nearly 10 cm wide – collected by René Gardi 1963 - III 16734

kunta as the Fulani say) into the marriage as a dowry. However, by the time of our visit, this custom had been abandoned. On one occasion we came across a splendid blanket that was being used as a rain-cover for a leaking grass roof (fig. 22).

BURKINA FASO

Shortly later we arrived in Dori, the capital of the Liptako region in northeastern Burkina Faso. The rains set in dramatically, killing in the floods many young animals still weak from the drought.

In and around Dori, wool was common too; more than a hundred years ago Fulani families from Mali had moved to this area. Mallere was the name of a weaver's village outside Dori. *Malle* (pl. *malleebe*) is, up to this day, the term used by the Fulani of Mali to designate all weavers who are not weavers by birthright, that is, do not belong to the *maabuube* 'caste' (sing. *maabo*). In Mallere there were quite a few weavers (originally slaves or serves, i.e. non-*maabuube*) who mainly produced blankets with rectangular patterns, the white parts of which (including the warp) being of cotton, the coloured parts of wool. In general, rectangular motifs are typical for cotton blankets from Mali, especially from the Banamba area. In Mallere the weavers had taken over the rectangles but retained the wide strips, often 20 centimetres and more, which is a typical feature of wool weaving.

In western Burkina Faso, in the area of Bobo Dioulasso, namely in the village of Darsalami, we again came across the technique of ikat weaving. In difference to Igara and Somorika, here it was the men – Dyula – who prepared the warps and were responsible for the indigo-dyeing. Later on, in Côte d'Ivoire, we again would come across marvellous ikat cloths in large numbers.

In Bobo Dioulasso we noticed a group of weavers who used very slim and long shuttles. They were young weavers from Senegal – Wolof men – who had left their country and come to Burkina Faso due to lacking perspectives at home. Actually, we found that in the towns the weavers were often very young, a fact that is true of Nigeria as well. As a rule, a weaver works on order for a female patron who provides the yarn and daily meals – thus solving the common problem of finding food. The weaver was paid directly in exchange for each finished strip. For young men skilled in weaving this was easily earned money.

In the Mossi area in central Burkina Faso where we stayed for six weeks we came across impressive dye workshops where the dyeing with vegetable indigo was done in deep pits in the same way as we had seen in northern Nigeria among the Hausa. In the small Mossi village of Waghien near Boussouma, outside Kaya, we counted 27 looms in one location. [28]

CÔTE D'IVOIRE

We stayed for seven weeks in Côte d'Ivoire. [29] Here we encountered weavers mainly along the main north-south road. We came across several villages with magnificent cloths for sale at roadside outlets. Usually the weavers were young Baule men. As against the northern regions where we had just come from, the cloths here were large-sized and very colourful. They were made for and worn by men. Among the Guro too we met remarkably skilled weavers with superb textiles.

In Bouaké, the largest town in the Baule region, we went in search of Baule weavers – but found none. All the weavers we met were from Senegal (Wolof), Mauritania (Fulani) and Mali. Strangely enough, however, the market offered a large selection of hand-woven Baule cloths.

22 — An old *arkilla kunta* marriage blanket now serves as cover for a leaking grass roof (Sawani, Niger).
See fig. 69

Photo B. Gardi 20.6.1974 – (F)III 101068

23 — At the market in Bouaké, Côte d'Ivoire: a selection of Baule cloths

Photo B. Gardi 17.9.1974 – (F)III 101455

The origin of weaving was a recurrent theme in our conversations, in all countries and regions. The local people usually had a general clue as to the origin of cloth. In Niger, for example, they said that the richly patterned cloths came from the west, in other words from Mali; in Côte d'Ivoire they said that weaving had come from the north. Thus, all clues pointed to Mali, our next stop on the journey, to which we looked forward.

MALI

At the time of our visit, the National Museum in Bamako had not yet been built, so their collection was stored at the Institut National des Arts. Yaya Coulibaly, the museum's multilingual interim director, accompanied us on our journey which took us to Ségou, Djenné and Mopti. Here we hired a pinnace and travelled to Niafounké.

On the two-week river journey, during which we stopped off at several villages on Lake Debo, we were especially interested in gathering information on Fulani wool weaving and the related terminology. During the two weeks our collection grew considerably. [30] At the time I was not aware of the fact that a few years later, from 1978 to 1982, I would be spending 18 months in this area doing research (see Gardi 1985).

Back in Mopti, we parted company at the end of November 1974: I returned to Basel to continue my studies, Renée travelled on with her new companion Ibrahim Guindo, the chauffeur of the Institut des Sciences Humaines. They first visited Sanga in the Dogon area, before returning to Bamako from where they continued via Nara and Nioro du Sahel to Kayes where they loaded the Landrover on to a train and travelled to Dakar.

SENEGAL

During the last two months of the expedition Renée concentrated on the weaving of the Mandjak and on indigo-dyeing. The only purpose of her journey to the arid northern part of Mali – to Nioro du Sahel – was to meet women indigo-dyers. The indigo produced by the Soninke women of Nioro is legendary throughout West Africa; the same is true of the women dyers of Bakel in Senegal. However, Renée never got to Bakel because in Matam, only a few kilometres short of Bakel, there was no fuel to be had. [31]

Renée's notes from Senegal and northern Mali are rich in information on indigo-dyeing but her real obsession – ikat – was nowhere to be found: according to her theory, there must have been a connection between the ikat of the Dyula in Côte d'Ivoire and the great dyers of the north, the Soninke women. However, there is no such link.

IN RETROSPECT

Looking back on our journey through West Africa, many and mixed memories come to my mind. There was something very archaic to our expedition. Renée was usually busy mulling over her hypotheses and communicating these to me. My role was to listen and help her think, which was not always easy. I certainly enjoyed collecting cloths more than I did compiling and supplementing word lists. The textile field is a public sphere and textiles are made for the public. Most of the fabrics we purchased were bought at markets. Throughout the journey, weavers, village chiefs and state officials welcomed us with open arms. We would have liked to do some collecting for national museums as well but we had no suitable contacts, and apart from Nigeria practically none of the young nations had a national museum at the time.

At the markets we had to do a lot of bartering, from which many interesting personal contacts grew. I enjoyed this part of the work. Approximately 80 percent of the total 1,000 purchased textiles were bought at markets, 10 percent we obtained straight from the producers (i.e. patrons and weavers), while the remaining 10 percent were worn cloths which we purchased from women. In addition, we gathered hundreds of weaving samples which we listed in inventory lists. Especially this part of the collection provides detailed information on the craftsmen and -women. Weavers often retain small strips of cloth – 20 to 30 centimetres in length – as mental props for later jobs. We purchased such samples by the bundle – much to the pleasure of the weavers.

At the time in the 1970s, our expedition was registered as being something 'special'. In Switzerland a few people voiced criticism, claiming that we were pursuing old-fashioned travel ethnography. In the United States the project gained the attention of a number of specialists, after which Renée received several invitations to visit the States: in 1977 she gave a talk at the fourth Triennal Symposium of African Art in Washington DC; in 1980 she spent three months as visiting professor at the University of Minnesota in Minneapolis where she organized a small exhibition (including a catalogue) showing textiles from the Basel collection; and in 1985/86 she conducted research at the National Museum of African Art in Washington DC for eleven months.

Indirectly, her activities also had an effect on the setting in Mali, in the sense that it was through Renée's work and lectures – and her enthusiasm for the subject – that the American academic audience 'discovered' African textiles. The publication of *African Textiles* by Picton and Mack in 1979 also contributed to this growing interest, with the result that money from American foundations began flowing into research and collecting expeditions. In 1983, on the initiative of Claude Ardouin, director of the new National Museum in Bamako, the first own collection project in Mali was launched. It was supported by WAMP (West African Museum Project) and funded by the Ford Foundation. Salia Malé, Yaya Coulibaly (who had been our companion in Mali in 1974) and the photographer Georges Meurillon travelled to the Niger Inland Delta and the Guimballa region east of Lake Debo where they assembled a magnificent collection which was shown in an exhibition a year later in Bamako. This was an absolute novelty: an own collection, own research and own photographs! In the following year a workshop was held in Bamako, focusing on the restoration and conservation of textiles for members of the technical staff of museums from all parts of West Africa; it was organized by ICCROM, based in Rome (a branch of UNESCO).

Five further collecting expeditions in Mali followed between 1987 and 1991, funded by the Fowler Museum of Cultural History in Los Angeles.[32] The altogether six collection projects resulted in a textile collection at the Musée National du Mali numbering roughly 1,500 items, making textiles the most important department. When the MNM in Bamako was extended in 2000, the museum celebrated the occasion with an exhibition on their textile treasures. Once again I came full circle in life when Samuel Sidibé, director of the MNM in Bamako, approached us with the suggestion that the Museum der Kulturen should participate in the event. Of course we agreed. In 2003 the project led to the publication of the exhibition catalogue *Textiles du Mali d'après les collections du Musée National du Mali* – a co-production between Basel and Bamako, printed in Bamako.[33]

40

MUNNYUURE

Bernhard Gardi

Many textile fragments found in the Tellem burial caves provide evidence that this type of blanket is based on an extremely old tradition. It is worth taking a closer look at.

Munnyuure is a Fulfulde word. The stem *munny* means 'patience', and *munnyuure* 'to patiently endure' (Seydou 1998: 468), implying that only a very patient weaver is capable of producing this type of blanket without making a mistake. Actually, flaws in *munnyuure* blankets are to be found quite often. [34] The number of strips is not pre-given; usually a blanket consists of ten to eleven strips but fabrics containing only five or six strips are not un-heard of. The blanket is named after the weft float patterns that come in the shape of diamonds or hourglasses.

In the old Fulani society of the Macina area, *munnyuure* blankets were a part of women's dress. Women from good families and a Muslin background were expected to wear such a garment over their shoulders and head when leaving the house.

In 1974, *munnyuure* blankets were still sold at most markets in the western Sudan, from Ouagadougou to Bobo Dioulasso, across Mali as far as Senegal. They were produced in many places and belonged to the distinct cultural heritage of the western Sahel.

In Bamanan the blanket is called *koso kalan*, from 'blanket' (*koso*) and 'stem' (*kalan*); the Dogon call them *uldebe*, further east they are called *gammba*.

The Dogon *munnyuure* – or *uldebe* – are a special case. To date they are still made from hand-spun yarn. Without exception they consist of nine strips and are decorated with nine supplementary weft float patterns. The number nine appears to carry special meaning among the Dogon. [35] *Uldebe* blankets are produced only in a few villages of the Piniyari area, a region approximately 30 kilometres east of Mopti; these include Pinia, Kowa, Tangadouba and Kansila. In 1979 they were sold at the weekly market in Somadougou at a fixed price of FM 12,500 (CHF 50). [36]

Uldebe blankets have special significance throughout the Dogon plateau. It is said that people travel more than 100 kilometres on foot to Pinia to purchase such a blanket, [37] they are also commonly found in the Seno Mango, the great plain that extends into Burkina Faso. They are used as male insignia of rank but, above all, they serve as shrouds for both men and women. The bodies of the deceased are wrapped in such blankets and carried to the grave in a public procession. The shrouds tend to be very large-sized, measuring approximately 2.8 by 1.6 metres. The body is then buried, but without the shroud. Many Dogon families own *uldebe* blankets only for this purpose. [38]

It is the only type of blanket that is of real significance to the Dogon. They are preferably shown in public in the context of rituals and ceremonies – marking their presence, so to speak, either open or folded. If you look at old photographs you never see an *uldebe* blanket being worn as dress or for protection by a living person. [39]

Going by Griaule, who knew and wrote so much about the Dogon, nine is a symbol for the first human being and, concomitantly, stands for the most prominet member of society, the chief (1948: 58–69). Be that as it may, in Mali children learn from casual conversations in the evening and when solving riddles that human beings have nine body orifices. [40] Whatever the exact connotation of the number nine, one thing stands for sure: *uldebe* blankets are an inherent part of Dogon culture.

Furthermore, we find that all the weft float patterns found on *munnyuure* – and *uldebe* – blankets also feature on the marriage blankets *arkilla kerka* (fig. 67). The dark patterns woven with wool stand out clearly against the light cotton ground.

Among the oldest textiles to be found in a European museum we have two *uldebe* blankets, collected in Sierra Leone in 1851. They look very much like the modern blankets. [41]

One of the two tunicae in the Weickmann collection in Ulm is even older; it was collected in what is today the Republic of Benin before 1659 (Gardi 2000: 46–51). It contains typical strips decorated with motifs from Mali.

It becomes apparent that various significant dimensions meet in *munnyuure* blankets: historical depth, social significance, religious meaning, in combination with unchanged technique and appearance.

One final aspect deserves comment. This refers to the archaeological Tellem textile complex which is of far-reaching significance because it provides clues to a number of changes encounted in the field of textiles. Tellem wom-

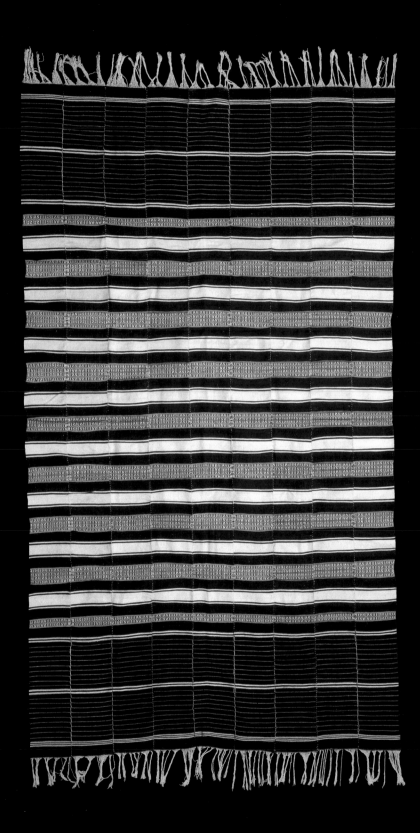

24 – COTTON BLANKET *ULDEBE*. DOGON. MALI.
Produced and purchased in Pinia

290×154 cm. 9 strips, each 17 cm wide – coll. by B. Gardi 1978 – III 21671

en, for example, did not wear 'pagnes' but so-called cache-sexes instead; and textiles with blue and white warp stripes did not exist. At the same time, the Tellem complex shows – and now with specific reference to the *munnyuure* blankets – that certain features remained stable and were hardly ever subject to change; these include, for example, the dark weft float patterns on a light ground. Of course, immediately the question arises: why is this so? Why did some things change and others not? Export might be an answer. Cotton blankets were not only produced for local use, but for export as well. Mali had always imported cola nuts from the rainforests on the Guinea coast in exchange for salt, glass beads and also cotton blankets. The Dogon had a great fancy for kola nuts but had neither salt of their own nor access to cheap glass beads. All they had was their industriousness as farmers – and their cotton blankets. With the arrival of European goods in the area, which on the coast were cheaper than the merchandise that reached Tombouctou via the Sahara, the production of, and trade in, cotton textiles increased markedly in the West African savannah (Roberts 1980). Cloths worn in the coastal areas were made of raffia, a rather coarse material, so soft cotton textiles were in great demand. Since the textiles had to be transported over long distances – covering an area from the Republic of Benin (but not Nigeria) to Ghana as far as Sierra Leone – the fabrics needed a fixed and clearly recognizable style, a brand identity so to speak. It is because the blanket in question remained unchanged over a long period of time, and thus identifiable in all areas, that it experienced such popularity and success.

42

25 – FRAGMENT OF A COTTON BLANKET OF THE *MUNNYUURE* TYPE. 15TH CENTURY. MALI.
Similar patterns have been documented for the 11th century.
The two plain weft bands originally contained red-dyed animal-fibre material (wool, silk?). Now only the white warp threads are visible; the animal fibres were eaten away by insects

3 strips, each 20 cm wide – Musée National du Mali, Bamako – 92-05-513 = Y 74-22
Photo Alioune Bâ

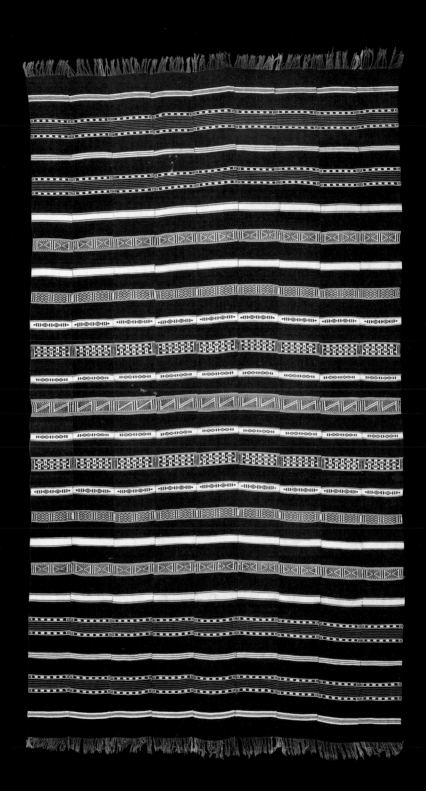

26 – COTTON BLANKET *MUNNYUURE*. FULANI. MALI.
Purchased at the market in Attara, north of Lake Debo. Produced in Attara

240 × 140 cm. 9 strips, each 15 cm wide – coll. by Boser/Gardi 1974 – III 20408

REFLECTIONS ON THE HISTORY OF WEST AFRICAN LOOMS

Bernhard Gardi

It is worth taking a look at the various looms used in West Africa. We can distinguish between three types that are based on different functional principles; next to that we have a fourth, hybrid type. The first three models are also found outside West Africa.[42]

The likelihood that a long time ago a certain type of loom was introduced to Africa is greater than the other way round. However, the diffusion of a specific type of loom in sub-Saharan Africa cannot be explained by trade with North Africa alone, as many authors have suggested. Techniques and technological equipment travel with migrating groups in possession of specialized knowledge who become integrated – as a social entity – into a new host society. This argument was always of primary significance to Boser-Sarivaxévanis: neither the plough and the wheel nor the potter's wheel, she maintained, reached the regions south of the Sahara through 'trade with North Africa'. The field of textiles constitutes a technological complex involving numerous factors requiring consistency in order for a fabric to be produced. Manufacture consists of chains of processes which are taken over as a whole and which cannot diffuse separately through 'trade'. There must be more to it than that. Not to forget, when speaking of weaving in West Africa we are dealing – for pre-industrial times and conditions – with a highly complex technology.

Undoubtedly, one could dismiss Boser-Sarivaxévanis' diffusionist hypotheses as mere speculation. The principle of diffusionism (i.e. the spread of cultural constituents to new geographical areas – as against multiple discoveries/innovations) can never be proven as such, merely made plausible through presenting sufficient and convincing comparative data. On the other hand, one can take the hypotheses as a heuristic tool with the aim of acquiring a better understanding of the overall relationships and interactions in the field of West African textiles as regards style and/or technology.

Two of Boser-Sarivaxévanis' hypotheses read as follows:

- The Fulani introduced the double-heddle loom found throughout West Africa.
- In terms of functional principle the upright loom used by women in Nigeria is simpler than the men's double-heddle loom, which means that the former must have been invented and in use in West Africa prior to the latter. [43]

When Boser-Sarivaxévanis speaks of 'migrating people' who had command of specialized knowledge and were in possession of the double-heddle loom, she is not referring to the Fulani as a whole, but to the Fulani weavers in specific, the *mabuube* (sing. *maabo*). They constitute a clearly defined, endogamous, professional group within Fulani society. The women are potters. At the same time, the *maabuube* serve as griots to aristocratic families. As to the question of how the upright loom reached Nigeria, Boser-Sarivaxévanis had no answer.

Before going on to describe the different types of loom, there is room for a brief sidetrack.

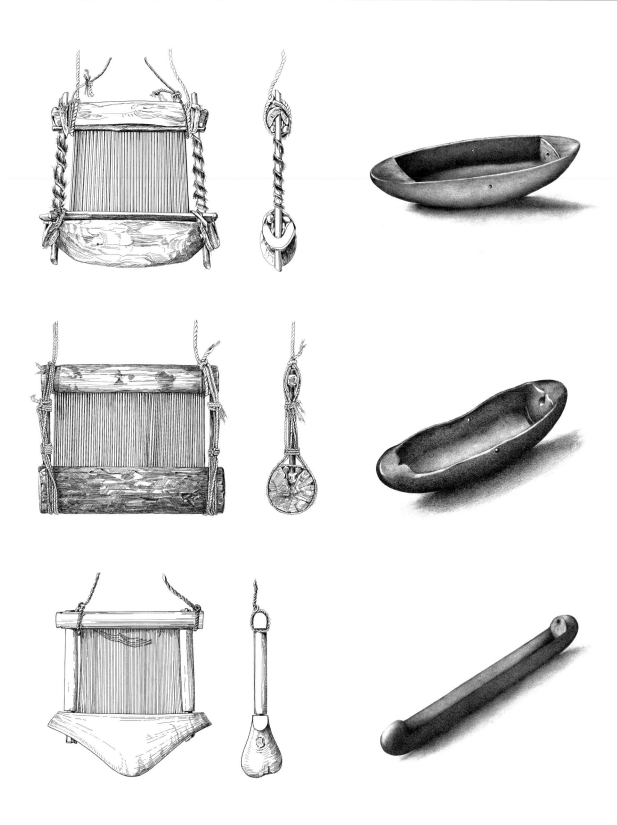

27 – WEAVERS' BEATERS AND SHUTTLES

Beaters, from the front and from the side, from top to bottom: Mossi, purchased in Kaya, Burkina Faso, width 25 cm; Dogon, purchased in Pinia, Mali, 23 cm; Baule-Nanafue, purchased in Menou, Côte d'Ivoire, 19 cm.
Shuttles, from top to bottom: Yoruba, purchased in Ilorin, Nigeria, 19.5 cm; wool shuttle, Fulani, purchased in Youvarou, Mali, 19 cm; Asante, purchased in Bonwire, Ghana, 13.5 cm

Beaters: coll. by Boser/Gardi 1974 – III 20877; coll. by B. Gardi 1979 – III 22026; coll. by Boser/Gardi 1974 – III 20890
Shuttles: coll. by. Boser/Gardi 1974 – III 20870; coll. by Boser/Gardi 1974 – III 20894; coll. by Paul Hinderling 1950 – III 11059

ARCHAEOLOGICAL FINDINGS

West Africa's textile culture is very old. In southern Nigeria, weaving is documented for the 9th to 10th century, in Mali it was flourishing at latest by the 11th century. The ten textile fragments found in Igbo-Ukwu (southern Nigeria – see p. 32) were not made of cotton or raffia, but of bark fibre. Admittedly, there are only few and small fragments, but alone the fact that they were found in this part of West Africa makes them significant pieces of evidence. Moreover, the largest piece is 25 centimetres in width not counting the borders, which we can take as a token that it was manufactured on an upright loom. [44]

In Mali the situation is slightly different: in the Tellem burial caves in the Falaises de Bandiagara hundreds of cotton fabrics were found (Bolland 1991). Wool fabrics existed at a very early age too, and wild silk was also processed. Indigo-dyeing had already reached a very sophisticated level. This whole textile complex dating from the 11th to 16th century is actually a unique stroke of luck. Although we do not know with certainty who actually manufactured these textiles, and where – neither whorls nor fragments of looms were found in the caves – we may assume that most of them were produced somewhere nearby. A few fragments were imported, probably through the well-documented trans-Saharan trade. [45]

The distance between the two discovery sites clearly suggests that, a thousand years ago, there existed two types of loom in West Africa, and that yarn was spun from different fibres.

In addition, even older clues indicating that weaving in Africa goes back even further in time were found in the Sahara. However, a systematic analysis of the great rock paintings found there, many of them going back as far as the Neolithic age and showing detailed scenes of human beings wearing garments, is still pending.

HUMANKIND'S FIRST MACHINE – THE LOOM

The first loom must have been invented many thousands of years ago somewhere in the Middle East. The yarns were made from animal fibres. [46] In the course of time, new and better looms were designed – for example in China for weaving silk (Kuhn 1977; Lamb 2005) – resulting in alternate and probable simpler work processes, and a higher output.

Whatever functional principle a specific weaving device is based on, looms must always be able to provide solutions as to how two different yarn sets – warp and weft – can be mechanically interworked so that a textile is created.

Weaving is only possible if the warp is stretched tight. The number of warp threads defines the width of the weave strip. In order to insert the weft an opening has to be produced mechanically. This opening is called shed and counter-shed respectively. To open a shed one needs a heddle. Taken together the heddles form the shaft. Only with the help of heddles is it possible to pick up all even-numbered – or odd-numbered – warp threads simultaneously and lift them so that a neat opening – the shed and counter-shed respectively – is created through which the weft can be passed. Following this work-step, the inserted weft is beaten in with a beater or, depending on the type of loom, some other tool. [47]

Thus, the basic elements that in the end make up a loom are not the many vertical and horizontal beams and sticks, threads, knots, spools and rods that an observer notices first, but the heddles (or shaft), a tool for beating in the weft and some device to keep the warp taut. Ultimately, weaving is not possible without heddles. Thus, the heddles constitute the main component of a loom.

I shall be returning to this point below. But let us first take a look at West African looms.

THE FOUR TYPES OF LOOM IN WEST AFRICA
Type 1: Horizontal ground loom with fixed heddle

This is probably the oldest type of loom ever invented. It is still found today in Mauritania, across North Africa, the Near and Middle East, and as far as the Himalayas. It is usually worked by women using animal fibres (sheep, goat, yak). [48]

In West Africa use is restricted to a small area on the border between Nigeria and Cameroon, south of Lake Chad. The men do the weaving and also spin the yarn; in all other parts of West Africa this latter task is performed by women. The cloth strips, attaining a width of up to 30 centimetres, serve as bride wealth but are also used as shrouds in the context of funerals. Apart from occasional warp stripes in different colours, no patterns are woven.

Next to cotton, at least one other type of vegetable fibre was – and still might be – spun and woven (see fig. 32).

This loom has only one heddle rod, which means that only a single shed can be formed automatically. The counter-shed is opened with the help of a shed rod. There are no treadles. The pick is not inserted with a shuttle but with a weft rod and beaten in with a wooden sword. In the process of work the weaver moves forward, advancing the heddle rod and the supporting frame at the same time. [49]

Type 2: Vertical loom

In sub-Saharan Africa this loom is found mainly in Nigeria, and in Benin and Togo. It is operated by women. The loom has only one heddle rod to work the shed. The counter-shed is opened with the aid of a shed rod, which means this loom functions on the same principles as the ground loom described above. However, often, additional heddles (or pattern heddles) are used for creating patterns. Again the pick of the weft is inserted with a weft rod. Weaves of up to a width of 80 centimetres can be produced, with two or three such units forming a cloth. The length of the fabric usually does not exceed three metres. [50]

Next to cotton, a further, historically older type of vegetable fibre is spun for weaving on this loom (see above pp. 44, 46).

The warp runs continuously over both warp beams, thus forming two planes. When the fabric has progressed to a certain point, the weaver detaches one of the beams and draws down the entire warp. The maximal length of the weave measures twice the distance between the warp beams. This makes this loom different to the device used by the Berber women of Morocco where a simple warp is mounted between two warp beams, forming only one plane. Similar vertical looms with a fixed heddle and a continuous warp are to be found in the Orient (Lamb 2005: figs. 138, 157).

Type 3: The double-heddle loom

This type of loom is common to all countries in West Africa. It is used by men to weave narrow strips ranging from two to twenty-five centimetres; these are then sewn together to form a cloth. The West African double-heddle loom is sometimes also called narrow-strip loom. [51]

This loom represents the most sophisticated, pre-industrial loom. The heddles are not fixed, instead they can be lifted and lowered with the help of treadles, thus creating shed and counter-shed. The woven cloth is wound around a breast beam. The weft is inserted with the aid of a shuttle. The mechanical principles of this loom are identical to the ones on European looms. It is to be assumed that this loom was being used in Mali – and probably also

28 — A Koma weaver sitting at his horizontal ground loom with fixed heddle. The weaver sits *beside* the loom and moves forward in the course of weaving together with the frame that holds the heddle rod (Bimba, Alantika Mountains, Northern Cameroon)

Photo Harald Widmer 1958 – (F)III 21149

29 — Mrs Grace Akpata working at her vertical loom. Benin City, Nigeria. One can see the heddle rod (below) and three shed rods above

Photo B. Gardi 30.11.1973 – (F)III 10097

30 — A Bamana weaver working at his double-heddle loom. He is weaving with cotton yarn. The historical photograph is posed. Several details are to be seen, for example, the treadles, the shuttle, the beater and the pulley. The wood required to construct the loom is to be found everywhere. The important part is the harness.

Postcard Edmond Fortier 1905 – (F)III 25355

31 — A tripod loom, Sierra Leone. This hybrid type is difficult to explain. The weaver sits *beside* the loom and moves forward in the course of weaving

Postcard W. S. Johnston & Sons (detail), around 1906 – private collection

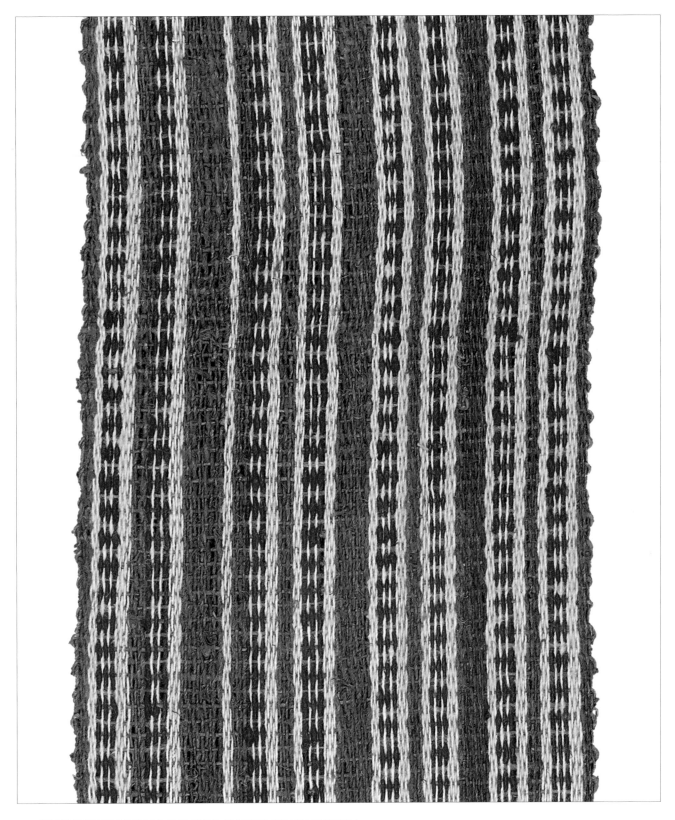

32 – SINGLE STRIP (DETAIL). DOWAYO. NORTHERN CAMEROON.
Unknown plant fibre. Strips like this were used as bride wealth and to wrap the body of a deceased person

280 × 25.5 cm – collected by René Gardi 1955 – III 14215

adjacent areas – more than a thousand years ago, at a time when a very much more simple device, the warp-weighted loom, was still being worked in Europe. This loom was actually already being used by the Ancient Greeks and by lake dwellers in the Bronze Age in Northern Europe. [52]

Type 4: The so-called tripod

This is a hybrid device, a crossover between Type 1 and Type 3, found in Liberia and Sierra Leone. The weaver actually uses a pair of heddles with treadles and a beater, but he sits or stands beside the loom. In the process of work, the weaver has to move forwards with the heddles and the supporting frame.

Most likely people in this area once also used a smaller version of the ground loom for weaving raffia. The introduction of cotton and the double-heddle loom at a later stage probably led to the development of this crossover version which is found nowhere else. [53]

In the following we shall be dealing exclusively with the double-heddle loom, in other words Type 3.

BOSER-SARIVAXÉVANIS' HYPOTHESIS AND THE FULANI

Boser-Sarivaxévanis put forward the rather daring hypothesis that the double-heddle loom had been invented in China shortly before the birth of Christ for weaving silk. According to her theory the narrow strip format was an adaptation to a nomadic way of life; the functional principle, however, remained the same. The Fulani, the hypothesis continues, being the last to leave the Sahara which was gradually running dry, introduced this nomadic loom to the Western Sahel in the course of the second half of the first millennia AD, above all to the humid area of the Niger Inland Delta in Mali and to the upper Senegal River. While still dwelling in the Sahara the pastoral Fulani had adopted the loom from neighbouring groups who were in contact with peoples in the Near East.

Admittedly, the hypothesis contains a number of ifs and buts. What the various specialists do agree on, however, is the fact that the Fulani were actually the last group to leave the drying-out Sahara and to move into the Sahel. When, where and how is a different matter. As last to arrive, and not owning the land they came to, they still live very dispersed, usually as a minority among other groups, even though in the meantime most of them have become sedentary. Especially in the Niger Inland Delta they still own many zebu and sheep herds.

Several facts clearly support the Fulani hypothesis:

– There is a breed of domestic sheep whose wool is processed which is only found along the Niger bend; otherwise it is not encountered in sub-Saharan Africa. The Fulani are the only people to breed this type of sheep. Their neighbours, the Songhay, not only adopted the sheep from the Fulani but also took in Fulani men as weavers. It follows that, next to the loom, the Fulani also introduced a specific fibre to the sub-Saharan areas. [54]

– In Fulfulde – the language spoken by the Fulani – woollen blankets are called *kaasa*. Any textile containing wool may be called *kaasa* in Fulfulde. The neighbouring Bamana have adopted the term *kaasa* to designate their cotton blankets, modifying it to *koso*. *Kaasa* is intimately linked to weaving among the Fulani, but is it not remarkable that

33 – Zarma weaver with his loom. Shafts, beater and treadles – the harness –
together with the breast beam weigh no more than two kilos. The West African
double-heddle loom was a device originally designed for mobile pastoralist
groups (Dosso, Niger)

Photo B. Gardi 7.6.1974 – (F)III 8495

34 – A Baule weaver, Côte d'Ivoire, with a pair of heddles. In the
threads' geometric middle are the heddle-eyes that control the even
and odd-numbered warp threads

Photo B. Gardi 9.9.1974 – (F)III 101445

linguists claim that the term *kaasa* is actually a loanword in Fulfulde? [55] And, is it not astonishing that two thousand years ago in the Eastern Mediterranean – when Greek was sill the common lingua franca – the term *kasson* or *kassopoioi* was used to designate a 'cloak made of coarse wool'? [56]

– *Kaasa* blankets display technical features otherwise not found in West Africa (see fig.65). [57]

This ingenious type of West African double-heddle loom is, ultimately, a model ideally adapted to a nomadic way of life. Why, in Africa, it is the men who operate this loom and not the women, as elsewhere, begs an answer. The narrow strip – a feature that has always rather irritated European observers – is actually an advantage in a nomadic way of life: the heddles with its system of treadles, the narrow and therefore light beater as well as the breast beam can be tied into a small bundle weighing no more than two kilograms. The sticks required for a frame are to be found everywhere. According to Boser-Sarivaxévanis, the Fulani loom was increasingly used for weaving cotton in almost all parts of West Africa as this material began to spread in the 9th and 10th centuries gradually replacing the previously common ground loom with fixed heddle (Type 1). In addition to this, it can be assumed that cotton weaving proliferated with the diffusion of Islam, similar to the spread of the *boubou* garment (Gardi 2000).

COMPARATIVE LINGUISTICS

A further argument in favour of Boser-Sarivaxévanis' hypothesis lies in the distribution and use of the term for heddle, the core mechanical device on every loom. In West Africa, across all languages and language families, one finds only two terms: one term – *asa* – is used for the upright loom worked by women, and therefore found mainly in Nigeria, the other – *ni-ire* or *niiri* – refers to the double-heddle loom and is encountered wherever this type of loom is used. [58]

Examples of the term *asa* describing fixed heddles on the female vertical loom: (transcription without regard to pitch)			
Yoruba	asa / ara	Ebira	aya
Nupe	esa / essa / assa	Igara	aya
Edo	aha / ayia	Igala	aya
Fon	asa	Igbo	èya / aya / afia
Northern Edo	ahiise		

The internal relationship is astonishing.

Male weavers among the Yoruba, Nupe and Hausa do not refer to the heddle on their double-heddle looms as *asa*.

Examples of the term *niire* describing the heddles on male double-heddle looms:
(transcription without regard to pitch)

Bamanan (Mali)	*niiri*	Mendi (Sierra Leone)	*nini / inini*
Baule (Côte d'Ivoire)	*nzaliè*	Mossi (Burkina Faso)	*niiri*
Bissa (Burkina Faso)	*niiri*	Nupe (Nigeria)	*niraa*
Bwa (Bwa)	*lila*	Fulani (Mali)	*niire / niiri*
Dogon (Mali)	*liiri / niili*	Serer (Senegal)	*asik*
Dyula (Burkina Faso)	*niiri*	Songhay (Mali)	*daange / dangay*
Dyula (Côte d'Ivoire)	*niiri*	Soninké (Mali)	*niiri*
Guro (Côte d'Ivoire)	*libi / liri*	Tucouleur (Senegal)	*niire*
Hausa (Nigeria)	*andiira / alliira*	Wolof (Senegal)	*mbad / bad*
Igbo	*aya*	Yoruba-Egba (Nigeria)	*omu*
Limba	*nere*	Yoruba-Oyo (Nigeria)	*omu*
Maninka (Côte d'Ivoire)	*niiri*	Zarma (Niger)	*danga*
Mano (Liberia)	*nini*		

There are divergences – namely in Yoruba and Igbo – but, overall, the list displays a very close relationship pattern within the terminological range.[59] The main point here is that two completely different terms are used for 'heddle' on the female upright loom and the male double-heddle loom respectively. As the two types of loom function on completely different principles, the differing vocabulary is a clear indication that, in the West African context, we are dealing with very distinct histories of invention and diffusion.

In the wordlists we compiled in 1973/75 a relationship pattern could only be established for the term for 'heddle' – also for 'indigo' – but not for 'whorl', 'beater' or any other part of the loom.

Let us remain with the term *niire* for a moment. As in the case of *kaasa*, the term *niire* – i.e. its stem *nir* – points beyond West Africa! In Algeria, *nîra* has been documented as the Arabic term for heddle (Golvin 1950: 114, 131), while in Yemen, also Arabic, we have the term *nirim* (Klein 1974: 229). In the region on the border between Egypt and Libya we find *nair*, and in southern Tunisia *nira* (Lamb 2005: 16, 77). Thus we have the same meaning of *nir* in West Africa as we do in North Africa. In Arabic *nir* also means 'yoke', the device for joining two animals together for ploughing, but this does not apply to Africa south of the Sahara since the yoke was not common to that region.

'Yoke' and 'heddle' – this makes sense. Both terms join together two entities. But it would be oversimplifying matters if we were to say that the Fulani loom had its 'roots in Islam'. Certainly Arabic is the language of Islam but, as we know, this religion incorporated at an early stage in time many languages, cultures, ethnic groups and minorities. Craftsmen and -women from many areas and languages became Muslim.

Moreover, the Arabic language goes back further in time than the age of Mohammed and uses many loan words that predate the time of the Prophet.

However, this simply shifts the problem of the term *niire* for heddle to the next level of complexity. Allow me to quote from a letter that the linguist and Old Testament scholar, Professor Ernst Jenni of the University of Basel, wrote to Boser-Sarivaxévanis:

The Word-stem *nir* and its Linguistic Origins

"Basel, 1 July 1982

Dear Mrs Boser

In answer to your question as to the origins of the word *nir* – 'yoke' or 'loom heddle' –
I can confirm that the term originated in the Middle East, although, I must
confess, I understand little about looms and weaving. [...] The term is first documented for Akkadian, i.e. the Semitic language of the Babylonians and Assyrians,
in the third millennium BC; from there it found its way into Sumerian spoken in
the Ur III-Period [...]"

Jenni goes on to quote various sources with the corresponding references. The letter, by the
way, is reproduced in full length in the notes at the end of the book. Summarizing, he writes:
"... what is more important for your research is the fact that, according to all leading specialists, the word *nir* was adopted into Arabic as a loan word from Aramaic, in both senses of the
term, i.e. 'yoke' and 'crossbeam of the loom'." [60]

Thus, fishing in the sea of West African linguistic terms provided a catch after all. *Nir*,
the word stem of the term for heddle, dates back to the pre-Christian era and has its origin in
one of the Semitic languages of the Ancient Middle East. This by no means proves the Fulani
hypothesis right, but at least it makes it look less speculative. Still, the equation of 'yoke' and
'heddle' really only makes sense if one takes the whole 'heddle rod' into consideration, including the frame that goes with it as found on the ground loom with fixed heddle (Type 1),
the oldest type of loom. In this case the heddle rod and the two supports resemble a yoked
team of oxen, with the warp threads representing the furrows. An apt image, easy to grasp!

But where do we stand now? Are we not ending the chapter on a note of contradiction?
Are we not applying the term *nir* which was used for the oldest type of loom – Type 1 – to a
loom that was invented only a few thousand years later – Type 3 – and which is fitted out
with a differently constructed heddles? Yes, we actually are. Some contradictions simply remain standing.

In the end, all we have been able to show is that, in West Africa, we have a very common
and widely distributed term that is associated with a clearly defined technical device. Both –
term and device – are very old and reach back to pre-Islamic times. The term has Semitic
roots and has its origin – together with the 'object' itself – in the Ancient Middle East. One
can only assume that the term *nir* was later also applied to the next generation of looms – the
double-heddle loom.

At least these findings invalidate other, frequently presented theories – 'the trans-Saha-
ra trade', 'Islam', the 'Berbers of Morocco'. All these forces might have played a part in the
diffusion of certain patterns or design elements, but not compellingly so. There are other
approaches, other ways of tackling the problem.

Possibly one could make similar comparisons with the Yoruba-term *asa*. What the
wordlists actually do show is that – in conjunction with other factors – the Fulani certainly
played an important role in the diffusion of weaving in West Africa.

What, in the end, is the purpose of writing a chapter that leaves so many matters unan-
swered? This is a legitimate question. I think we have been able to show that an interconnec-
tion does or at least did exist, which means that we are treading on the ground of verifiable
facts. Maybe the above findings will encourage someone to compile a systematic word list
containing the terms for 'heddle' and 'heddle rod', including all the smaller devices used for
weaving raffia along the Guinea coast and in Central Africa.

35 – Mrs Mercy Ebun Balogun working on her vertical loom. The fixed heddle rod is about in the middle of the picture. Below are the pattern heddles with which the patterns seen at the bottom and at the top are created (Okpe near Igara, Nigeria)

Photo B. Gardi 1.1.1974 – (F)III 100623

WEAVE STRIPS

Bernhard Gardi

56

European authors have often described the double-heddle loom as 'archaic' or 'primitive', just because – unlike in Europe – the strips need sewing together before the cloth can be said to be finished. These travellers – all men – usually knew very little about textiles as against the first Portuguese to visit the Congo more than five hundred years ago who left behind very competent reports on the textiles found there. In this context it should not be forgotten that in pre-industrial Europe spinning and weaving were common in nearly all households, while to later travellers, having grown up in the industrial age, weaving in the narrow strip format implied inferior technology and quality.

In actual fact, the West African double-heddle loom is the most developed and sophisticated, pre-industrial loom ever to be invented! The mechanical principles are the same as on the looms used in European.

From a technical point of view, having to sew together the strips is a disadvantage. It is time- and work-intensive and if the seam is not sewn neatly, the cloth easily tears. But there are advantages as well. Thus, for example, a damaged cloth is easy to mend: you simply remove the damaged strip and you still have a viable cloth, albeit a little smaller – or the damaged strip can be replaced by a new one. A further advantage is that patterns are possible which could not be produced in a broad weave format. For example, a blanket with a chequerboard pattern with identical front and reverse sides cannot be manufactured in one piece (fig. 51).

In the course of the last few decades the strips have become broader on average. Time is money: the broader the strip, the less strips are required for a wrap cloth, or 'pagne', which means weaving takes less time. But one should be careful when making generalizations; as we know from the Tellem textile complex strips measuring 20 centimetres were being woven already eight hundred years ago.

One should also make a distinction between large cloths and blankets for covering more or less the entire body, and the smaller wrap cloths, or 'pagnes'. In general, blankets have wider strips, while a statistical survey would probably show that the strips produced in the Sahel are wider than the ones manufactured further south.

The narrow strip format, found at all times in history, probably has something to do with prestige and social status as well, true to the motto, the narrower the strip, the greater the work input, the higher the price and, therefore, the more prestige for the man or woman wearing it.

Across West Africa one frequently encounters the same pattern formation in different settings, for example, four blue warp threads followed by two white ones, with the same sequence in the weft. Very fine chequers are often likened to the plumage of the guinea fowl in the respective language. Often – usually by order of the woman patron who has spun the yarn and hired the craftsman – the weaver uses two shades of blue for the yarn. This automatically enhances visual impact and makes even the basic pattern look really elegant.

Strips with alternating blue and white stripes often contain different shades of blue. One of the longitudinal edges is woven white because this is the side where the seam will be. When the strips are joined together the white stripe is more or less hidden.

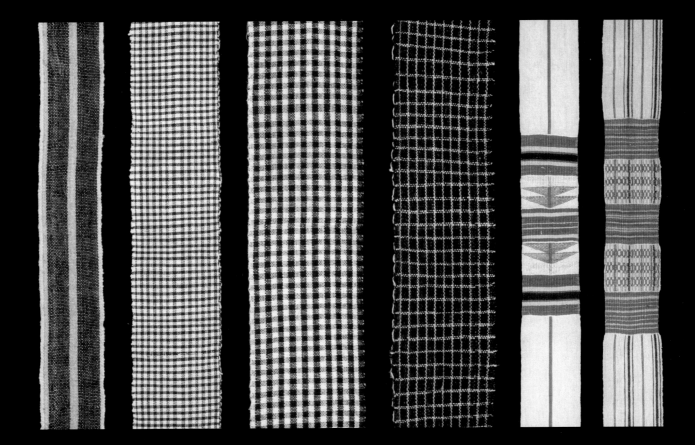

36 – EXAMPLES OF SINGLE STRIPS. FROM LEFT TO RIGHT:
Width 7.5 cm. Mali, purchased in Bankass. The two brown warp stripes are made of wild silk; 10.5 cm. Mali, purchased in San; 13 cm. Mali, purchased in Téné near San; 12 cm. Côte d'Ivoire, purchased in Bouaflé; 6 cm. Ghana, before 1888; 6 cm. Ghana, before 1900

Collected by B. Gardi 1979 - III 21645; coll. by Boser/Gardi 1974 - III 20830; coll. by Boser/Gardi 1974 - III 20835; coll. by Boser/Gardi 1974 - III 20826; Basler Mission Collection in the MKB - III 23353; Basler Mission Collection in the MKB - III 23362

OLDEST ARCHAEOLOGICAL EVIDENCE OF WEAVING IN WEST AFRICA

Annette Schmidt, Rogier M. A. Bedaux

The question as to how long people have been weaving in West Africa is not easy to answer. Usually textiles decay in the ground, and so do looms as they are made almost completely out of perishable materials. Nevertheless, archaeology is able to provide a few answers because spindle whorls, pollen and carbonized cotton seeds have survived and serve as indirect evidence of the early existence of weaving.

There are two theories dealing with the import of textile garments to West Africa.

The first is based on Arabic sources and maintains that in the old Ghana Empire people went either completely naked or wore animal skins (Levtzion 1973: 179). These sources suggest that the wearing of textiles only commenced after the decline of the Ghana Empire in the 11th century and that the practice must be seen in connection with the introduction of Islam to the region. Levtzion argues that the spread of Islam in the western Sudan established a market which not only spurred the import of cloths from the north, but also stimulated local production. According to this theory, weaving commenced in West Africa in the 11th century.

The other theory dates back to Mauny (1961: 59, 245). This author believes that weaving in West Africa predates Islam and can be traced back to contacts established through the trans-Saharan trade. Thus, according to this theory, weaving in western Sudan reaches back beyond the 11th century.

Mauny's theory is corroborated by the textile fragments from the 11th to 12th centuries found in the area of the Tellem, definitely a non-Muslim people. In addition, there is sufficient evidence to prove the existence of the spindle whorl in the western Sudan around AD 800.

Numerous whorls were discovered during excavations in the West African savannah, and the fact that many of them were embedded in a sound archaeological context seems to confirm Mauny's theory. [61] The oldest spindle whorls ever to be found in West Africa come from the well-documented archaeological excavations in Djenné-Djeno and Dia. Both sites are located in the southern part of the Niger Inland Delta in Mali. Some of the whorls found there definitely predate AD 1100; interestingly enough they are undecorated, which seems to be typical of spindle whorls for the period between AD 800 and 1100. It was only after the 11th century that the people began embellishing their whorls. At the two excavation sites in Dia (Bedaux et al. 2005) 50 spindle whorls were found in total. Most of them are black; the decorated ones display

incised, carved or stamped patterns, the notches have white in-fills. They are very small, measuring between 1.8 and 4.5 centimetres. Their size and weight indicate that they were used for spinning cotton, but not for wool. Cotton fibres are short and fragile, and when heavy whorls are used the thread tends to tear (Barber 1991: 33, 52). Thus, we have good reason to believe that these small and light whorls were used for spinning cotton, but not any other kinds of fibre.

Arabic sources mention the cultivation of cotton in the southern part of the Niger Inland Delta for the Middle Ages (Robert-Chaleix 1983: 501). Lab tests on the carbonized cotton seeds found in Dia-Mara and Dia-Shoma show that cotton was being cultivated there very much earlier than the written sources claim, that is, already in the archaeological horizon I (800 BC to AD 1). Recent research has shown that the earliest evidence for the cultivation of cotton predates the oldest spindle whorls by 1,500 years. Very much later, in archaeological horizon IV (AD 1000–1600), a tremendous increase of cotton seeds was noted (Murray 2005), indicating a rapid expansion of cotton cultivation from the 11th century onwards. Moreover, the quantity of cotton seeds discovered suggests that cotton was not only cultivated for local manufacture.

These short remarks show two things: cotton spinning was common to Mali prior to the 11th century, thus predating Islam in the area, but the golden age of weaving only began after the advent of Islam in the 11th century. By this time, cotton had been around for approximately 2,000 years.

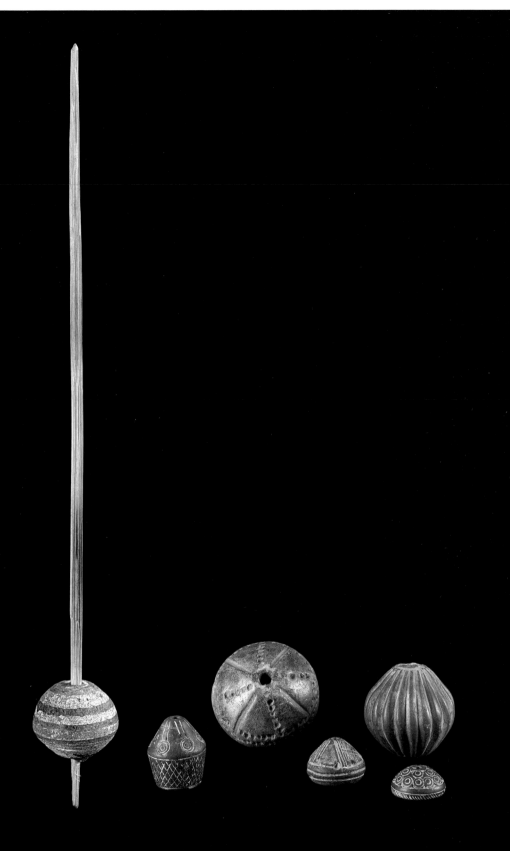

37 — LEFT: **SPINDLE FOR SPINNING COTTON YARN. ISEYIN, YORUBA.**
Spinning wool requires larger and heavier weights

RIGHT: **ARCHAEOLOGICAL WHORLS. MALI**

From left to right: collected by Boser/Gardi 1974 – III 20905 / III 20942, 20940, 20971, 24695, 20953.
Collected by Boser/Gardi 1974, Youvarou, and B. Gardi 1987, Bamako

— 38 —

SUSPENDED *ARKILLA KERKA*.

In a square room in a rectangular-built house an alcove has been constructed, the bedroom of the newly-wed couple. What we see here is the bed hidden behind a suspended blanket (*arkilla*) which serves as a mosquito net (N'Gouma in the Guimballa region, Mali)

Photo B. Gardi 1982

MALI

Weaving with Wool and Cotton
Bernhard Gardi

Mali is a land of transitions, a cultural hub between North Africa and the Guinea coast, with old trade routes running northwards from Tombouctou to Morocco, and to Ghana, Guinea and Sierra Leone in the south and west respectively. The town of Kong in Côte d'Ivoire played an important part in this network.

Soft cotton fabrics were extremely popular among the people on the Guinea coast, as their own raffia cloth tended to be rather coarse; and Mali was an exporting country. Rare goods worth transporting were carted – on the heads of carriers and by donkeys – down to the Guinea coast where they were traded in for cola nuts and other items. These valuable and rare goods – salt, glass beads, gold and indigo – also included textiles which played an important role, not only cotton but, interestingly enough, also woollen fabrics.

Cotton textiles look different from woollen fabrics; here I will be dealing with both traditions. Wool comes from the north of Mali, from the Fulani and Songhay, while cotton is typical for the central part of the country, the home of various Mande-speaking peoples.

Today it is hard to imagine how deeply embedded weaving in Mali used to be in earlier days. Just about every woman knew how to spin yarn, and among the Mande groups most of the farmers were also weavers, time permitting. Woven strips of ecru cotton equalled money. Folded by the cubit or in the form of large rolls, cloth was transported over long distances. Woven strips were items of exchange, trade and sale.

In Mali weaving was still very common up to the 1990s, even in towns. In the rural hinterland yarn was spun by hand, in the towns the weavers used *bolooti* – industrially spun yarn (from the French 'la pelote', meaning a ball of yarn). After the overthrow of dictator Moussa Traoré (1991) the country went through a period of economic growth and democratization creating new styles of living. By and by hand-woven textiles lost their significance, and wool weaving, unique to Mali, was practically given up completely.

WOOL
The wool sheep is common to the area along the Niger River from Diafarabé to Tillabéry (Republic Niger).

It may sound surprising that woollen fabrics were in demand in a sub-tropical region, but they actually played a very important role for the people living in reach of the Saharan climate, since temperatures vary strongly, with a cold wind blowing from the north-east in the cooler months, and night temperatures falling close to freezing point in January. Woollen textiles also provide better protection against mosquitoes than cotton fabrics do. A further advantage of wool is that it contains proteins, which makes dyeing a lot easier. While cotton is almost exclusively dyed with indigo, woollen fabrics were dyed with black, yellow and red pigments, apart from indigo.

One can distinguish between two broad categories of woollen textiles that look distinctly different: on the one hand the woollen *kaasa* blankets, and, on the other, the *arkilla* blankets, some of which reach a length of over five metres.

Especially the *kaasa* blankets were extremely popular among all groups in the area, and they were in great demand. They were never made of camel hair – although this is what many vendors tell the tourists – and they were not produced in Tombouctou, but in the many small villages between Diafarabé and Lake Debo, in other words, in the area around Mopti.

In the old trade between Mali and present-day Ghana woollen blankets played an important role. In the Asante kingdom they were called *nsa*. Still today one finds important power insignia such as war horns and drums sewn in to Malian woollen textiles, and the Asante kings who on the occasion of religious festivals are carried in palanquins like to have their litters padded with *kaasa* and *arkilla* blankets. The Asante believe that woollen textiles from Mali are imbued with special power. [62]

THE WEAVERS *MAABUUBE* (SING. *MAABO*)

The Fulani weavers south of the Niger bend form a highly specialized artisan group. Apart from being weavers, the *maabuube* are also griots, that is, they are the local historians, keepers of tradition, musicians and mediators. In the Niger Inland Delta of pre-colonial days every aristocratic Fulani family is said to have been linked with a *maabo* family. The relationship was reciprocal. The *maabuube* women are potters. Fulani and *maabuube* do not intermarry. In Fulani society, the status of the *maabuube* is comparable to that of the blacksmiths (*numu*) among the Manding whose wives are also potters. Just as in the old days the Manding farmers required iron to work their fields, the pastoral Fulani were dependent on woollen blankets to protect them against the cold and the mosquitoes. Thus, similar to the *numu*, the *maabuube* enjoyed high status.

THE MANUFACTURE OF *KAASA* BLANKETS

The conditions of production are worth taking a look at. Spinning yarn and dyeing was women's work, weaving and joining the finished strips were done by the men. It was fascinating to watch the weavers throwing their shuttles to and fro with stupendous skill and confidence, and to see how they measured out each pattern which had to tally with the adjoining weave strip with the help of a piece of string. A small lance-shaped piece of wood (*alluwal*) was used to separate and count the warp threads needed to create a pattern. In earlier days up to six thousand metres of yarn were required for a top-quality *kaasa* blanket; in the year 2000 the amount was down to three thousand metres. This meant that the blankets were lighter and thinner but they provided less warmth and wore out more quickly. [63]

In the 1970s Fulani weavers still used to move from village to village in search of work in order to earn enough money to start a family, or to pay their taxes. They were hired by women who had sufficient spun yarn at hand.

The yarn needed for the pattern weaves had to be dyed. Red was produced from the flowers of a bush (*Hibiscus sabdariffa*) that was grown outside the village, or from the stems of a certain type of millet (*Sorghum caudatum, var. colorans Snowden*); yellow was extracted from the spores of a mushroom (of the phylum *Basidiomycetes*); black from a mixture of vegetable and mud pigments. [64] Indigo blue is never found on *kaasa* blankets.

Patron and weaver were bound by an agreement: the weaver was contracted to weave six strips in a pre-arranged design; in return the woman offered him a place to sleep, gave him a small present each morning (five cigarettes, two cola nuts) and cooked two meals a day for him, one in the morning, one at lunchtime, but no evening meal since the weaver did not work at night.

When he was finished, the woman paid him a fixed amount, approximately a quarter of the blanket's sales value. This does not sound like very much but one should not forget that the weaver received two meals a day (not a matter of course to all people in Mali) and, above all, that he did not produce the cloth all by himself. In fact, the weaver's work equalled roughly a quarter of the total work input. By far the most work hours went in to spinning the yarn, which is why the finished product belonged to the woman patron.

The weaver delivered the rolled strips to the patron. A least ten more hours of work were needed to finish the cloth; this comprised the following steps: sewing together the strips including a separate, specially woven band which was inserted down the middle; twisting together the projecting warp threads; attaching decorative tassels; attaching a plaited supportive band to each long side of the cloth. Only now the *kaasa* was really finished. [65] These finishing touches, applied nowhere else in West Africa, made *kaasa* blankets unique textiles. It also explains why a proper *kaasa* could only be produced in a functioning rural Fulani milieu. Each blanket was the product of a collaboration between men and women from different social classes that did not intermarry.

DIFFERENT *KAASA* TYPES

There are various types of *kaasa* blankets. [66] One of the differentiating criteria is the dominating ground colour. A plain white blanket, i.e. with no patterns, is called *kaasa daneewa* (*kaasa* 'white'). The term for a blanket dyed black is *kaasa baleewa*. If the yarn is naturally dark-brown or blackish it is called *kaasa Allah duuri* ('God given').

Otherwise blankets are named according to the dominant pattern. *Kaasa ndaakaka* is the oldest known type of *kaasa*. It has just one rust-coloured weft band running across the entire width (fig. 43), and not two. Two other old types are *kaasa njowaaka* (with large diamond-shaped patterns *jowal*, pl. *jowe*) and *kaasa lanndaaka* (the most refined of all *kaasa* blankets).

Later creations include *kaasa Samba lobo* ('the beautiful Samba'), *kaasa maliiwa* (since 1960, the year of independence) and *kaasa munnyuureewa* (in the style of the cotton blanket *munnyuure*).

The *sakkalaare* blanket is mainly of cotton, but the patterns are made of wool. It too appeared for the first time around 1960; it consists of seven strips. [67]

No matter what a *kaasa* or its design are called, the diamond-shaped patterns *jowal* always include small, pea-like motifs called *cukke* consisting of yarn strands inserted into the fabric by hand. During the process of weaving, by the way, the weaver faces the reverse side of the fabric, the same as when producing the large *arkilla* blankets. Protruding weft threads are carefully clipped so that the reverse side also looks tidy.

Every *kaasa* and each weft float pattern (*cubbe*) is symmetrical in design; the weft float pattern itself consists of individual elements such as triangles, diamonds or double lines (finer lines are called *nyaawe*, thicker ones *coppe*), allowing for an almost endless combination of patterns.

The classic *lanndal* motif, which gave the *kaasa lanndaaka* its name, is said to show the reflection of a mosque in the water.

Wool came in different qualities. A wealthy family was in a position to order a *kaasa 'petit mouton'* which required for the yarn the wool of 20 to 30 or even more lambs. The wool of fully-grown sheep was coarser and tended to be rather dirty, making the blanket scratchy, at least when new. The village of Dialloubé was legendary for the best and most beautiful *kaasa* blankets.

ARKILLA

Arkilla blankets occasionally measured up to six metres; when being produced for an upcoming wedding they were woven under special ritual conditions. In their function as bed curtains (fig. 38) they radiated pure luxury. Until roughly 20 years ago they were still woven in northern Mali, on the fringe of the Sahara, between Lake Faguibine in the west and Gao in the east, in other words, in a territory roughly five times the size of Switzerland. However, in Tombouctou, *arkilla* blankets were of no significance. Apart from cotton the blankets also contained wool. *Arkilla* blankets served as the chief symbol of marriage and were the property of the wife. *Arkilla* means 'mosquito net'. [68]

Weavers skilled in making *arkilla* blankets enjoyed high reputation. Many of them came from Ata, an unspectacular place near Tonka. They were called by their patronyms Saré, Sango or Daou.

ARKILLA KERKA

Let us take a look at the marriage blanket *arkilla kerka*, the best known and most frequent type of *arkilla* (see also Gardi & Seydou 1989).

Due to the fact that it was for a wedding, weaving had to be done very diligently, in other words, manufacture was time- and work-intensive. First the yarn had to be spun and, considering the amount required – five to seven kilos – the job took several women a few months to complete. Then a certain quantity of the yarn had to be dyed; especially the red had to be beautiful and vibrant. As against *kaasa* blankets, where black yarn was used, a *kerka* required indigo-blue. [69] Then the search for a good *maabo* weaver began. Not every weaver had the skill required for a *kerka*, and possibly the only suitable one lived miles away. It was up to the bride's father to work out the details of the arrangement, after which the weaver, together with his whole family, came to live in the compound of the bride's family for the period of weaving (30 to 60 days), at the latter's expense. If the *maabo* owned a horse, he brought it with him, which meant that the animal had to be fed too. Only the best meals were good enough, cooked with ample milk and butter. The *maabo*'s wife was spared work in the kitchen. The patron went to great lengths to keep the weaver content so that he could concentrate on the weaving and so that, later, he would tell around how well he had been treated by the bride's family. The patron also made sure that everybody got to know how much he had paid the *maabo*; thus the news about the upcoming wedding spread automatically.

Back in 1974, the *maabo* Sambalday Daou from Niafounké told me what he had been given two years before for an assignment: 100 kilos of rice, a goat and the equivalent of 150 Swiss francs. As an incentive, and in the hope of getting an especially beautiful blanket, the patron also gave him a small present in money after completion of a specific pattern. Each morning he also received two cola nuts and a beer-bottle filled with butter. As Sambalday was working in his home-compound two meals were delivered to him every day.

39 – Woman holding a finished roll of cloth consisting of ten decorated strips for a simple *arkilla jenngo* (M'Bouna on Lake Faguibine)

Photo B. Gardi, January 1980 – 45/28

40 – The tent of a Tuareg chief roughly 150 km north of Gao (near Agamor, Mali). Several *arkilla jenngo* blankets are to be seen

Photo Harald Widmer, January 1952 – (F)III 18570

Expenses were not high; the great drought that ravished the area in the 1970s had already set in. In better years, 40 to 60 sheep were the average investment that went into the manufacture of *kerka*, spinning the yarn not included.

In pre-colonial days, clients had usually ordered two *kerka* at a time, the second blanket being of lower quality. The latter was then either given to a poor Fulani family who could not afford to produce a blanket of its own, or sold to Ghana (fig. 68).

GOUNDAM

Among certain groups living in the far north of Mali there was great demand for certain types of *arkilla*; they constituted an important aspect of the people's identity.

The three most common *arkilla* blankets – *kerka*, *munnga* and *jenngo* – came from the Cercle de Goundam, an area the size of Switzerland. And it was here that, in the 1950s, modern weaving began with colourful, machine-spun cotton yarn. Ungrudgingly the *maabuube* wool weavers acknowledge that it was not they who had launched this innovation, but the *malleebe*, in other words, weavers who did not belong to the *maabuube* 'caste' and whose fathers had probably still been serfs to Fulani and Songhay masters. The *maabuube* claim that the *maalleebe* learnt weaving from them. Again it was *malleebe* weavers who, relying on their knowledge of wool weaving from the region around Gao, invented the modern Zarma blankets in the Niamey area (Niger) where some of them moved to in the 1940s.

In 1980 there was wide consent on one matter in the Mopti area: everyone agreed that modern weaving in Mali had commenced in the Goundam region.

Although the large prestige blankets which were often given away as presents at weddings in fact contain all the techniques and pattern elements found on the other *arkilla* blankets, the adaptation of new designs and colours had practically created a new type of blanket. The great tradition of woollen marriage blankets – which today has almost disappeared – actually stands at the beginning of modern weaving in the Sahel, which is itself now gradually dying out. I have more to say about the modern cotton blankets below.

COTTON

European-style clothes – 'les friperies' – have flooded the entire African continent. Industrial textiles such as Wax, Fancy or bazin, produced in distant countries such as China, Germany, the Netherlands, Czech Republic and, more recently, Côte d'Ivoire, clearly dominate the scene today. In Mali, COMATEX (Compagnie Malienne de Textiles, since 1967) and ITEMA (Industrie des Textiles du Mali, since 1970) produce printed cloths (Traoré 1999). Cotton weaving has always been practiced in Mali – but not everywhere. Neither the Tuareg nor the Bwa and Bobo were into weaving, the Samogo probably only a little. Where weaving was practiced, white, plain strips were the norm. Textiles were embellished using indigo-resist dye methods or mud dyes, *bogolan*, or else the entire cloth was dyed brown or yellow. [70]

But in the great majority of the hundreds of villages, weaving meant producing white or blue-and-white-striped strips of cotton without weft patterns.

With regard to cotton textiles one has to distinguish between two kinds: on the one hand 'pagnes', or wrap cloths, on the other, various kinds of blankets.

'PAGNES'

Next to blue and white warp stripes, 'pagnes' were often decorated with very small chequer patterns – for example, by having four blue warp threads following four white ones, with

41 – THE OLD *MAABO* KOLOUROU SARÉ AT WORK.
He is weaving a *kaasa*. In place of a pulley, *kaasa* weavers use two plates of soft wood
(*tonngi*), connected by a hardwood stick. The strings that connect the heddles run
over this stick. Through the torsion the stick gradually eats into the soft wood, creating
a special sound: the loom sings. The weaver is sitting very low, operating the treadles
with outstretched legs. During weaving he is facing the reverse side of the fabric;
he must think of the front of the textile in mirror-image (Sindégué Ouro Boulo, Mali)

Photo B. Gardi 1979 – 37/22

the same sequence in the weft. This created many possible combinations, especially if the weaver was using two yarn sets in different shades of blue. Such cloths are called *buguni*. Fine chequer patterns in many variations are found on cloths reaching as far as Nigeria; they were also found in large numbers on the Tellem textile fragments found in Mali. This implies that we are dealing with a very old pattern. These 'pagnes' are manufactured in plain weave, the basic weaving technique; when a few wefts of red yarn are woven in, the cloths look even more splendid.

We found the most beautiful 'pagnes' along the Niger-Bani river system – here most of the weavers were Maraka or Fulani – but also in the Seno Mango, the sandy plain that reaches as far as Burkina Faso; here the weavers were Dafing people. In this area, occasionally warp stripes of wild silk were incorporated. [71]

As regards the 'pagnes' there is, however, one exception: this is the cloth called *baayon* (fig. 60). In the 1970s it was worn as festive dress by many women in all larger villages and towns in Mali. The narrow strips measuring five to seven centimetres as well as the finely woven patterns, offset against the background by the colour contrast, lent this cloth great elegance.

It is the only 'pagne' in Mali that I know of with supplementary weft float patterns. It is possible that in earlier days this cloth consisted of dark and light-coloured strips only, but by 1949 supplementary weft float patterns had been added (Meyerowitz 1949: fig. 26). Interestingly, the *baayon* 'pagnes' disappeared in the 1990s. They were simply no longer made! But then they reappeared, simply in different form: with woven strips in light colour, and dark strips consisting of coloured damask (bazin) in vibrant colours. But the textile had its disadvantages too because the seams appear to have been susceptible to tear, with the result that, today, the *baayon* 'pagne' is back to what it looked like fifty years ago: made of narrow woven strips with beautiful supplementary weft float patterns. [72]

BLANKETS

The generic term for cotton blanket is *welimaare* among the Fulani, and *koso* among the Bamana. These light blankets were not only used for sleeping, they were also worn over the shoulder and served various other functions too, and actually belonged to the standard accessory of a man dressed in a boubou. Figures 52 to 59 show variations of light cotton blankets called *sagiire*.

The travel literature of the late 19th century often mentions blankets from Ségou called *dampe*; these were traded as far as the Guinea coast. However, they were not, or at least hardly ever, produced in Ségou itself, but further north in the region around Banamba, Nyamina and Sansanding which was inhabited by Bamana and Soninke. Ségou was simply the main trading place for these blankets. [73] Today they are known under the Bamana term *koso walani* or *koso damye*. Among the Fulani, who also produce them, they are called *sudumaare walaniyeeri*.

Their design consists of a chequer pattern of dark indigo-blue and ecru, or a mix of chequer patterns and weft bands. They too are manufactured in plain weave. Occasionally they display small weft float patterns.

The tightly woven and rather heavy Banamba blankets strike the eye by their modern elegance. Like the blankets called *munnuyuure* – see Story 4 – the *dampe* blankets were also produced for export (fig. 51).

42 – View of a bedroom. The ceiling and walls have been white-washed with lime.
A colourful *tapi* blanket decorates the wall. The bedcover is embroidered (Niafounké, Mali)

Photo B. Gardi 31.10.1974 – (F)III 101876

INNOVATIONS

Let us return briefly to the innovations of the 1950s. It is interesting to see how new types of blankets evolved from the large plain-coloured *arkilla*; with their jazzy colours they looked completely different, although they were still woven in the old technique. The first new creations were called *tapi*, from the French word 'tapis' meaning carpet (fig. 42). The makers adopted from the *arkilla jenngo* the chequer pattern and the strip width, but changed the colours. The width of the strips matched the side length of each square and because the strips were sewn together, the blankets looked the same on both sides. This thread is followed up in Story 15.

Independence in 1960 brought on many innovations. There was a spirit of optimism everywhere, and the people were looking forward to a bright future. In 1970, the government organized the first *Biennale Artistique et Culturelle* with the aim of promoting the arts in general, and weaving in particular. Competitions between the regions were staged, and prizes were awarded. One of the most prestigious prizes was the one for weaving.

Today, weaving in Mali has lost much of its significance although the capital Bamako still ranks as an innovative textile centre, and the fashion business provides jobs for thousands of people. The focus is on synthetic dyes for damask textiles (bazin), the export of these textiles and the haute couture sector.

43 – *KAASA NDAAKAKA*. FULANI. MALI. PURCHASED IN GHANA IN 1913.
Rust-coloured weft bar without diamond-shaped motifs at the top end. No patterns on the main surface. Small *biccircgal* motifs. There is no *bidinol* in the middle and no protective bands down both lengths. Only plain white *kaasa* (which actually do exist) have a more simple design

215 × 130 cm – collected by Dr. med. Rudolf Fisch, mission doctor. Purchased 1913 – III 4206

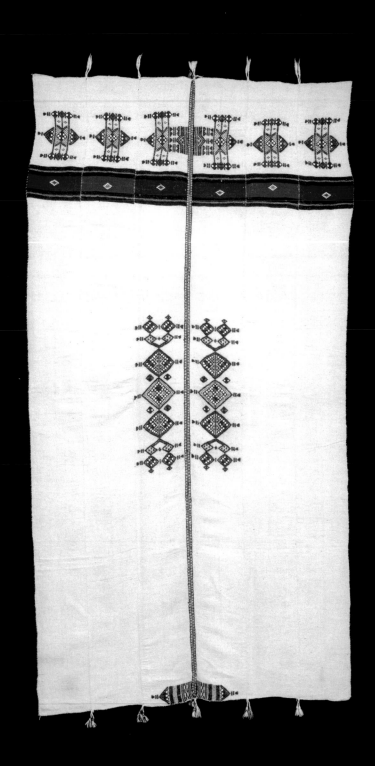

44 – *KAASA NJOWAAKA* FROM DIALLOUBÉ. FULANI. MALI

238×126 cm – collected by B. Gardi 1982 – III 22166

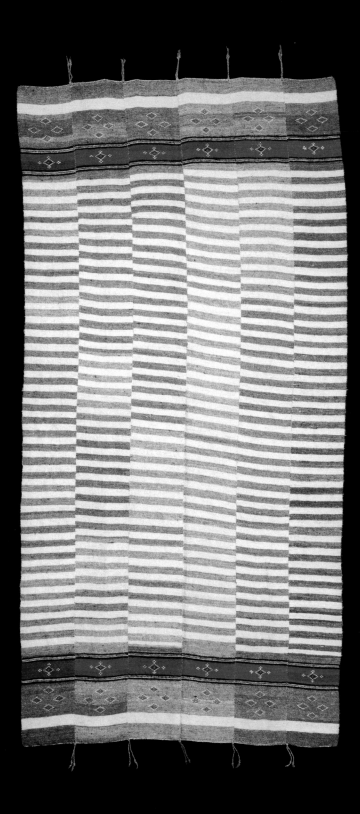

45 – *KAASA MBUNAAWA*. FULANI. MALI.
The idea of having weft bars in the central section is an innovation
of the 1980s inspired by the cotton blankets from the area around
Banamba. Purchased in Bamako

260 × 135 cm – collected by B. Gardi 1987 – III 24918

46 – *KAASA ALLAH DUURI*. FULANI. MALI.
Used blanket. Cotton warp. The rather irregular arrangement
of some of the diamond motifs (bottom left) is due to a mishap
on the part of the weaver

244×132 cm – purchased by Kolado Cissé, Bamako 1991 – III 25951

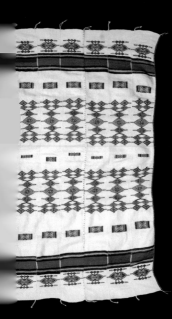

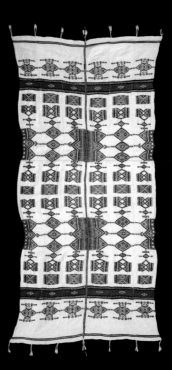

EN BLANKET *KAASA NJOWAAKA*. FULANI. MALI.
f purchase the blanket was new, which is why
s rumples. It has never been washed. It is a *kaasa*
'; the yarn was spun from the wool of young
 cyadugol embroidery in the two russet weft bars.
r in the middle by coarse stitches and not by a
bidinol)

llected by Boser/Gardi 1974 – III 20467

48 – WOOLLEN BLANKET *KAASA LANNDAAKA*.
FULANI. MALI.
Eight *lanndal* motifs ('mosque') in total. The wool of
young lambs has been used which is why the blanket
looks fleecy. Purchased in Youvarou

260 × 122 cm – collected by Boser/Gardi 1974 – III 20468

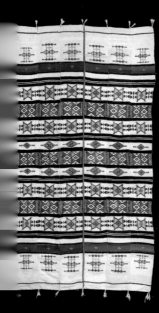

EN BLANKET *KAASA MALIIWA*. FULANI. MALI.
s unfinished: the two protective bands *sembiyawol*
n both lengths. Produced in the Guimballa
ased on the market in Ambiri Abe on Lake Debo

llected by Boser/Gardi 1974 – III 20464

50 – *SAKKALAARE*. FULANI. MALI.
Hand-spun cotton and wool yarn. *Sakkalaare* blankets
always have seven strips – and not six like the *kaasa*
blankets. Purchased in Bobo Dioulasso

244 × 144 cm – collected by Boser/Gardi 1974 – III 20471

51 – COTTON BLANKET *DAMPE* OR *DAMIYE*. BAMANA/SONINKE. MALI. BEFORE 1862.
Thick fabric. Hand-spun cotton. In the records of the Basler Mission noted as 'cotton cloth from Yoruba land'. Probably the blanket was purchased in Badagry, west of Lagos, where other items of the collection are from too. Ten strips are left; there must have been more at some point in time. Today these blankets go by the name of *damiye* (from French 'damier', chequerboard pattern)

206 × 84 cm. 10 strips, each 8.5 cm wide – Basler Mission Collection in the MKB – III 23337

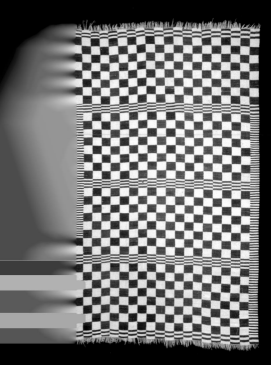

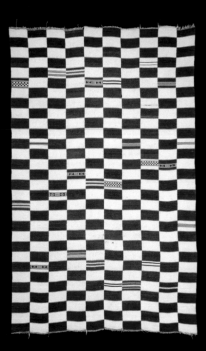

**COTTON BLANKET *DAMPE* OR *DAMIYE*.
ANI. MALI.**
Fulani call these blankets *koso walani*. Washed-
Hand-spun cotton yarn. Purchased on the
ket in Youvarou

150 cm. 20 strips, each 7 cm wide – collected by
r/Gardi 1974 – III 20423

**53 – COTTON BLANKET *DAMPE* OR *DAMIYE*.
BAMANA/SONINKE. MALI.**
The Fulani call these blankets *koso walani*. Washed-
out. Hand-spun cotton yarn. Single weft float patterns.
Purchased in San

239 × 150 cm. 10 strips, each 15 cm wide – collected by
Boser/Gardi 1974 – III 20424

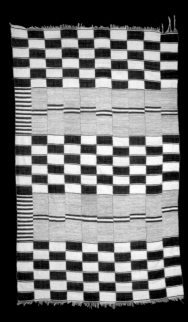

– LIGHT COTTON BLANKET *SAAGI*.
chased on the market in Dori, Burkina Faso

114 cm. 7 strips, each 15.5 cm wide – collected by
er/Gardi 1974 – III 20505

55 – LIGHT COTTON BLANKET *KOSO WELIMAARE*.
Purchased on the market in Attara, Mali

224 × 139 cm. 10 strips, each 14 cm wide – collected by
Boser/Gardi 1974 – III 20500

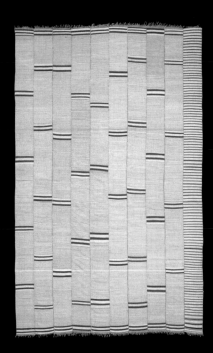

56 – LIGHT COTTON BLANKET *SAAGI*.
Purchased on the market in San, Mali

244 × 132 cm. 10 strips, each 13 cm wide – collected by
Boser/Gardi 1974 – III 20502

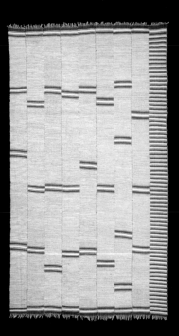

57 – LIGHT COTTON BLANKET *SAAGI*.
Produced in Fatoma near Mopti, Mali

221 × 125 cm. 9 strips, each 14 cm wide – collected
Boser/Gardi 1974 – III 20495

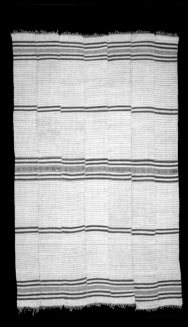

58 – LIGHT COTTON BLANKET *SAAGI*.
Purchased on the market in Dori, Burkina Faso

191 × 120 cm. 7 strips, each 17 cm wide – collected by
Boser/Gardi 1974 – III 20501

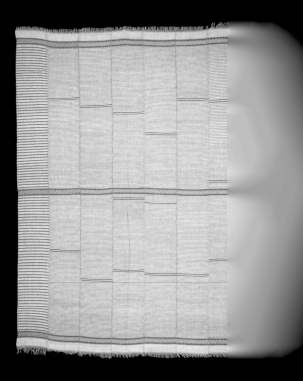

59 – LIGHT COTTON BLANKET *SAAGI*.
Purchased on the market in Ségou, Mali

226 × 158 cm. 7 strips, each 22 cm wide – collected
Boser/Gardi 1974 – III 20503

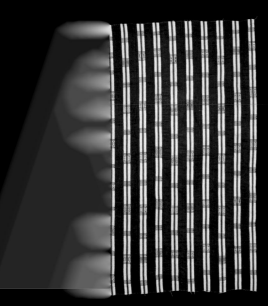

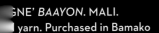

'GNE' *BAAYON*. MALI.

yarn. Purchased in Bamako

m. 10 strips, each 5 cm wide, and 10 strips,
wide – coll. by Boser/Gardi 1974 – III 20547

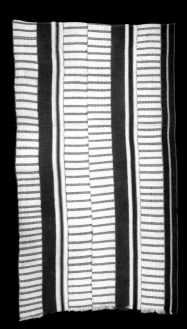

61 – 'PAGNE' *TUMU TUMU*. BAMANA/SONINKE. MALI.
Small 'pagnes' like this are typical for the San and Djenné
regions where they are worn by unmarried girls. The
Bamana name ('little worm, little worm') derives from the
simple pattern. Produced in Konani near Banamba, Mali

159 × 90 cm. 9 strips, each between 6.5 und 13.5 cm wide – coll. by
Boser/Gardi 1974 – III 20610

'GNE' CALLED *KOSO WALANI* BY SOME,
BY OTHERS.
ed in San. Mali. Industrial yarn

m. 20 strips, each 5 cm wide – coll. by Boser/Gardi 1974 – III 20447

63 – *KOSO WALANI* **BLANKET OF INDUSTRIAL COTTON YARN. FULANI/SONGHAY. MALI.**
It is evident that the blanket has never been washed. All the motifs also feature on the *arkilla kerka*
marriage blankets. Purchased in Mopti

245×150 cm. 15 strips, each 10 cm wide – collected by Boser/Gardi 1974 – III 20433

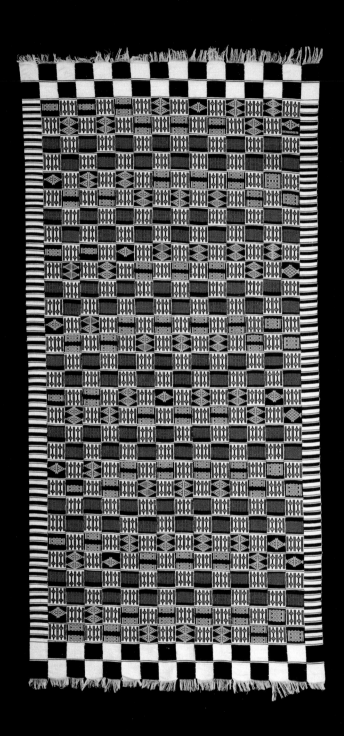

64 – *KOSO WALANI* BLANKET OF INDUSTRIAL COTTON YARN. FULANI. MALI.
Purchased from the producer, the master weaver Hammadoun Daou in Niafounké

235×108 cm. 16 strips, each 7 cm wide – collected by Boser/Gardi 1974 – III 20448

KAASA BLANKETS

Bernhard Gardi

Below I explain the design of a *kaasa* blanket. The terms given are in Fulfulde, the language of the Fulani. [74]

① Without exception six strips: *lefol* (pl. *lepi*).
② Down the middle there is an inserted band that is woven separately: *bidinol* (pl. *bidini*).
③ Narrow braided bands sewn on to both long sides: *sembiyawol* (pl. *sembiyaaji*, from *sembe*: strength); for protection of the selvedge.
④ Border in shape of a cord consisting of projecting warp threads twined to groups of four: *karrol* (pl. *karri* from the verb *harrude*: weave).
⑤ Tassels: *wukkuru* (sing. *buuki*).
⑥ The *biccirgal* motif features on every *kaasa* displaying patterns (from the verb *wicude*: to shake off, to spill water).
⑦ Rust-coloured weft band: *daakol* (pl. *daaki*). The term *daakol* refers to a distinct colour pattern on the neck of a cow. On this weft band there are no small diamond motifs (*paalel*, pl. *paaloy*), but small embroideries called *cyadugol* instead.

The selected piece shows a blanket with a single rust-coloured weft band. Normally *kaasa* blankets have either two *daakol* or none at all.

It appears that, in the past, *kaasa* blankets only had one *daakol*. The upper end of the textile could be sewn together, forming a hood to cover the head. In this form the blankets served as sleeping bags for the herdsmen, but not every blanket designed like this was actually used for this purpose – but at least that was the original idea. These blankets are considered as cut open at the top (*yooboodu*). The concluding motif at the lower end is also a *jowal* containing pee-sized *cukke* made of light-coloured cotton.

Today's *biccirgal* motifs – meaning 'sprinkled water while watering the cows' – at the top end of the blanket are about twice the size of what they used to be fifty years ago. The connecting patterns on the strips three and four are called *biccirgal bohe* (*bohe*: something half-done, or, to be more precise, a colour pattern that only features on one side of a cow's neck).

A comparison with old *kaasa* blankets [75] reveals two things:

For one, the general design of the blanket has remained more or less unchanged. Each patterned *kaasa* blanket consists of six strips, in a combination of four and two strips; this means the weaver produces two kinds of strips, fourfold in the one case, twofold in the other. The two strips usually feature on the outside (i.e. strips one and six) but occasionally one finds them located on the inside too (strips three and four, as in the present example).

The second aspect: in the past *kaasa* blankets had fewer patterns; they were also smaller and more densely woven than in the 1970s. The patterns always come in the shape of either diamonds or triangles, but in almost endless variations, which is why one never sees two absolutely identical *kaasa* blankets. However, the weaving technique and the concluding work on the borders and fringes, so typical of *kaasa* blankets, has not changed over time.

The blankets were named after a number of classical patterns. In the present case the *jowal* diamond pattern served as the name giver for the *kaasa njowaaka*. There must always be three diamonds and they have to contain bright *cukke* made of cotton.

In the 1970s it became fashion to produce *kaasa* displaying several patterns which otherwise served as eponyms for other blankets. The allegedly 'strongest' motif that was incorporated almost always was the *lannde* motif, said to represent the reflection of a mosque on the water. It gave the *kaasa lanndaaka* its name.

Before the First World War a *kaasa* blanket cost more than a sheep on average. Later, the ratio was reversed as *kaasa* blankets gradually lost in value.

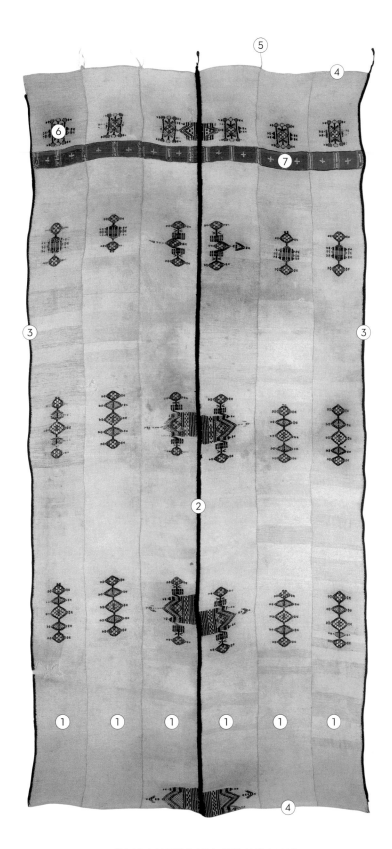

65 – *KAASA NJOWAAKA*. FULANI. MALI.
Classical complete blanket with very finely woven
patterns. Almost certainly woven before 1930

233 × 111 cm – purchase 1963 – III 16228

GREY *KAASA* BLANKETS

Kolado Cissé, Bernhard Gardi

When I discovered, and immediately bought, a plain grey *kaasa* blanket on the market in Mopti in 1982 (today it is in the Historisches Museum Bern, B.G. 82.313.6) I was unable to know that I was contributing to the creation of a new – albeit also the last – generation of woollen blankets. Moreover, I only got to know this many years later, in the autumn of 2008.

At the time in 1982, I was fascinated by the blanket; I had never seen such a type before although I had been collecting *kaasa* blankets for years. I especially liked the blocks of varying grey created by the use of different shades of yarn which themselves corresponded to the length of yarn on the spool in the shuttle. My old friend Kolado Cissé who at the time was still working as an embroiderer on the market in Mopti, told me in Basel in 2008 that he had been surprised by the enthusiasm I had shown for this specific blanket. He added that grey blankets like this had always existed, not many, and most of them rather ugly, but usually of good yarn quality. The blankets were mainly used by herders while tending to their flocks.

When he went back to his village Sindégué Ouro Boulo in 1982 he placed an order for more grey *kaasa* blankets. The first one produced was a plain grey textile without *daakol* and patterns. He sent it to Switzerland and I bought it for the Museum der Kulturen (see fig. 66). It is, so to speak, the second grey *kaasa*. Later, weavers also began incorporating patterns on the blankets. The new grey woollen blankets sold like hot cakes, for almost twenty years. They were usually bought by tourists, who thought that grey blankets were something 'special', probably because they were rarer than other textiles. Due to this popularity other vendors on the market also started ordering grey *kaasa* blankets in their home villages. In the course of time, new patterns found otherwise on light-shaded *kaasa* began to appear on the grey blankets, especially designs that feature only on cotton blankets, for example, the basic pattern consisting of light and dark squares, typical of blankets from the Banamba, Nyamina and Sansanding regions.

The proliferation of grey blankets was as if wool weaving in the Niger Inland Delta had risen to fight a last desperate stand before succumbing to the tides of time. Today, proper *kaasa* blankets are no longer produced.

During his visit to Basel in 2008 Kolada Cissé told me that the occurrence of grey wool was in actual fact already a sign of the decline of wool weaving. In the past, the owners of the herds had taken great care to keep the different kinds of sheep separated, thus preserving distinct categories of white and dark-brown wool respectively. This was an important aspect in breeding too. However, there was such a thing as grey wool, but it was quite rare and only found on the bellies of dark-brown sheep. This wool was softer and produced very warm blankets. Grey wool was often dyed black because it meant less work than dyeing white wool black. Dark-coloured blankets were more expensive than white ones due to the soft quality of the wool.

The decline of the *kaasa* blankets went hand in hand with the decline of sheep breeding. Cross-breeding became more common, even between wool- and hair-sheep, thus generating more animals with unspecific colouring, in other words, more grey wool.

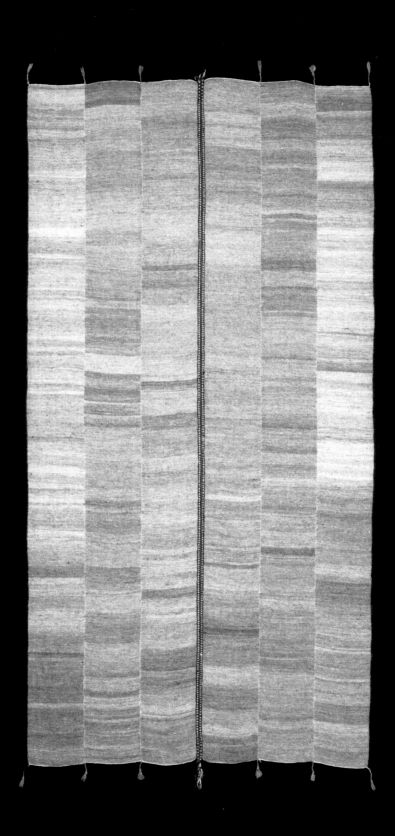

66 – *KAASA MBUNAAWA* FROM SINDÉGUÉ OURO BOULO. FULANI. MALI

250×134 cm – purchased by Kolado Cissé, Mopti, 1982 - III 22165

ARKILLA KERKA

Bernhard Gardi

The *kerka* is the 'mother of all *arkilla*'. They are no longer produced today. A *kerka* consists of six patterned strips, occasionally a seventh strip, striped black and white and called *sigaretti* (from French 'cigarette'), is added und used for hanging up the blanket. [76] The white sections and the warp are made of cotton, the rest is wool. Black is never applied, only dark indigo-blue. A *kerka* blanket of the finest quality requires between 25,000 and 30,000 metres of hand-spun yarn. [77]

Kerka show a very strict symmetrical overall design; the same applies to the motifs. These basically consist of diamond and triangle motifs in various shapes and combinations.

The sequence of the motif blocks – always running across the six patterned strips – reflects the sequence of the weaving techniques applied: supplementary weft float patterns (*cubbe*) are followed by tapestry weave patterns (*tunne*), with narrow strips of plain weave – the basic weaving technique – in between.

A red weft block forms the blanket's central axis. Thus, tapestry weave stands at the centre. The main motif here is called *lewruwal* ('moon') surrounded by 'stars' (*kode*) by some people, others call it *tiide eeda* ('the forehead of the wild buffalo').

Each half of the blanket contains in the middle again a red weft block with tapestry weave patterns. Here the diamond patterns formed from triangles are referred to as *gite ngaari* ('eyes of the bull').

It takes an experienced and diligent weaver half a day to weave a single *lewruwal* pattern.

The projecting red fringes are considered beautiful. They possess no intrinsic meaning, but come in handy in

67 – *ARKILLA KERKA* FROM THE GUIMBALLA REGION, AROUND 1978. FULANI. MALI.
I was offered this blanket in 1979 on a market north of Konna. The dealer was the brother of the woman who owned it.
Like many of her peers, the young woman wanted a modern mosquito net and a metal bed with a soft foam mattress.
The white-coloured sections as well as the warp are made of cotton, the coloured parts of wool

440 × 150 cm. 7 strips, each 21.5 cm wide. Weight: 4,500 g. Total yarn length: approx. 25,000 m. Collected by B. Gardi 1979.
Acquired by the MKB 1998 – III 27026

a technical sense: before the single strips are sewn together, they are joined by these fringes in proper order.

The Fulani distinguish between different qualities of *kerka*. Although each type has three red weft blocks with tapestry weave patterns, a quality distinction is made according to the number of supplementary weft float patterns (*cubbe*). A top-quality blanket must have twelve weft bars with supplementary weft float motifs (six on the left, and six on the right of the central tapestry weave), as shown in the figure above.

With regard to the names of the patterns one has to distinguish between two levels. The first level is entirely technical: *cubbe* always refers to supplementary weft float patterns, *tunne* to tapestry weave motifs.

The second level is idiomatic and relates to the pattern's appearance, for example: 'teeth of an old woman' (black-white-black in reference to gaps between the teeth), 'tracks of a rabbit in the sand', 'hoof of a gazelle', 'star', 'ear of the second wife', or 'upturned calabash'. It seems that the Fulani and Songhay have a preference for names of patterns that refer to the humorous or at least pleasant aspects of everyday life.

The weaver always finishes the work by weaving the sixth patterned strip. It has a special name – *bippol* – and displays a more simple design: the patterns are smaller, and some may even be missing. When I asked the people why this was so, I always received the same answer: "Because the weaver was tired." But I believe there is another reason: when the blanket is suspended, the lowest strip, the *bippol*, touches the bed. This means, this section is not only less visible than the rest, it also frays more quickly than the other strips.

88

ARKILLA KERKA FOR GHANA

Bernhard Gardi

Since the manufacture of an *arkilla kerka* was time- and work-intensive, customers often ordered two at the same time: a good and expensive one for their daughter, and slightly cheaper and inferior one for sale. The expensive version usually became the talk of the town very quickly.

The *arkilla kerka* shown here is of the cheap kind; it was purchased in Ghana in 1950. Clearly the work input was held in limits, which means that the blanket was produced for sale. Nevertheless, judging from the fact that the blanket includes twice six weft bars with supplemen-

tary weft float patterns, we are still dealing, from a Fulani point of view, with a first-quality *arkilla kerka*. However, a closer look reveals that the patterns are quite small and less finely woven; the wool is rather coarse and not as finely spun as in other cases; in addition, the textile has only a single cotton warp, and not a double warp. The important thing was that the blanket looked good and colourful.

The *sigaretti* strip used for hanging up the blanket is missing, and the weave on the sixth, and final, strip is distinctly simpler than on the other five strips.

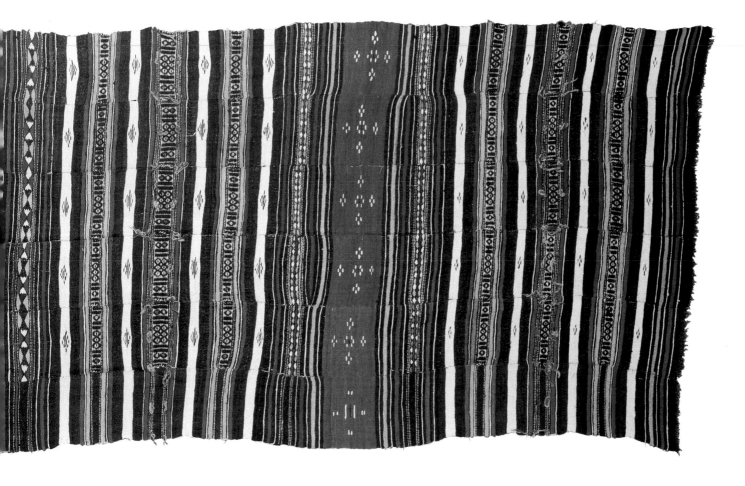

68 – *ARKILLA KERKA*, AROUND 1950. FULANI. MALI. PURCHASED IN GHANA.
The seventh strip *sigaretti* **is missing**

472 × 126 cm. 6 strips, each 21 cm wide. Weight: 2,500 g. Total yarn length: approx. 11,000 m.
Collected by Paul Hinderling 1950 – III 11078

ARKILLA KUNTA
Bernhard Gardi

The resemblance to a *kerka* is astonishing. The striking bright motifs on the red ground – the 'moon' and the 'stars' and the 'bull's eyes' – are very similar. However, a *kunta* consists of only five strips (and not six), but these in turn are very wide, measuring up to 32 centimetres. As on a *kerka*, the fifth, and lowest, strip is simpler in decoration than the other four. The viewer senses quickly that a *kunta* has something rather brittle to it; this is because it consists to nearly 100 percent of sheep's wool. Even the warp is made of wool. Only the small bright tapestry weave patterns – stars, moons or eyes – are cotton. With its roughly 10 kilos a *kunta* is about twice the weight of an *arkilla kerka*. *Kerka* and *kunta* actually look so alike because the tapestry patterns (*tunne*) on the red ground dominate the picture. The weft float patterns compare less clearly.

But what really distinguishes the two is the sequence of patterns and their different emphasis. The *kunta* has four red weft bars (compared to three in a *kerka*) from which follows that a *kunta* displays a higher rate of red, apart from being shorter than a *kerka*. Moreover, the large band of motifs that forms the geometric centre is not executed in tapestry weave – as is the case on a *kerka* – but in the supplementary weft float technique.

What is also striking is that the single strips of a *kunta* measure over six metres in length. But only a part of the blanket is richly decorated; the other part is plain dark brown with occasional red and yellow weft bands. The dark-brown half is turned over or folded, while the slit at the upper selvedge is stitched up so that a kind of tent emerges. This tent is then hung up in the round-shaped

69 – *ARKILLA KUNTA* FROM THE VILLAGE SAWANI. WOGO. REPUBLIC OF NIGER. BEFORE 1960.
Complete. Tent-shaped. All five strips woven in one piece. Only the small white sections are
made of cotton, the rest is wool. Warp probably made of goats' hair

375 × 164 cm. 5 strips, each 32.5 cm wide. Weight: 9,500 g. Total yarn length: approx. 30,000 m. Collected by
Boser/Gardi 1974 – III 20462

house which is covered with mats. Whereas a *kerka* is merely used as a sort of bed curtain (in a usually futile attempt to keep the mosquitoes away), the *kunta* actually forms a closed tent and provides effective protection.

The Wogo people, as well as inhabitants of the small village Sawani where we purchased this *arkilla kunta*, originally come from the Lake Debo area. Their ancestors emigrated from there about 200 years ago, gradually moving down the Niger River. [78]

Had these people retained an early form of *arkilla kerka*? Did they forfeit the prevalent fashion trends of their old home area in the west when they migrated to the east? Is it possible that they even kept up some of the marriage ceremonies that were abandoned elsewhere? Olivier

de Sardan tells of a custom that was continued up to the beginning of the Second World War, which I encountered in Mali nowhere else. According to this custom, the weaver received in payment for his artwork, among other items, one head of cattle designated as *kunta kuru*, 'the hide of the *kunta*'. The tent-like blanket was first displayed publicly for three days in the compound of the bridegroom's family, during which the visitors were entertained with food and drink. After that the women of the village erected the *arkilla kunta* in the round-shaped straw hut in the bride's compound, decorating it with especially finely woven and colourful mats. Following this, the newlywed couple remained seven days and seven nights in their new house. [79]

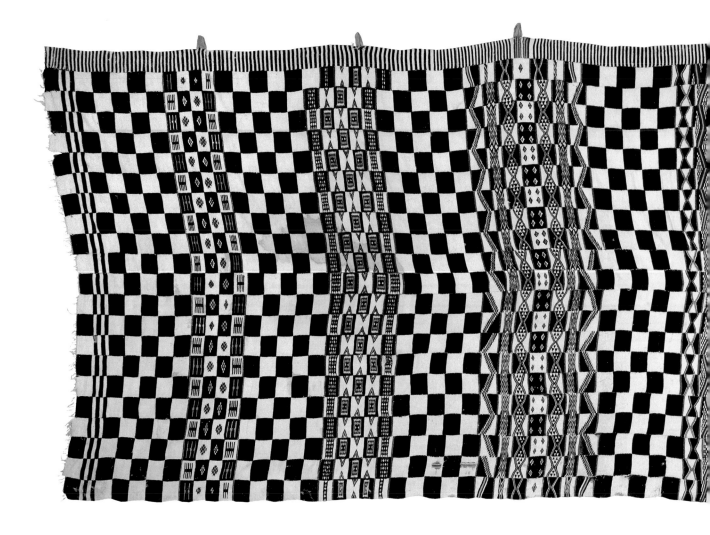

ARKILLA JENNGO
Bernhard Gardi

Jenngo blankets were woven in the area west of Tombouctou near Lake Faguibine by Songhay-speaking *maabuube* weavers. The Songhay call these blankets which were produced for the Tuareg *jonngo arkilla*. In 1980, the market of Adarmallen in the Arondissement de Gargando west of Goundam was the trading centre for these textiles, next to Goundam itself. A *jenngo* consists mainly of cotton; only the dyed parts are made of wool. The arrangement is completely symmetrical. The basic design is a chequerboard pattern. The single patterns are woven in tapestry technique; supplementary weft float patterns are not applied. As against *kaasa*, *kerka* and *kunta* textiles, *jenngo* never played a role in the trade with Ghana.

I make the distinction between a simple (frequent) and a refined (rare) version.

In the simple version the strips are approximately 12 centimetres wide. It takes a weaver six to seven days to finish a blanket. Approximately 12 – 15,000 metres of yarn are required. Similar to the *kerka*, two textiles were produced for a wedding in the past. The bride's blanket consisted of 16 strips, the simpler version made for sale had 14 strips. [80]

The finer version is special to Niafounké, and within Niafounké, a speciality of the family Gaata, the traditional chief-family in the Canton de Souboundou. [81] These finely-woven *jenngo* blankets are very rare. Featuring up to 30

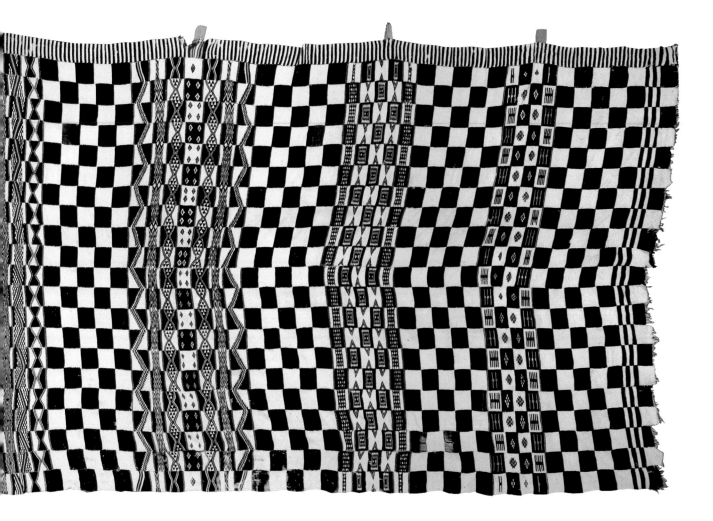

70 – *ARKILLA JENNGO* FROM NIAFOUNKÉ. SONGHAY/TUAREG. MALI. AROUND 1968.
The blanket was made for a granddaughter of Ayssata Babakar from the Gaata family. When the said Ayssata Babakar got married in 1921 she was presented with an *arkilla jenngo* (today in the Museum der Kulturen Basel III 20460); it probably served as a model for the blanket shown here.

535 × 174 cm. 22 strips, each between 7 and 9 cm wide. Weight: 5,800 g. Total yarn length: approx. 40,000 m.
Collected by Boser/Gardi 1974 – III 20454

strips, each measuring between six and eight centimetres in width, these blankets rank among the masterpieces of African craftsmanship. A single piece requires up to 40,000 metres of yarn. The fine weave as well as the number of patterns incorporated in a rectangle are astonishing. It takes a weaver about 60 days to produce such a blanket.

The high-quality *jenngo* are outstanding and unique specimens; one never sees two identical textiles, but they nearly always display seven symmetrically arranged pattern units. The design positioned in the midsection, ide-

ally showing seven different patterns, clearly dominates the overall picture.

The names given to the various designs reflect the significance that weddings and bride wealth have in social life: we have, for example, 'cushion', 'bedposts', 'money', 'board game', 'leather fringe' or 'calabash' (with and without lid). The frequently shown diamonds are described as 'bowls' or 'dishes', this includes calabashes and wooden containers as well as enamel dishes.

Similar to the *kerka*, here too the patterns reflect pleasant and delightful things in everyday life.

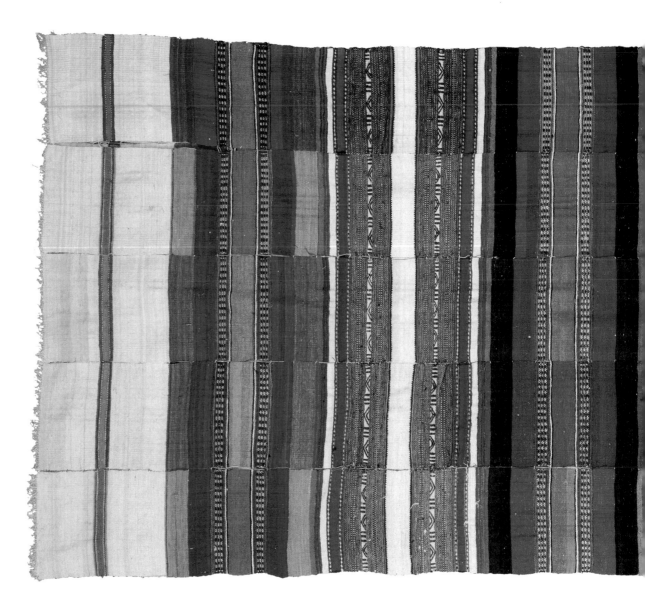

ARKILLA MUNNGA

Bernhard Gardi

Munnga blankets, produced mainly for trade with the Moors, were manufactured by Songhay-speaking *maabu-ube* weavers in the villages of Mbouna, Bintagoungou and Tukabango near Lake Faguibine. These *arkilla* weigh up to 10 kilos and were used as sleeping-blankets or as carpets in the tents of the nomads. The Songhay call these blankets *amunnga arkilla*. To the Fulani they are the '*arkilla* of the poor' due to their rather dull patterns. Only the

warp is made of cotton yarn, the rest is wool. What is striking are the bright indigo colours. Supplementary weft float patterns are sparingly distributed over the ground weave. There is no tapestry. In principle, a complete *munnga* blanket consists of 10 strips each measuring 25 centimetres in width, amounting to 'twice seven cubits' (2 × 7 × approx. 30 cm = 420 cm), as the master weaver Mohammadu Ali Fofana dit Mayga explained to me in

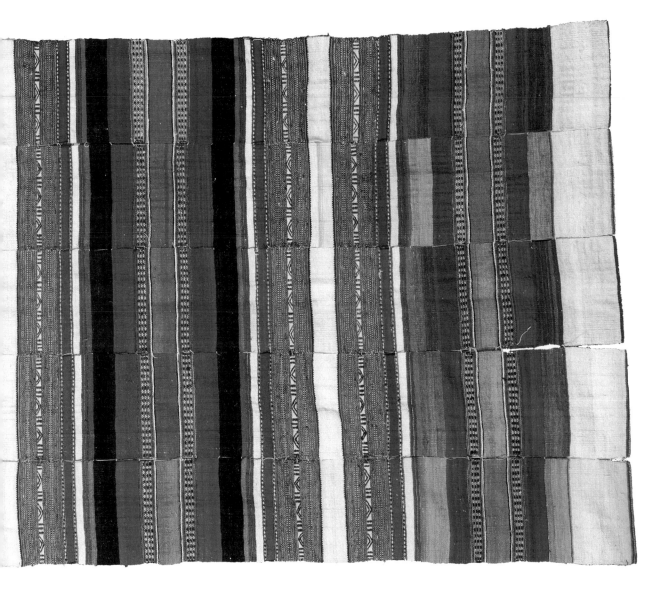

71 – *ARKILLA MUNNGA* FROM GOUNDAM. SONGHAY. MALI. 1942.
Cotton warp, woollen weft. At the time of purchase the blanket had not been used yet,
which is why the strips are only joined together with provisional stitches

320 × 125 cm. Total length: 640 cm, then folded once. 5 strips, each 24.5 cm wide. Total yarn length:
approx. 17,000 m. Collected by Jean Gabus 1942. Acquired by the MKB 1946 – III 9365

Goundam back in 1980 (see fig. 141). It takes an efficient weaver ten days at most to produce a *munnga* of this kind. But there are variations – depending on how the blanket is to be used. The *munnga* shown here consists of five long, folded strips.

When sewn together it produces a kind of tent similar to the *arkilla kunta* in fig. 69. For many years Râs el Mâ, located at the western end of Lake Faguibine, was the place that camel herders (Moors, Berbers) visited regularly to buy blankets or trade them in for sheep, dates and salt. During the great drought of the 1980s many of the herders lost everything they owned and were forced to move to the towns. This spelt the beginning of the end for *munnga* weaving. During the First World War, the people were conscripted to produce *munnga* blankets for the French troops (Seydou 1998: 468).

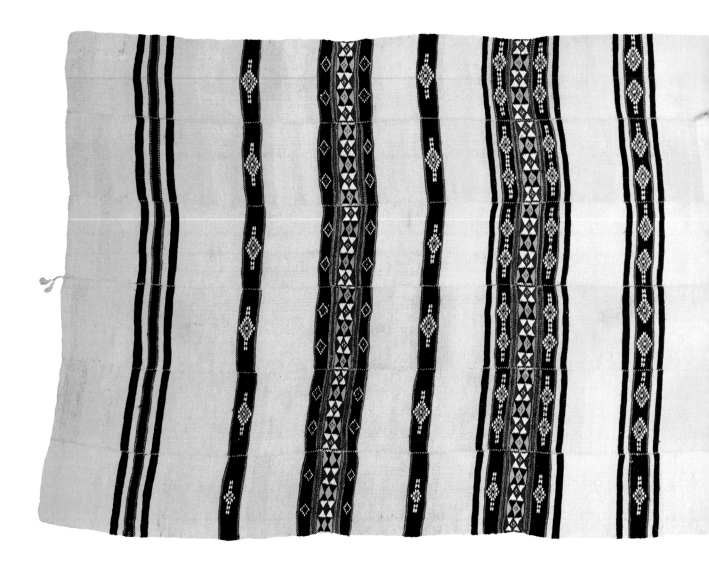

ARKILLA BAMMBU

Kolado Cissé, Bernhard Gardi

Nothing is known about this rare kind of *arkilla* except that, among the Fulani, it was destined for an orphan. One gets the impression that, in principle, it is just a very large-sized *kaasa*: the blanket is quite light, the warp is made of wool, and the protruding warp threads are twined at both ends, in the same way as on a *kaasa* blanket.

The patterns one finds on an *arkilla bammbu* are the same as the ones to be found on an *arkilla kerka*, as are the protruding fringes.

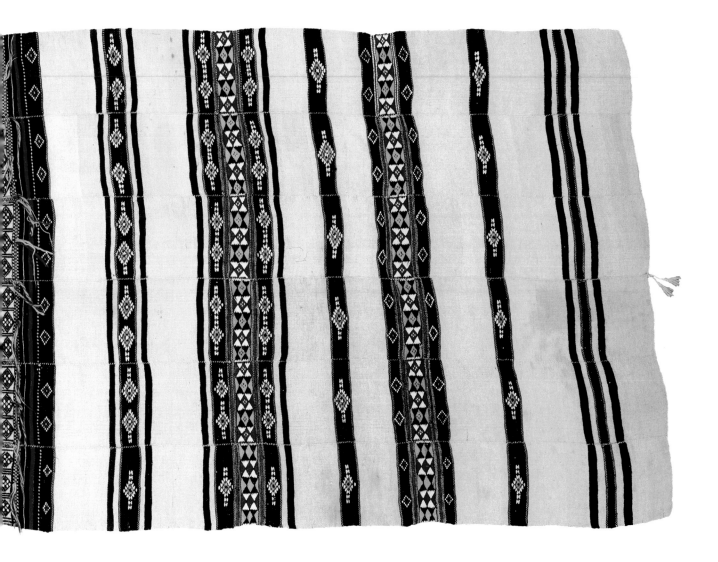

72 – *ARKILLA BAMMBU* FROM SARÉ DEMBA, A PLACE BETWEEN
KORIENTZÉ AND N'GORKOU IN THE GUIMBALLA REGION, EAST OF
LAKE DEBO. FULANI. MALI. AROUND 1980

395×138 cm. 6 strips, each 23 cm wide – collected by B. Gardi
(through Kolado Cissé, Mopti, 1983). Acquired by the MKB 1998 – III 27027

'COUVERTURE PERSONNAGES'

Kolado Cissé, Bernhard Gardi

A comparable blanket was published by John Picton (1995: 65), together with the weaver's correct name: Oumar Bocoum. Bocoum is a typical *maabo* name from northern Mali. Large-sized blankets of this kind are more common than one might expect. However, they rarely get to be sold on a public market, usually they are commissioned straight from the weaver and presented to the bridal couple at their wedding. In most cases they are used to decorate the inside walls of a house – especially in the bedroom – as well as the bed itself.

Let us take a look at the tradition behind this blanket. Kolado Cissé pursued the question as to who began producing this type of textile. He told me his story that spans three generations in Basel in November 2008.

These 'couvertures personages', as they are called in Bamako, evolved from the so-called *tapi*, themselves a creation of the 1950s shortly before independence. The first weaver to produce *tapi* was a man called Ousman Baba Dramé, better known under his professional name Gwòòtal Bambara. [82] He must have been an absolute master weaver. Sometimes he worked for the 'Commandant de Cercle' in Mopti. His date of death is not known (but it was before 1970). Certainly a significant event in his life was his encounter with the Ghana's charismatic president, Kwame Nkrumah on the occasion of the latter's visit to Mopti in November 1960 (Konaré 1983: 164). The *kente* cloths worn by Nkrumah and his entourage made a deep impression on Ousman Baba Dramé and encouraged him to continue weaving colourful squares spread over a large surface – in fact very similar to the design of Asanti *kente* cloth.

This reference to *kente* cloths is of interest because, within the tradition of Malian weaving, *tapi* blankets constituted an innovation with regard to their large-sized format – again not unlike the *kente* cloths – but with the difference that *tapi* blankets were not used as dress, but as bed covers for the modern double beds with steel tubing instead. The rectangular motifs in the textile's design were not a new invention. They were already in use, for example, on the *arkilla jenngo* marriage blankets and on cotton blankets from the area of Bamenda. What was new was the colourfulness.

Thus, three factors must have coincided: a new type of colourfulness on the basis of an old chequer-pattern design; the visit of a charismatic head of state dressed in a hereto unseen cloth; and the advent of new, modern beds. [83]

Let us move on to the second generation: Abdurrahman Bura Bocoum is said to have been the first to copy Ousman Baba Dramé's alias Gwòòtal Bambara's *tapi* textiles. Pushing the development of the *tapi* ahead he is said to have been the first weaver to include images of human figures and animals in the design, distributing over the different strips. After the coup d'état of 1968 when the army took over power in Mali he also began weaving soldiers in uniform. It is told that he gave the first blanket decorated with human figures to the regional office of Air Mali as a present. One of his specialities was the depiction of lions, especially in the shape of two maned lions facing each other, occasionally with a figure standing between them. For many years Bocoum worked in Sokura, a well-known village near Mopti. Abdurrahman Bura Bocoum, who is said to have earned quite a lot of money, is regarded as first weaver to have included figures in his designs. He is no longer alive. [84]

In the third generation we are talking about two of Abdurrahman Bura Bocoum's followers. Both of them still produce these 'couvertures personages', or, at least, they did so until a short while ago.

One of them is the above-mentioned Oumar Bocoum. He lives in Ségou but has given up weaving. He too is from the Guimballa region, a relative of Abdurrahman Bura Bocoum, his teacher. The second apprentice, about the same age as Oumar Bocoum, lives in the Badalabougou quarter of Bamako and is still engaged in weaving. His name is Jaara Ila Jigannde alias Maabel Jiga. He is from the village of Bokoré near Korientzé. [85]

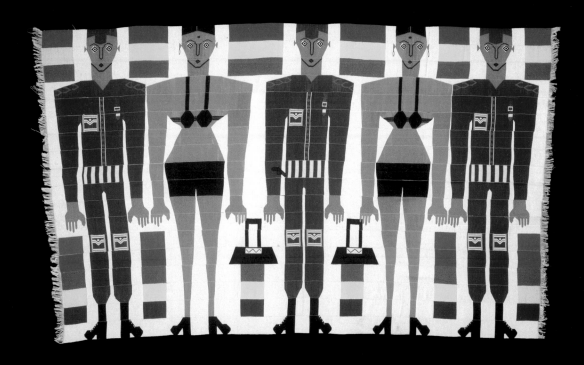

73 – 'COUVERTURE PERSONNAGE'. MALI.
Produced by the master weaver Oumar Bocoum

Purchased by Kolado Cissé, Bamako, 2008 – III 27542

A CLOTH DEALER IN HIS SHOP.
The hand-woven cloths: each set including a woman's wrapcloth, a head-tie and a shawl is wrapped in plastic.
Iseyin, Nigeria

Photo Duncan Clarke 1997

NIGERIA

Women Weave – Men Weave
Duncan Clarke

The extraordinary richness and diversity of textile traditions in Nigeria reflects its varied ecology, its very large and ethnically diverse population, and the complex histories of its component peoples. Local and long distance trade, warfare, migration, religious conversion, the rise and fall of kingdoms and caliphates, the slave trade, colonization, independence and modernization have all played a role in shaping these histories, as have local ideas about status, personal and group identity, appropriate dress, fashion and tradition.

Today documentation of many of these Nigerian textiles remains sporadic. Although field research, museum collections, the archives of missionaries and colonial administrators, along with study of early images in photographs and postcards, have provided a basis for a growing body of academic research by both local and international scholars, much remains to be discovered and undoubtedly much has already been lost. The collection of Nigerian textiles assembled by Renée Boser-Sarivaxévanis and Bernhard Gardi in 1973/74 provides a vital contribution to this growing body of knowledge. By documenting and collecting the ordinary and even mundane cloths then still being woven for everyday use in the key towns along their route, as well as the better-known styles made for prestige dress, they have provided a unique record assembled at a time of unusually rapid change. Nigeria in the 1970s was in the midst of the so-called 'Oil Boom' years. Expensive imported 'lace', often from Switzerland, became essential for fashionable dress among the newly rich – a craze Wole Soyinka satirised in his play *Opera Wonyosi* (premiered 1977). This growing wealth, along with such factors as the spread of primary education, the expansion of local factory-based textile production, and the rising availability of alternative occupations led to a rapid decline in many but not all Nigerian weaving traditions.

In this chapter, we will look at traditions that have continued into the 21st century. Two main forms of weaving technology were present in Nigeria: the narrow-strip, double-heddle loom found throughout West Africa and, in the past, operated only by men; and an upright single heddle loom found only in Nigeria and areas of neighbouring countries that was used by women. Today each technology sustains only one single thriving tradition that contrasts with the more general pattern of gradual decline. Among the Yoruba [86] people of the southwestern states of Nigeria large numbers of both men and women use the double-heddle loom to weave a fashionable and prestigious fabric called *aso oke*, meaning 'high status cloth'. In Okene, a town in central Nigeria, Ebira women using the upright single-heddle loom produce large quantities of a competing fashion-inspired cloth.

ASO OKE

Almost uniquely among African textiles there is sufficient data preserved to begin to trace a history of *aso oke* design dating back several hundred years, in which changes in cloth design and use can be located alongside far wider issues of social change. Moreover this is a living, ever evolving history, extending into the present, with far reaching changes in the design, production and use of *aso oke* continuing to this day as it retains its crucial role in Yoruba ceremonial life. The number of full-time professional weavers is certainly higher today than it was 25 years ago, and perhaps the highest it has ever been. [87] As elsewhere in West Africa, the double-heddle loom was operated in the past exclusively by men. Yoruba women participated in *aso oke* production by cultivating cotton, spinning the yarn and dyeing both threads and completed cloths. Since the late 1980s however large numbers of women have also begun to weave using the double-heddle loom.

The history of *aso oke* is closely associated with that of the Oyo Yoruba. In the 18th and early 19th century Oyo-ile was the capital of a large and expansionary empire controlling key trade routes. A slave ship captain called Adams, who visited the coast on several voyages between 1786 and 1800, wrote that "the cloth manufactured in Hio [Oyo] is superior, both for variety of pattern, colour, and dimensions, to any made in the neighbouring states." (Adams 1823:93) The sack of Oyo-ile in the Fulani Jihad of the 1830s led to the dispersal of this weaving community as part of the general southerly movement of the Oyo, with large numbers of weavers moving in particular to Ilorin and Iseyin, as well as the re-established town of Oyo. Weavers in the Fulani-ruled city of Ilorin were able both to supply the more southerly Yoruba markets and to compete with the Nupe for trade within the Sokoto Caliphate. A contemporary account records that over 150 weavers were seen at work in the course of less than an hour's ride through the town (Campbell 1861:86). Weaving lineages in most of the major Yoruba towns today trace back their origins to Oyo-ile, either directly or through later moves via Ilorin or Iseyin.

What did the cloth woven by these weavers look like? As far back as 1858 the Baptist missionary William Clarke (1972:273) commented, "scarcely any two pieces of cloth are found of the same size and colour, as each weaver is continually striving to turn out something extra or fanciful." We can begin to piece together a picture of what *aso oke* looked like in the past 200 years by a combination of approaches. Elderly informants have their own recollections of the cloths they wove or wore in the early part of the 20th century. Old cloths that have been handed down through the generations can still be found. There are a few brief comments in contemporary accounts on Yoruba dress. A few photographs survive from the final decades of the 19th century and many more from the early 20th. However the most important resource is cloths with recorded accession dates in museum collections outside Nigeria (see Clarke 1997, chapter 2). The collection of the Museum der Kulturen Basel, and in particular the group of *aso oke* assembled during the 1970s by Renée Boser and Bernhard Gardi add more detail at the later stages of this sequence.

EARLY *ASO OKE*

Three cloths, *etu*, *sanyan* and *alaari*, dominate the picture of early *aso oke* that emerges from interviews with elderly weavers, cloth traders and other local sources. *Etu*, named for the speckled plumage of the guinea fowl, is dark indigo cotton with a fine check of narrow white or pale blue threads. *Sanyan* is natural beige wild silk spun from the cocoons of moths of the *Anaphe* family. *Alaari* is magenta silk imported from southern Europe for at least two centuries until the early decades of the 20th century via the trans-Saharan caravan trade routes into northern Nigeria. Although today they are regarded as fundamental to Yoruba cloth culture, the evidence suggests that their prominence is largely attributable to their role in a sphere of high-status dress associated with the dominance of the Sokoto Caliphate in the 19th century, with its emphasis on 'robes of honour'. Both Yoruba and Nupe weavers wove these three fabrics, and were key participants in a shared sphere of prestige textile production and use that extended to the Hausa emirates and beyond (Perani 1977).

Looking more closely at old cloths themselves allows us to move beyond this emphasis on three prestige cloths and see aspects of the pattern diversity and design experimentation that so amazed William Clarke in the 1850s. At least by 1900, and perhaps even several decades earlier, Yoruba *aso oke* weavers had essentially the same repertoire of pattern techniques that they would be using at the start of the 1990s. These were: warp stripes down the cloth strips; weft stripes across the strips; warp ikat; supplementary weft float, that is patterns created by extra weft threads across parts of the strip; and openwork, rows of holes across the strip created by tying together groups of warp threads. The last two techniques were until the 1950s at least, particularly associated with Ilorin weavers and were only rarely used elsewhere. Both have been documented in use far earlier for women weavers on the upright single-heddle loom and it is likely that their use in *aso oke* derives from design interaction between the two traditions. In combination with the raw materials, namely cotton and silk, both local and imported, and very occasionally raffia, and the repertoire of colours available through local dyeing and imports, this small set of techniques opened up a vast range of different designs.

ASO EBI

These different designs arose in part from experimentation by the weavers themselves, eager to produce novel variations that would catch the eye of a buyer. Equally important however were two other key participants, namely cloth traders and cloth consumers. Fashion was a key factor in this interaction between cloth consumers, traders and weavers, particularly after the emergence of the custom of *aso ebi* in the early decades of the 20th century. *Aso ebi* or *aso egbe* (meaning 'family cloth' or 'group cloth') involved key guests at an event demonstrating allegiance to the celebrants by dressing in the same cloth. This could be European dress or African styles using imported fabrics, but increasingly from the 1930s onwards it involved the wearing of hand-woven *aso oke*. Groups of up to twenty or more guests at a funeral, wedding, child's naming or a chieftaincy ceremony, all wear the same design of cloth selected and distributed by the event organizer. Today at a society wedding one might see six or more sets of *aso ebi*, representing the bride's friends, the groom's friends, the bride's mother's friends and so on.

The production of *aso oke* to supply these events is organized primarily by master weavers in Ilorin, Iseyin, or Oyo who obtain orders from event organizers or women cloth traders in Lagos and other cities. The family compound forms the basis of weaving organization, with one or more master weavers controlling a small group of apprentices and dependent weavers. He supplies the thread to the weavers, tells them what designs to produce, makes small payments to dependent weavers, and owns the finished cloth. Most cloth is woven directly to the order of traders, but master weavers who can afford to also weave cloth for stock. This is carried to one or two of the three regular wholesale markets held every sixteen days in Ede, Ibadan and Oyo. At these markets the master weavers meet traders to hand over completed orders and solicit new business.

Cloths worn by prominent individuals at major events often set a base from which new modifications are spun off. For the women who organize events at which *aso oke* is worn, the key issue is to select a design that is new and distinctive while at the same time is recognizably within the fashion set by recent similar events. Lagos society women attend such events several times a week and develop a keen sense of the latest developments. In choosing a cloth most will select one that was widely admired at a recent event and suggest minor modifications, such as changing a colour or rearranging the stripes. The result is a continual process of incremental change, interrupted more rarely by major alterations we can regard as innovatory changes. Some of these have been the result of newly available materials, such as imported thread, which largely displaced hand-spun local cotton in the 1950s, or metallized plastic lurex called *shine-shine* in the mid-1970s. The leading cloth traders, who are part of the same social network, compete to secure orders by encouraging this process of gradual change and, where possible, introducing more dramatic innovations. In the mid-1990s one trader initiated a process of radical change that transformed the look of *aso oke* almost beyond recognition. This is the story of *Super Q*, as told by Malika Kraamer (see p.180).

Thereafter the pace of innovation slowed and in the early years of this century, while *aso oke* continued to be worn, it was less fashionable than imported damask. Around 2007, however, another new *aso oke* style emerged in which thin weft-faced cloths using a tapestry weave technique to produce 15 centimetre wide strips with geometric patterns in the weft became increasingly popular. The result of this continual change is that *aso oke*, almost uniquely among African textile traditions, exhibits a combination of novelty and continuity at any given point that results in a recognizable time sequence, at least in outline. The remarkable contemporary vitality of *aso oke* stems from its ability to be fashionable yet at the same time to draw on longstanding ideas about the salience of cloth. As with European fashions, there are fashion leaders and a continuous cycle of emulation and distinction. Yet, at the same time, there is a real and widely shared sense that in wearing *aso oke* on appropriate occasions Yoruba people are dressing as their forefathers did.

NORTHERN NIGERIA

Today none of the other traditions of male weaving using the double-heddle loom in Nigeria continue on anything like the same scale as that of *aso oke*. Nupe men were once famous for their weaving but aside from a few Yoruba migrants I have seen no trace of men's weaving on repeated visits to the Nupe capital of Bida and other Nupe towns. There are a very few Jukun weavers in villages around Wukari in the Benue River valley of eastern Nigeria, and a larger number, maybe a few hundred, Tiv weavers near Gboko, mainly weaving ceremonial cloths in warp-striped patterns of brown, black and white. The distinctive indigo-dyed openwork wrappers of the Gwari women around Abuja are still woven in small quantities by weavers of Hausa descent. [88] Some Kanuri men still make plain white strips in villages near Lake Chad in the extreme northeast of the country. Elsewhere in the northern half of Nigeria small numbers of Hausa weavers are scattered among the villages, supplying both local demand and the pastoral Fulani with a wide variety of wrapper cloths and blankets. However, even around Kano only a few traces remain of the great trade that was the economic mainstay of the Sokoto Caliphate in the 19th century.

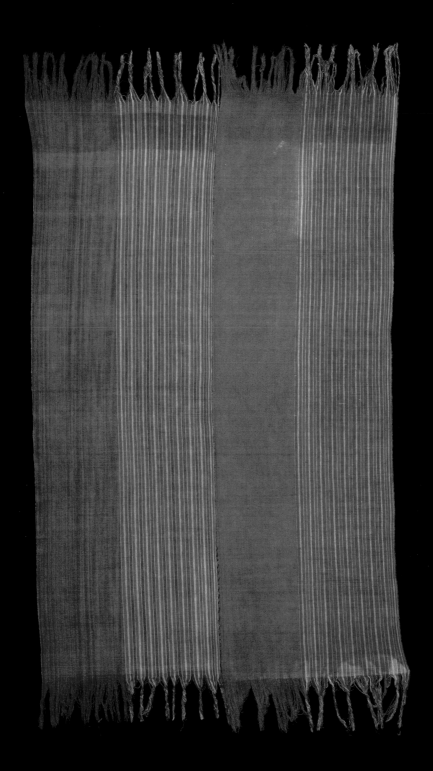

75 – WOMAN'S WRAP CLOTH. YORUBA. NIGERIA. AROUND 1900.
The extensive use of trans-Saharan magenta silk in this wrap cloth is indicative of an exceptional and prestigious cloth woven for a wealthy woman in the 19th century. Woven in two panels by a female weaver using the vertical single-heddle loom, it was collected in the port town of Loko on the Benue River in eastern Nigeria, but was probably the work of a Yoruba weaver

214 × 114 cm, 2 panels – collected by Hanns Vischer 1902 – III 1398

In the 1850s, the explorer Heinrich Barth noted a vast trade in textiles from Kano extending as far north as the shores of the Mediterranean – estimating that Tombouctou alone imported over 300 camel loads of cloths a year from Kano. The most highly valued cloth was the shiny glazed indigo fabric called *turkudi*, woven in very narrow strips of about one centimetre in width, and worn as a turbans and veils by the Tuareg and other peoples of the Sahara. Today the village of Kura, a few kilometres south of Kano, remains the centre of *turkudi* production; traders still visit from Niger and Mali, but only a few elderly men still have the specialist expertise necessary to weave, dye and beat the cloth to a metallic glazed finish.

WOMEN'S WEAVE

In contrast to the double-heddle narrow strip loom, which was clearly introduced to Nigeria from the north, women weavers have been using the upright single-heddle loom since ancient times. On this loom the warp is mounted on a rectangular frame that is usually fixed to a wall and manipulated by use of a fixed heddle to create the shed through which the weft is passed back and forth by hand. If we look at continued use today a picture of current activity emerges similar to that we have already seen for male weaving.

Unlike their male counterparts, Nupe women are still quite active weavers, as are smaller numbers of Hausa women in Zaria and other northern Nigeria cities. In the north weaving by women tends to be an urban craft practiced largely by Muslim women in more secluded compounds. A few Igbo women near Asaba weave white cotton cloths decorated with patterns in openwork and silver lurex weft floats. The wide elaborately decorated cloths woven by women in the town of Akwete are still in demand as fashionable attire for ceremonies in the Niger Delta and the city of Port Harcourt. [89] In Igara and the nearby village of Somorika near the confluence of the rivers Niger and Benue, some women weave narrow cloths that are widely traded as baby-ties, as well as some wrapper styles for local use. Among the Yoruba, where single-heddle loom weaving was extremely widespread until the 1960s, there has been a dramatic decline. Today, aside from a few isolated village weavers, the only Yoruba women using this loom are small numbers in the cities of Ijebu-Ode and Owo, where there is still local demand for culturally specific ceremonial attire.

In all of these areas the numbers of women still weaving can be numbered in the tens or at most the low hundreds, with very few new apprentices. Thus, continued decline is likely. There is however a single exception to this pattern. At dawn on every fourth morning in the town of Okene, near the Niger-Benue confluence, the market place fills with several thousand women. Each carries the cloths she has woven, neatly folded and stacked on her head, as the press of the crowd leaves no space on the ground. Traders from Lagos, Kano, Onitsha and even as far away as Accra come to buy the cloths. The brightly-coloured pairs of rayon cloths they sell provide a cheap, fashionable and distinctive alternative to Yoruba *aso oke* for use in modern life-cycle ceremonies across Nigeria.

The Ebira [90] of Okene town have a long tradition of weaving cloths from local cotton and bast fibre both for daily wear and in certain patterns for funeral display, and for masquerades associated with the dead. In the 1930s, the local ruler introduced patterned silk weaving among the women of his household. By the early 1990s, however, local demand for hand-woven cloths was in decline and Ebira women mainly wove baby-ties, cheap imitations of Yoruba *aso oke* and Akwete patterns that sold largely in rural markets. Today's thriving new phase of Ebira weaving was an offshoot of the competition between Lagos-based cloth dealers that transformed the *aso oke* design in the mid-1990s. Soon after one dealer

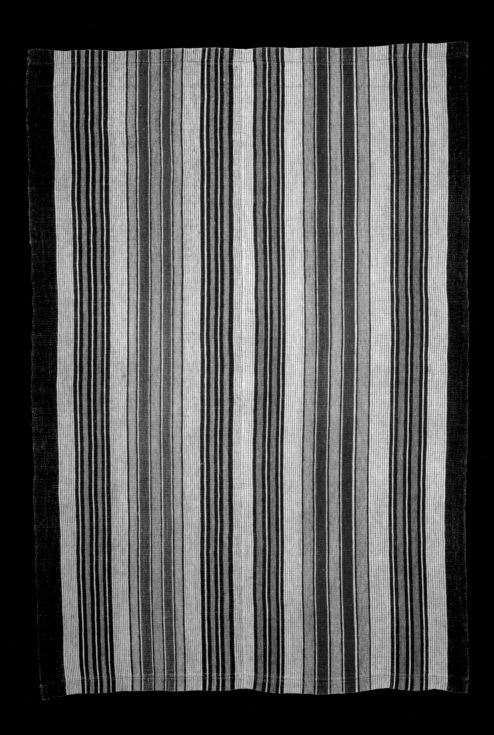

76 – WOMAN'S WRAP CLOTH. EBIRA. NIGERIA.
Good, heavy cloth. Hand-spun cotton yarn. Typical warp stripes in
two shades of blue and white. Women's work. Collected in Igara

170 × 122 cm. 2 panels – collected by Boser/Gardi 1974 – III 19863

introduced wider strips in the new *Super Q* style, a rival imported Swedish handlooms and began to sell hand-woven broadloom cloths decorated with *aso oke* techniques such as openwork and supplementary weft float. Other dealers who could not afford similar looms then turned to Okene women as a local source of broader strip fabrics. This new fashion-focused demand stimulated design innovation as it did in *aso oke*, with Ghanaian inspired float patterns and the Yoruba technique of openwork with overshot threads spreading to Okene. Other pattern innovations were introduced directly by weavers in conjunction with their patrons and although Okene cloths were only briefly at the forefront of fashionable taste they remain sufficiently in demand to sustain a large body of women in employment.

As we have seen, a minority of Nigeria's textile production traditions are continuing to flourish but with radically transformed styles of cloth being woven. Most others are in more or less gradual decline, although future events may perhaps transform their prospects in some cases. The nature of customer demand and the role played by traders in mediating and stimulating this demand have been important factors in the past. In tracing the diverse histories of these traditions a vital contribution is made by dated and documented museum collections, of which that assembled for the Basel museum by Renée Boser and Bernhard Gardi is of unique magnitude and geographic range.

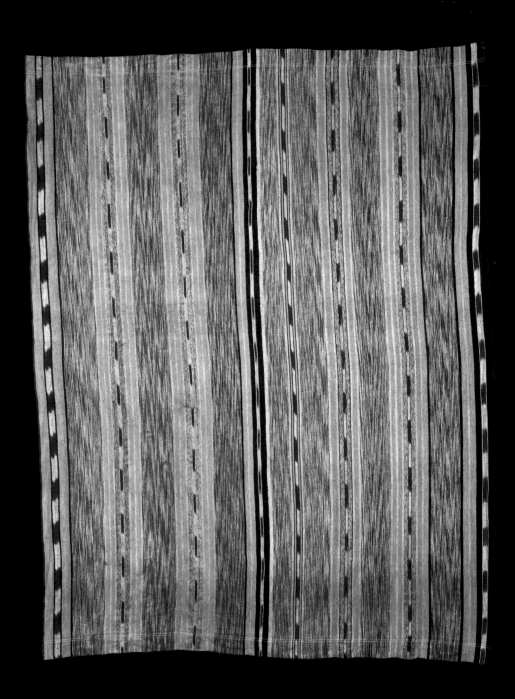

77 – WOMAN'S WRAP CLOTH. EBIRA. NIGERIA.
Heavy wrap cloth made of hand-spun cotton yarn. Simple but cleverly arranged ikat.
Various shades of indigo. Women's work. Produced and collected in Somorika

168×133 cm. 2 panels – collected by Boser/Gardi 1974 – III 20163

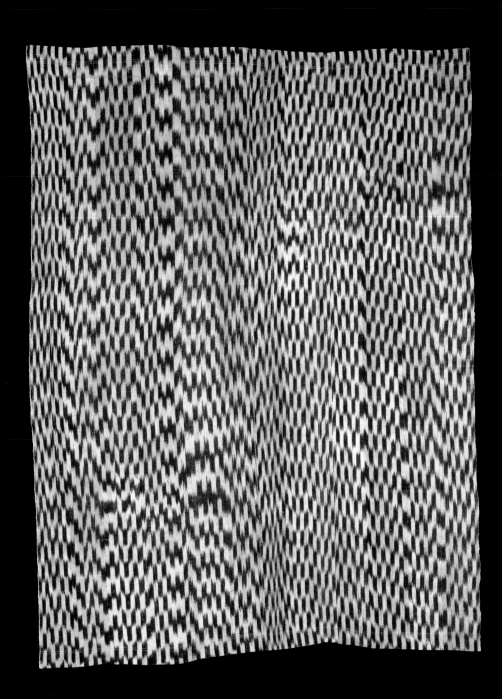

78 – WOMAN'S WRAP CLOTH. EBIRA. NIGERIA.
Heavy wrap cloth made of hand-spun cotton yarn. The simple but systematically offset ikat creates a strong visual impact. Women's work. Produced and collected in Somorika

177×134 cm. 2 panels – collected by Boser/Gardi 1974 – III 20165

79 – WOMAN'S WRAP CLOTH. EBIRA. NIGERIA.
Heavy wrap cloth made of hand-spun cotton yarn, with five different ikat patterns.
Women's work. Produced and collected in Igara

179 × 139 cm. 2 panels – collected by Boser/Gardi 1974 – III 20155

80 – WOMAN'S MARRIAGE CLOTH. IGBOMINA-YORUBA. NIGERIA.
Until the 1960s the Igbomina area southeast of Ilorin was a major centre of women's weaving. Around the
small town of Esie each locality had a distinctive variation of this type of marriage cloth in which the
indigo-dyed cloth was decorated with one or more panels of supplementary weft float weaving. They were
the most prestigious and complex of a set of up to five cloths which the bride's mother could weave

188 × 153 cm. 2 panels, each 76.5 cm wide - acquired from Duncan Clarke 2001 - III 27309

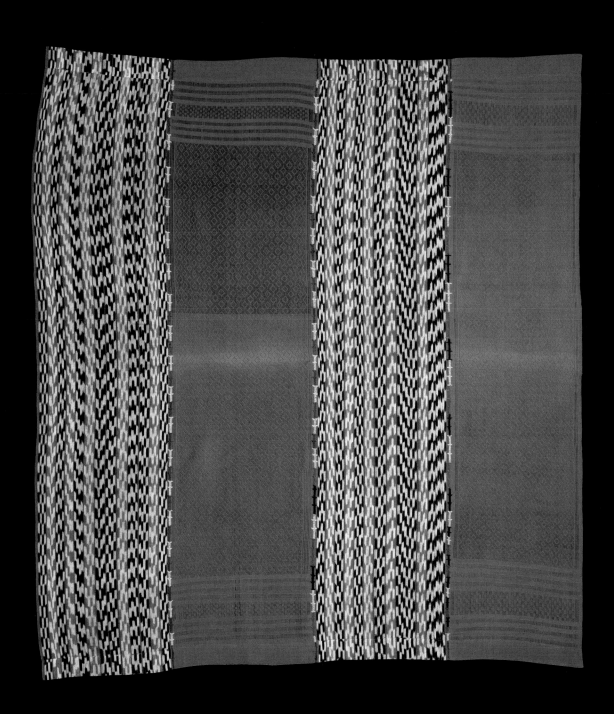

81 – LARGE-SIZED MAN'S CLOTH. EKITI-YORUBA. NIGERIA. BEFORE 1960.
Different yarn qualities. The green patterns are woven from industrial woollen yarn.
Produced in Owo. Purchased from Chief Oshendaiye (Mr Salami Ogundeji) in Isuada,
outside Owo. Women's work

220 × 202 cm. 4 panels – collected by Boser/Gardi 1974 – III 20166

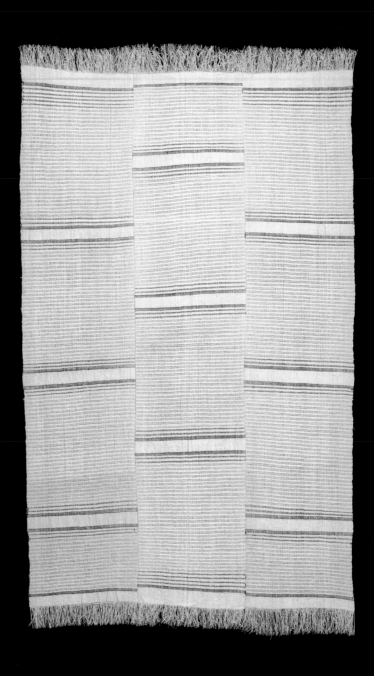

82 – WOMAN'S WRAP CLOTH. TOGO? REPUBLIC OF BENIN? AROUND 1900.
Three panels, each 31.5 cm wide. The panel in the middle is turned upside-down.
The cloth is made largely of raffia. The weft also contains cotton yarn. Open-work.

147 × 94 cm – Donation 1991, altes Schulhaus Reinach AG - III 25927

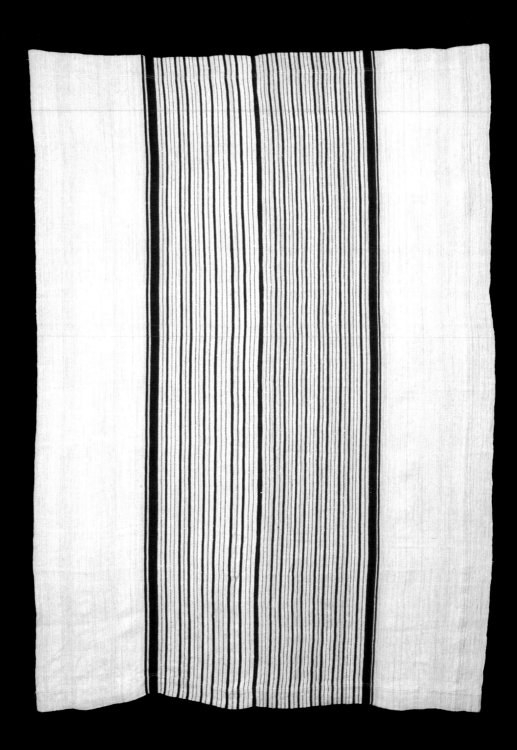

83 – WOMAN'S WRAP CLOTH. EBIRA. NIGERIA.
This is an *ebase* cloth: the white sections on the heavy cloth are not made
of cotton but of spun bast fibre (*ebase*) from a tree. Women's work

195×140 cm. 2 panels – collected by Boser/Gardi 1974 – III 20062

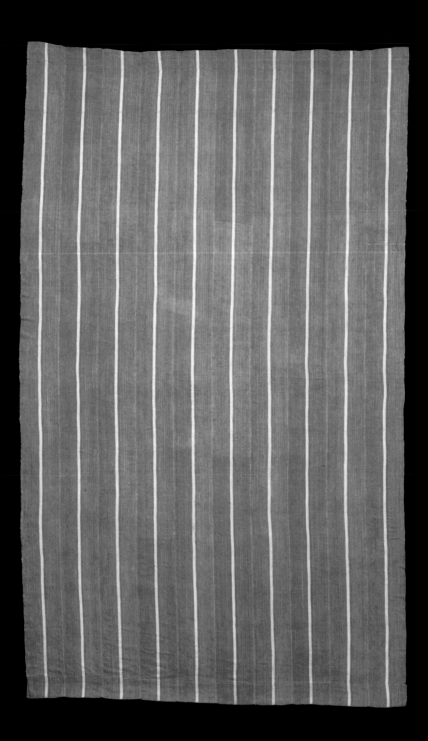

84 – WOMAN'S WRAP CLOTH. YORUBA. NIGERIA.
The brown sections on the cloth are made of natural-coloured
wild silk. Men's work. Produced and purchased in Ilorin

189 × 114 cm. 10 strips, each 11 cm wide – collected by Boser/Gardi
1974 – III 20058

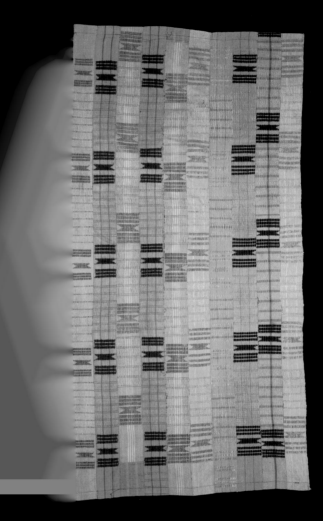

– SHAWL. YORUBA. NIGERIA.
is type of open-work in which the weaver draws in the
ft threads lengthwise in a float pattern mode in the
cess of weaving is a speciality of men's weaving among
Yoruba. Cotton and artificial silk. Purchased in Iperu

×95 cm. 10 strips, each 9.5 cm wide – collected by Boser/Gardi
4 – III 19957

86 – SHAWL *IPELE*. YORUBA. NIGERIA.
Worn for ceremonial events such as weddings, together
with a larger wrap cloth and a narrow head-tie of the
same material, and with a blouse tailored from imported
lace fabric. Collected in Ilorin

182 × 105 cm. 10 strips, each 10.5 cm wide – collected by Boser/Gardi
1974 – III 19959

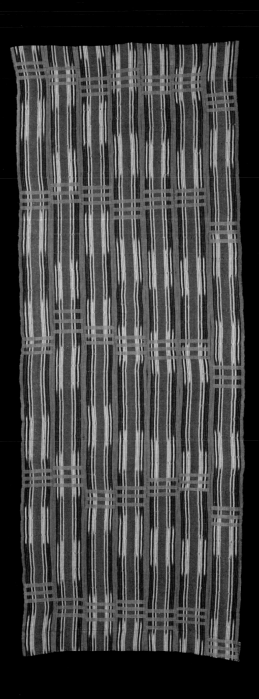

87 – SHAWL OR WOMAN'S HEAD-TIE. YORUBA. NIGERIA. BEFORE 1970.
Ikat. Cotton yarn, magenta-coloured silk. Purchased in Benin City

188 × 70 cm. 7 strips, each 10 cm wide – collected by Boser/Gardi 1974 – III 20130

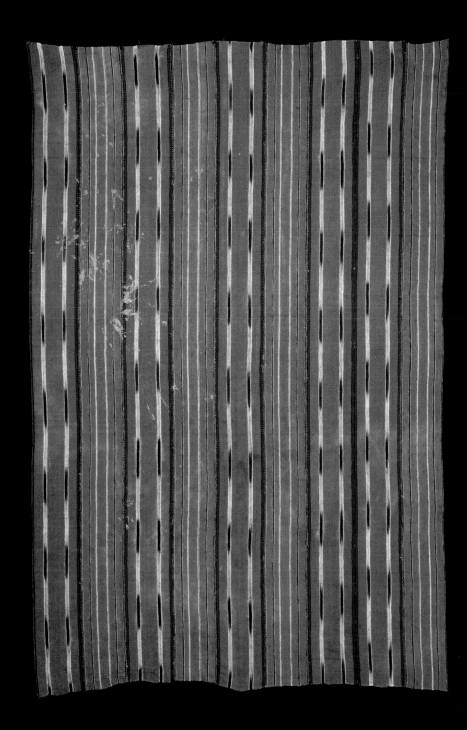

88 – SILK IKAT. YORUBA. NIGERIA. AROUND 1900.
In the 19th century silk cloths like this were among the most valuable textiles; the silk was
imported via Tripoli across the Sahara on the old caravan trade routes to Nigeria. The strips
on this rare cloth are wider than the 12 cm format usually found in Yoruba weaving

225×145 cm. 9 strips, each 15 cm wide – collected by Hanns Vischer 1902 – III 1397b

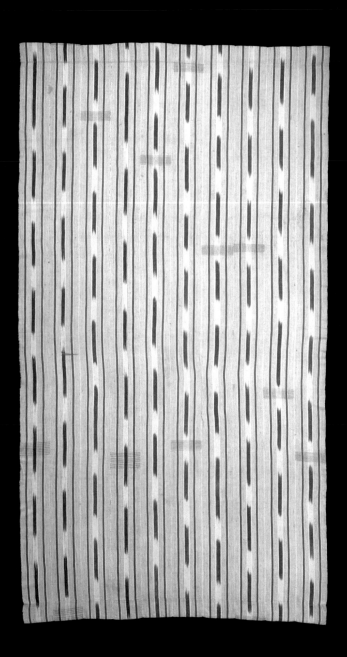

89 – WOMAN'S SHAWL *IPELE*. YORUBA. NIGERIA. AROUND 1930–1950.
Cloths like this were worn on ceremonial occasions together with a wrap cloth, *iborun*,
and a head-tie, *gele*, of the same design. Collected in Ilorin

192 × 108 cm. 10 strips, each 11 cm wide – collected by Boser/Gardi 1974 – III 20128

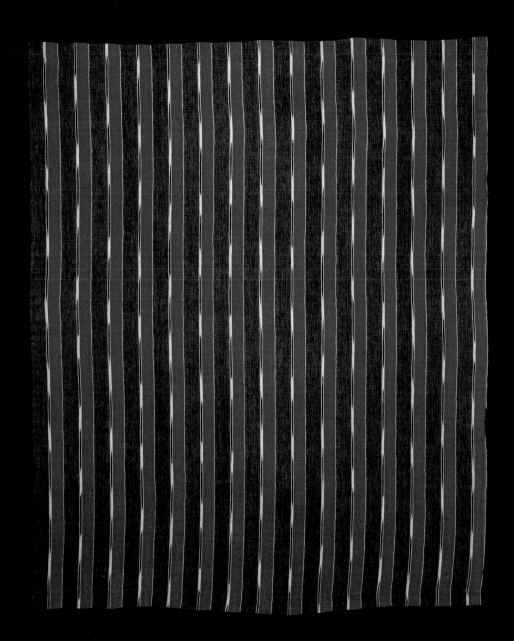

90 – SHAWL *IPELE*. YORUBA. NIGERIA.
Simple ikat patterns are typical for Yoruba men's weaving in the 20th
century. Produced and purchased in Ejigbo

176×147 cm. 15 strips, each 10 cm wide – collected by Boser/Gardi 1974 – III 20146

MIXED STRIP CLOTHS

Duncan Clarke

Yoruba *aso oke* cloths made up of more than one strip pattern were once quite common. Many cloths alternated two patterns while others had a repeat of four or as much as six different strips. However, we must distinguish these planned designs from a second type of mixed strip cloth, of which the piece shown here is an example. In this second type the cloth is composed of leftover strips and the overall effect is an incidental result. To understand the origin of this second type of mixed cloth we need to look more closely at the economics of cloth production within weaving compounds. Master weavers, who are usually men in their 40s or older, obtain orders from customers, buy the thread needed, and organize production, but in most cases do not actually weave the cloth themselves. The weaving is done by junior relatives, apprentices, and a few young men who have completed their training but lack sufficient resources to work independently. It is only this latter group of dependent weavers who receive any payment, getting an agreed sum of money for each set of strips completed. When the warp thread is set up to produce a set of strips the master weaver allocates sufficient thread to produce one more than is needed. If there is a problem with one piece during weaving this extra strip is taken as a replacement but otherwise it is retained by the individual weaver. Specialist traders regularly tour weaving compounds buying up these extra strips from the weavers. They then resell them, either individually at one of the periodic wholesale cloth markets or made up into cheap 'patchwork' cloths which are generally exported to northern Nigeria and sold in rural markets.

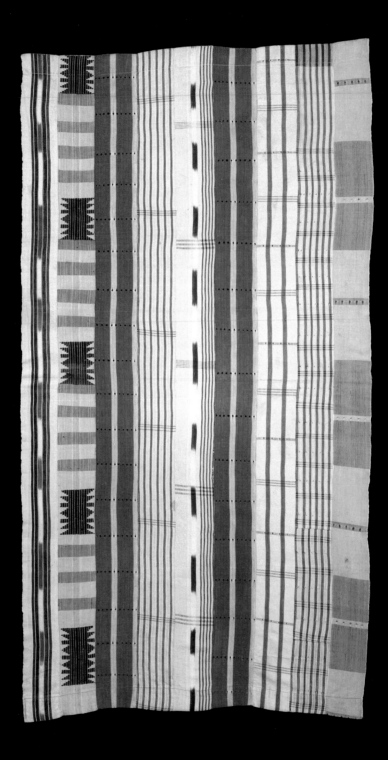

91 – OYO-YORUBA. NIGERIA. AROUND 1970.
Nine strips, eight different warps: only the two red strips were woven
with the same warp. Industrial cotton yarn. Purchased in Ilorin

165 × 91 cm. 9 strips, each 10 cm wide – collected by Boser/Gardi 1974 – III 20132

BABY-TIES

Duncan Clarke

Usually a woman ties the baby onto her back with the cloth wrapper she is wearing as a skirt, then positions the baby-tie around it as an additional support. Today the overwhelming majority of hand-woven cloth that one sees worn in non-ceremonial contexts, for example, by women in the market, will be these baby-ties. For many years the production of simple warp-striped and plain cloths for use as baby-ties were a main source of income for women weavers on the single-heddle loom in towns such as Okene, Igara and Ijebu-Ode. Thick nylon threads have largely replaced hand-spun cotton and many have a tufted pile area at the centre of the cloth band. Expensive imported velvet or brocade cloths serve as a more prestigious substitute.

Strip-weave *aso oke* cloth is also frequently used as a baby-tie as is illustrated by many pieces in the Basel Museum collection, and it is this usage that highlights aspects of the cultural and metaphorical significance of the practice. Among the Yoruba when a young woman has her first baby it is expected that her mother will give her the cloth she will use as a baby-tie to secure the infant to her back. The role of cloth in linking together generations through the female line is actualized in the practice of women giving to their daughters some of their old *aso oke*, if possible a piece from the set that they wore for their own wedding, to literally support the new born child. Elisha Renne (1995: 192–196) has provided us with a sensitive and nuanced account of the cultural salience of the practice of using cloth to 'back' a child, drawing on ideas that extend far more widely than the Bunu Yoruba region that was her primary focus. The imagery of 'backing' as protecting and sustaining is frequently invoked, as for example in the case of a major Iseyin master weaver who, when talking about the numerous less successful weavers who were reliant on him, told me "masters carry masters on their backs nowadays."

92 – BABY-TIE OJA. YORUBA. NIGERIA. BEFORE 1940.
This cloth served originally as a head-tie, or *gele*, being part of a three-piece ceremonial
outfit known as a 'complete'. The weft float design on a check ground is an unusually
complex example of a common style that is called *omolangidi*. Purchased in Ilorin

249 × 56 cm. 4 strips, each 14 cm wide – collected by Boser/Gardi 1974 – III 19962

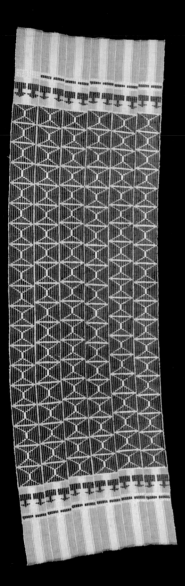
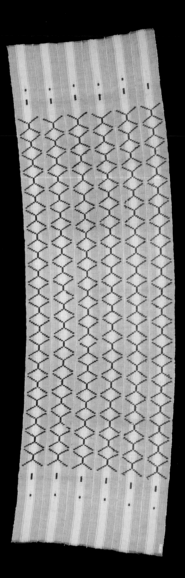

93 – BABY-TIE *OJA*. YORUBA. NIGERIA.

The elaborate style of weft float decoration that almost totally concealed the ground weave of the strip, dating from around the 1930s, was relatively unusual but Yoruba weavers were continually experimenting with new variations on patterns. Popular new designs were often given a name by the cloth dealers to promote sales. In this example the name *temi di ire*, 'what belongs to me is good', was noted when it was collected. Purchased in Ilorin

197 × 59 cm. 6 strips, each 10 cm wide – collected by Boser/Gardi 1974 – III 19968

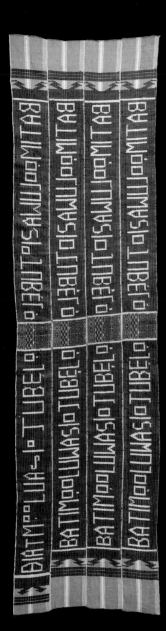
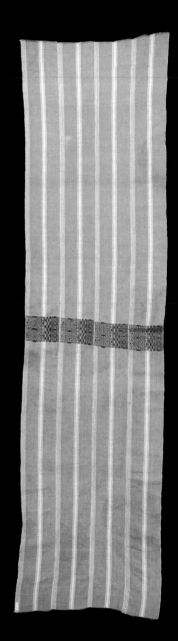

94 – BABY-TIE *OJA*. YORUBA. NIGERIA. AROUND 1920.
This is an early and unusual example of a style of cloth with written text created
by supplementary weft float. In a virtuoso display of weaving skill the text is
reversed so there is a mirror image at each side of the central block of geometric
pattern. It reads *Batimo Oluwa so, o jubelo!* which can be translated as 'God is
greater than we can say!' Purchased in Ilorin

209 × 56 cm. 4 strips, each 14 cm wide – collected by Boser/Gardi 1974 – III 19970

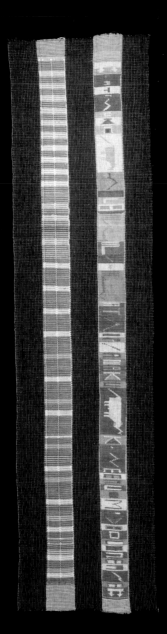

**95 – BABY-TIE OJA. YORUBA. NIGERIA.
AROUND 1920–1940.**
This design was normally found with the weft float motifs
in magenta thread rather than the vivid array of colours
seen here. Yoruba weavers liked to experiment, and designs
such as this were a response to the increasing availability
of imported, coloured yarns. Purchased in Ilorin

200 × 58 cm. 6 strips, each 10 cm wide – collected by Boser/Gardi
1974 – III 19969

96 – BABY-TIE OJA. YORUBA. NIGERIA.
AROUND 1920–1940.
By varying the colour within each pick of the weft the
weaver can create motifs that, in this case, include animals
as well as words in both Yoruba and Arabic. Although all
Yoruba male weavers are Muslims, the use of Arabic texts
on cloths is extremely unusual. Purchased in Ilorin

217 × 53 cm. 5 strips, each 10.5 cm wide – collected by Boser/Gardi
1974 – III 19971

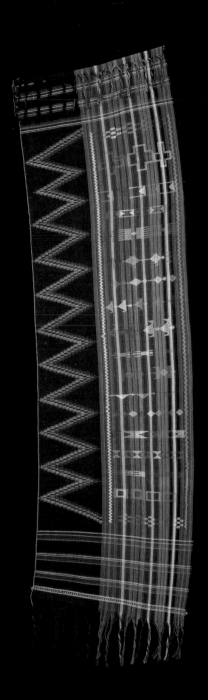

97 – SHAWL. NUPE. NIGERIA.
Most Nupe men's weaving was simple warp-striped patterns.
The more elaborate style shown here was clearly influenced
by Yoruba *aso oke* designs and was extremely rare. It may well
be the case that it was developed by the master weaver of
this example, Alhaji Sule of Umaru Majigi quarter, Bida (see
fig. 144). Purchased from the weaver

225 × 52 cm. 5 strips, each 10.5 cm wide – collected by Boser/Gardi
1974 – III 19985

98 – WOMAN'S CLOTH *FULANI*. NUPE. NIGERIA.
Single panel produced by Mrs Nana Al Hajj Sehu of Kutigi
(see fig. 143). Nupe women weave with machine-spun
threads and favour elaborate geometric patterning in supplementary weft float on a warp-striped background.
Purchased from the weaver

232 × 72 cm – collected by Boser/Gardi 1974 – III 19979

A TALE OF TWO SISTERS

Jean Borgatti

I first met Achetu Obamina during the Oghalo title festival of her stepson Idogu in 1972. She was one of the painters working on the exterior wall of his title chamber. Several days later, she strode into his compound, a leader among the group of female elders who performed and officiated during this ceremony along with their male counterparts (see Borgatti 1983). As I came to know her better, I discovered that she was a weaver and textile designer too, one specializing in the distinctive Okpella cloth called *omada* that designates a woman's status as female titled elder and serves as her shroud. [91] I met her sister Iyawo as a member of the women's sodality associated with Okpella's commemorative masks. She served as *inyilimi* (Mother of Spirits), and custodian of her Aunt Idegbuwa's memorial masquerade. [92] Iyawo, like Achetu – though somewhat in her shadow as a younger sister with a less flamboyant personality – sang, told stories, wove and designed cloth. She accompanied Achetu singing the songs of women's title taking in a private performance for the tape recorder; offered a story in a session organized by Achetu, again for purposes of recording; and sold the title cloth she had made to the Basel Museum at her sister's behest.

Achetu and Iyawo were Okpella women living in the rocky uplands of the northern part of Edo State in southern Nigeria,[93] in a rural community reached by travelling some miles over a rutted dirt road. Their lives bridged the colonial and post-colonial eras, and they saw dramatic changes in the worlds of their children and grand-children, although it did not seem to affect the lives that they themselves led, except to portend changes that distressed and disconcerted Achetu, at least, towards the end of her life.

Iyawo died between 1979 and 2002, but Achetu was still alive in 2002 when I returned to Nigeria after a 23-year absence. Achetu lived in the same modest quarters she had used when I first knew her, though her grandson lives in a fine multi-storied house, drives a Mercedes, and was said to own a cybercafe. As I walked towards her across the open courtyard of the compound in 2002, she said: "I wondered if I would see you again before I died." As part of our time together, I began collecting her family history. [94]

She and Iyawo were the two youngest of their mother's five surviving children. Their parents, Onebe and Obamina, belonged to the highest ranks of Okpella society, the body of titled elders who assume their place on the basis of achievement, birthright and generosity. Achetu described them as skilled artists and performers, noting their fine voices. Achetu followed her mother to the events where wall-painting and praise-singing took place, eventually taking title herself and assuming her mother's roles in these activities. Achetu maintained that of the five children, three girls and two boys, only she and the oldest brother showed interest in art and craft, and developed that interest into skilled execution. However, all five were performers. The oldest brother played an acrobatic masquerade and the others excelled at different named dances. Iyawo was Mother of Spirits, taking the title and its

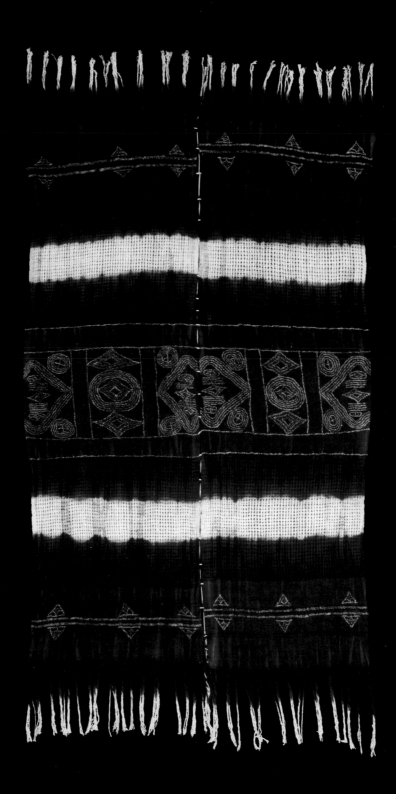

99 – *OMADA* CLOTH. OKPELLA, ETSAKO EAST DIVISION. NIGERIA.
These cloths were female insignia of rank. Some sections in openwork, indigo resist
dyeing, hand-spun yarn. The two panels have been sewn together provisionally.
Produced by Mrs Iyawo Obamina on order from Jean Borgatti for the Museum der Kulturen

150×101 (without fringes) – collected by Jean Borgatti 1979 – III 21498

responsibilities at Achetu's request. As the senior sister, it was her right to do this, but as a Christian, she chose not to participate in this particular cultural practice. All the girls tried their hands at wall painting, but neither sister was as good at it as Achetu. Presumably, they all learned to weave as well.

In the early 1970s, she and Iyawo were among the few women who continued to make *omada* cloth for female titled elders. This is an indigo-dyed resist patterned cloth that is woven of finely hand-spun cotton thread. Bands of openwork, loosely woven, separate tightly woven fields that are stitched with raffia to create designs. These designs recall the body-painting designs applied to a man's back and chest during his title ceremony, as well as designs painted on the walls of the title chamber. To be painted with this design is to be crowned. To sleep in the title chamber during the three-month transitional period from elder to living ancestor is to be imprinted with the values embodied by these designs. To wear cloth designed similarly is to show the corresponding status of a titled woman.

Achetu and Iyawo, belonging to an older generation, supported Okpella cultural traditions and derived a sense of identity and well-being from so doing. She lamented in 2002 that she had no lineal descendant to follow her in wall-painting and no one to sing funeral songs for her, as she had sung them for so many. Achetu Obamina passed away in November 2008, over 100 years old by her reckoning.

100 — Mrs Achetu Obamina, titled elder, textile artist, painter and performer. She is the sister of Iyawo Obamina who has produced the cloth on fig. 99

Photo Jean Borgatti 2002

132

101 – Mrs Achetu Obamina demonstrating the spinning of cotton

Photo Jean Borgatti 1974

— 102 —

HIS MAJESTY KING ANUBIL OF THE WAREBO IN SAKASSOU, CÔTE D'IVOIRE.
The king and his dignitaries are richly adorned with gold insignia and large-sized cloths. At the far right an ikat of the type *zaza* is to be seen. The man to his left is wearing an Asante *kente*.

Photo Urs Rahm, January 1957 – EIII-28

CÔTE D'IVOIRE

Textile Craft Between Success and Decline

Kerstin Bauer

Today's textile craft in Côte d'Ivoire is the result of a rich blend of practices and cross-cultural exchange. Appropriations and mutual influences have their origin in the mobility of people and goods, long-distance trade with cloths, cooperation between producers across ethnic boundaries and market preferences. In this context labour migration plays an important role in a double sense: one the one hand, migrant weavers introduced new technologies and designs to the areas where they settled down, either permanently or on a temporary basis; on the other hand, they themselves learnt new techniques on location which they were then able to incorporate into their own designs and manufacture, thus enriching the textile traditions of their home region upon return.

A look at textile manufacture in West Africa shows that occasionally the same types of cloth were produced by weavers from different ethnic backgrounds. Some of these textiles are actually so alike that even experts find it difficult to allocate them to a specific group. These overlaps are not necessarily the result of trade, the migration of population groups or the mobility of craftsmen, very often they ensue from interethnic collaboration. In the process of production, a fabric often passes through the hands of weavers and dyers from different ethnic groups. This kind of blending and interaction is encountered in many textile traditions of Côte d'Ivoire, for example between various Mande groups (Dyula, Maninka/ Koyara, Guro) and the Akan (Baule).

THE EARLY MASTERS: DYULA ARTISTRY

The Dyula people who, arriving from the north, began to settle in Côte d'Ivoire in the 16th century exerted strong influence on the textile traditions of various ethnicities. The Dyula are Muslim Mande-speakers who, in earlier days, used to be occupied mainly in trade, Islamic studies and textile production. They not only introduced Islam to the locations along the trade routes where they settled down, these towns grew to become actual centres of technological innovation and diffusion for industries such as weaving and dyeing.

The town of Kong in northern modern Côte d'Ivoire became an important textile centre and a hub in the trans-regional trade in fabrics, salt, cola nuts and gold. Kong was famous for the large variety and exclusive quality of the cloths produced in the local workshops. Binger, the first European to visit Kong in 1888, commented on the supreme craftsmanship of the Dyula weavers, dyers and embroiderers as follows: "Ces étoffes sont à juste titre les plus belles que produisent les noirs." (Binger 1889/90: 86) Next to the elaborate weaves, one of the main features of Dyula textiles from Kong was the early application of imported red yarn to produce prestigious red-patterned cloths. [95] Next to that the local weavers were renowned for their ikat cloths which date back to pre-colonial times (see fig. 119).

The exquisite pattern weaving and dyeing common to this West African region probably had their origin in Kong. However, the town's golden age came to an abrupt end when it was destroyed by the forces of Samori Touré; [96] changes to the economic geography during the colonial era led to the demise of this famous commercial centre. Nowadays Kong has approximately 4,000 inhabitants; it lies off the main travel and trade routes and has lost all its significance as a trade and textile centre. The Dyula, famous for their mobility, are now to be found in many West African cities and along the main routes of commerce where they brought their textile art to. Especially in the central part of Côte d'Ivoire the division of labour between craftsmen from different ethnic backgrounds has led to numerous mutual influences between Guro, Baule, Maninka and Dyula. Thus, for example, you have Duyla dyers working for Baule and Guro weavers, applying special resist-dye techniques to yarns and cloths.

The Dyula not only influenced the weaving and dyeing practices of other ethnicities, often they themselves took over designs from others and incorporated them into their repertoire, for example, the ikat patterns *dame* ('checkerboard') and *zaza* ('mixture of patterns') which evolved through the collaboration of Baule and Dyula craftsmen in the Baule region (see fig. *zaza*). It appears that the Dyula integrated the *dame* pattern into their repertoire at some time after the Second World War, the *zaza* design in the course of the 1950s and 1960s. Dyula weavers took with them from the Baule area the *dame* and *zaza* designs back to Kong in northern Côte d'Ivoire from where the designs spread as far as Burkina Faso. Today these ikat cloths are part and parcel of every Dyula wedding and belong to the standard repertoire of many Dyula weavers.

In earlier days Dyula hand-woven cloths were worn as everyday dress and also served as festive attire for rituals, ceremonies and on feast days. However, since the 1960s hand-woven fabrics have disappeared almost completely from everyday dress and today they are practically only worn for ritual and ceremonial occasions (weddings, funerals), with the result that demand has declined rapidly. Moreover, many of the traditional patterns have gone out of fashion and the old designs are no longer ordered with the result that when old weavers retire from work, knowledge as to how they were made is lost by and by. Considering the low level of income, very few young Dyula men are willing to go into weaving. Their only chance to stay in the textile business is to move to an area where tourism and the sale of arts and crafts have created new market opportunities.

GURO TEXTILES

The Guro are members of the Southern Mande language group. Arriving from the north, they settled in the central region of Côte d'Ivoire between the 13th and 16th century. In the face of Baule groups moving in from the east during the 18th century the Guro retreated to their present settlement area in the western part of central Côte d'Ivoire.

Guro weaving and dyeing bear clear reference to the textile traditions of the Manding groups in the north (Dyula, Maninka/Koyara) and to those of the Baule. In pre-colonial days, trade with the Dyula and neighbouring Maninka and Koyara groups was especially important for the northern Guro groups. Following colonial occupation and pacification by the French in the course of the 19th century, Manding craftsmen and traders began moving into the area where the Guro settled, and "[...] along with their trading activities they brought their looms and their different models of cloth to influence and be influenced by Gouro cloth." (Sumberg 2001: 80–81)

136

The Guro weaving tradition is probably quite old, but its precise history is not known. The Guro used cotton cloths for ritual and ceremonial purposes in pre-colonial times but we do not know whether they produced the fabrics themselves or whether they were traded in. Certainly they were cultivating cotton by the beginning of the 20th century, and nearly every village is said to have had its weaver (Tauxier 1924: 188), but it cannot be ruled out completely that the Guro adopted weaving from one of their neighbouring groups. What speaks for a strong influence from the north is the fact that the Guro use the same type of loom as their northern neighbours, and that there are distinctly more weavers in the northern Guro areas than in the southern and western region. Fact is also that the Guro did not do the dyeing themselves, instead they employed resident Manding craftsmen to do the task.

Guro textiles from the first half of the 20th century were usually made of local hand-spun cotton. Men and women wore the same cloths, distinct only in terms of size. Men's cloths consisted of 14 to 16 strips, the women's cloths of 10 to 12 strips. White and blue were the predominant colours; occasionally the weavers used imported red yarn. As among other groups, cloths decorated with patterns of red yarn were regarded as especially valuable. From the 1930s onwards, figurative motifs appeared in Guro weaving for the first time (as in Baule weaving) as well as textiles made of industrial yarn. In the economic boom years of the 1950s, industrial fibres increasingly replaced hand-spun yarn – a development that was not specific only to the Guro. Whereas early fabrics were hardly decorated, if at all, ornamentation increased in the course of the 1960s. The first time written words appeared on Guro cloths was in 1963. Since the 1980s the number of cloth types as well as the quality have noticeably decreased (Sumberg 2001), and today young Guro weavers limit production to very simple models with uncomplicated patterns.

The majority of the Guro textiles held in the Museum der Kulturen Basel were collected in 1974. They are chiefly from the northern Guro region and were probably produced sometime between 1946 and 1974.

THE NEW MASTERS: THE SUCCESS OF BAULE TEXTILES

The best-known textile manufacture in Côte d'Ivoire today is that of the Baule. The Baule are members of the Akan language group; they migrated to central Côte d'Ivoire from what is today modern Ghana in the 18th century, pushing out resident Guro and Senufo groups. The Baule appear to have been receptive to cultural imports from neighbouring groups right from the start, and this proved a highly successful strategy. Their weaving and dyeing display clear signs of Dyula influence, many of whom settled down, or at least worked temporarily, in the Baule area during the colonial era as traders, weavers and dyers. By the same token, Baule textile manufacture exerted noticeable influence on various other Ivorian textile traditions.

The Baule appear to have been familiar with weaving when they moved to their new settlement area in Côte d'Ivoire. Compared to the Dyula, however, their textile vocabulary is quite limited. And since the patterns they produced were still rather unsophisticated at the time of independence, the hypothesis has been put forward that the Baule are still quite new to weaving and that they adopted most of their techniques from resident and neighbouring groups after their arrival in Côte d'Ivoire.

We certainly know that the Baule often engaged craftsmen from other groups (mainly Dyula) for the dyeing of yarns and cloths. Cloths that the Dyula call *fani siri* were especially popular. These are hand-woven textiles often richly decorated with weft patterns and additionally coloured with indigo by the tie-dye method (figs. 113, 114, 120). This latter technique expands the design variation of already patterned cloths, thus enhancing and refining the quality of cloth. Fabrics of this type were being produced by Dyula dyers for their Baule patrons already during the colonial era (i.e. in the 1930s).

It was only in the course of the 1950s and 1960s that the Baule began to adopt resist techniques from local Dyula dyers: "Les Baoulé nous apportaient le fil et les étoffes à teindre, et aussi à ligaturer pour les *fani siri* [tie-dyed indigo cloths] et les *suruku kawa* [ikat]. Petit à petit les Baoulé ont aussi appris chez nous à faire du *suruku kawa* et les autres *fani siri*.» (Amadou Touré, Korhogo, 26 September 1974, fieldnotes Boser-Sarivaxévanis).
Due to the strong Dyula influence on Baule textiles, cloths produced by the two groups today look very similar. Some of the ikat patterns are manufactured by craftsmen from both ethnicities (see *zaza*, figs. 115–117). A further feature in common is the red border that is joined to one of the long sides of the cloth. Today, these two elements are considered typical of Baule textiles although they are actually of Dyula origin. Textile manufacture among the Baule was not only characterized by this form of appropriation but also because they were quick to adopt and incorporate all kinds of innovatory trends. Thus, for example, the Baule began using industrial yarn as early as the 1930s (Heuzey 1936: 7); by the 1950s the rate of hand-spun yarn had sunk to a mere 11 percent. The Baule also developed and adapted their looms to new standards. They used to operate the same type of loom as their neighbours but in the course of the last twenty to thirty years they have rationalized loom technology and, today, the Baule weavers adopt a nearly upright posture when working at the loom.

NEW AND OLD TEXTILE CENTRES IN CÔTE D'IVOIRE

The elaborate pattern weaving and indigo dyeing in Côte d'Ivoire almost certainly originated and spread from the old Dyula centre of Kong that had been famous for its textile art even before the colonial era began. During colonial days the Duyla brought with them their highly-developed weaving and dyeing technologies to the Baule region which, after independence, gradually grew to become one of the main textile centres in Côte d'Ivoire. From here, and as a result of cross-cultural exchange, new textile designs and cloth types began to spread to other regions. Thus, some Dyula returned north taking with them new ikat patterns from the Baule region; the same is true of Koyara craftsmen from the Mankono area who, after having mastered ikat techniques in the Baule region, returned with this new method to northern Côte d'Ivoire after independence (fieldnotes Boser-Sarivaxévanis, Mankono, 20 September 1974).

What are the grounds for the present success of the textile industry in the Baule region? One reason certainly lies in the fact that the Baule commercialized production at a very early stage. They not only produced on commission, they also sold their produce directly to walk-in customers, for example, hand-woven cloths at outlets along the main north-south road running through the Baule region. These textiles are very popular as souvenirs and presents among both European and African tourists and travellers, but they also serve as representative cloths for dignitaries and traditional chiefs and leaders.

A further reason is the flexibility that the Baule displayed in taking over ideas and elements from other groups, to the extent that new designs and dye methods which the Baule had adopted from neighbouring groups soon came to be seen as being of Baule origin: "Because the Baoulé are some of the most prolific and commercialized weavers in Côte d'Ivoire these cloths are associated with them now ..." (Sumberg 2001: 124). Thus, for instance, ikat cloths, which are actually of Dyula origin, are now regarded as typical Baule textiles. The patterns are used as imitation prints on cotton fabrics and even adorn souvenirs and web-sites. The popularity and renown of Baule textiles underlines the success story of Baule textile art. They have become the actual hallmark of Ivorian textile production, while the elaborate Dyula cloths have more or less faded into oblivion.

The vitality of the Baule weaving tradition also became evident during the civil war that broke out in Côte d'Ivoire in 2002, leading to a partitioning of the country with a practically closed frontier between the northern and the southern regions, and markedly reducing the mobility of people and goods. In the northern half of the country, which was dominated by the rebels, textile production and sales almost came to a stand-still since the people no longer had the money to purchase expensive cloths. After tourism and the sale of souvenirs broke down (for example in the Korhogo region) there were no more income opportunities and the weavers had to turn to new jobs for a living. In the south, which remained under government control, the production, distribution and sale of hand-woven fabrics continued almost unimpeded. In fact, Baule textile manufacture actually flourished. Today, hundreds of young men in the Baule region have moved into the textile business, forming the next generation of weavers. They certainly would not have done so if they had not sensed new income opportunities and anticipated a bright future for the textile industry.

103 – BALADJI BARRO (c.1905 – c.1985).
He was a weaver from Kong who is still famous for his skill. He came from
a family of weavers, traders and Islamic scholars, members of which
also lived in Burkina Faso (Darsalami). The Barro family owns a large compound in the Barrola quarter with a small mosque

Photo B. Gardi, 20.9.1974 – (F) III 101597

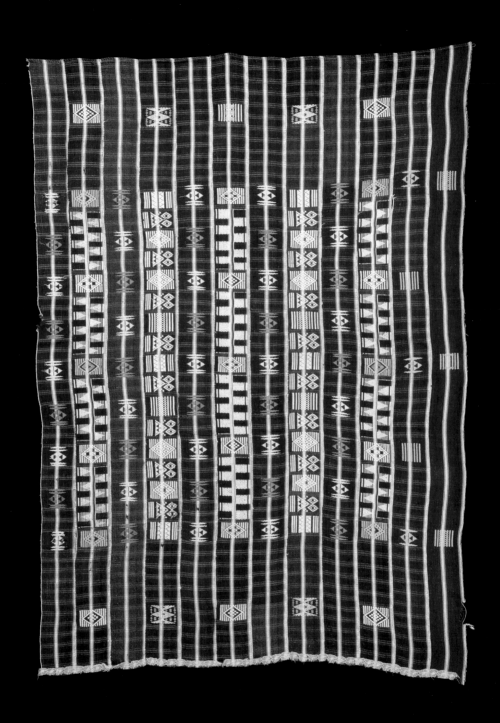

104 – 'PAGNE' *MALAKA KAWA* ('STAINS ON THE DYER').
DYULA. CÔTE D'IVOIRE.
Purchased from the master weaver Baladji Barro in Kong. Patterns
misiri ('mosque'), *sosira* ('track of the horse'), *foroto* ('spice')

160 × 116 cm. 12 strips, each 10 cm wide – collected by Boser/Gardi 1974 – III 20580

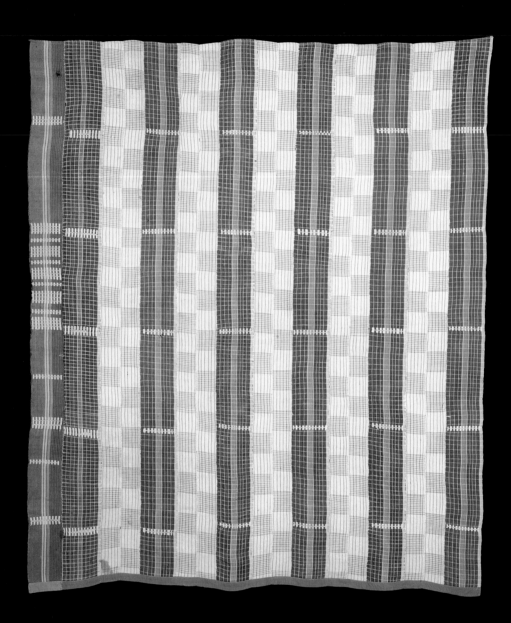

105 – 'PAGNE' *KORO FANI*. DYULA. CÔTE D'IVOIRE.
Narrow strips with red and white chequers: *koro fani*. They are only half
the width of usual strips. This pattern was probably already being produced
by the Dyula before the colonial era. Produced and purchased in Kong

136 × 119 cm. 6 strips, each 9.5 cm wide; 10 strips, each approx. 5 cm wide – collected by
Boser/Gardi 1974 – III 20577

106 – 'PAGNE' *AKUBE*. DYULA. CÔTE D'IVOIRE.
The cloth is richly decorated with white weft float patterns including *misiri* ('mosque'),
sosira ('track of the horse') and *foroto* ('spice'). At the centre the patterns are
arranged in diamond-shape. Cloths with central motifs like this are hardly produced
any more, except by Maninka and Guro weavers. Produced and purchased in Kong

151 × 112 cm. 13 strips, each 9 cm wide – collected by Boser/Gardi 1974 – III 20579

107 – 'PAGNE'. BAULE. CÔTE D'IVOIRE.
Ikat. Red warp stripe down one length. At both ends twined white threads
and white fringes decorate the borders. Purchased in Gouitafla

154 × 106 cm. 12 strips, each approx. 9 cm wide – coll. by Boser/Gardi 1974 – III 20196

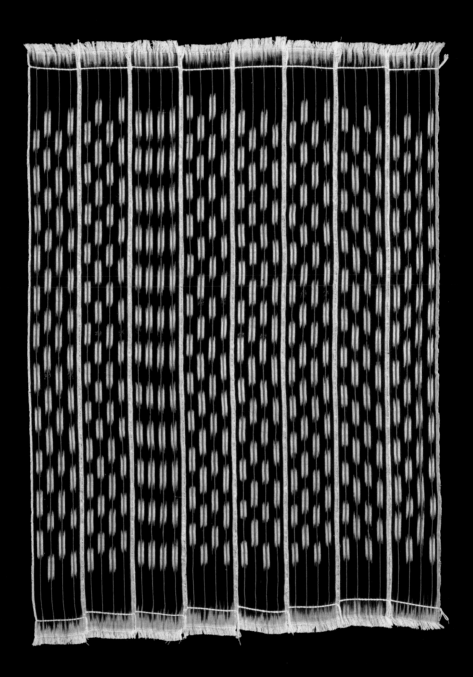

108 – 'PAGNE'. BAULE. CÔTE D'IVOIRE.
Ikat. Yellow warp stripe down one length. At both ends twined white
threads and white fringes decorate the borders. Purchased in Bouaké

145×108 cm. 8 strips, each 13 cm wide – coll. by Boser/Gardi 1974 – III 20200

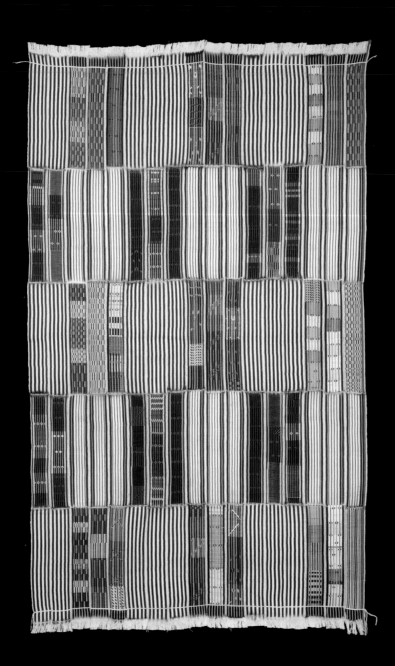

**109 – MEN'S WRAP CLOTH *ZAZA*, POSSIBILY *MONEKENYAN* ('DEUX DIMANCHES').
BAULE. CÔTE D'IVOIRE.**
Purchased from the producer, the master weaver Akoumbi Kouamé in Bomizabo.
Ikat, weft float patterns. Red warp stripe down one length. At both ends twined white
threads and white fringes decorate the borders

264×164 cm. 17 strips, each 10 cm wide – collected by Boser/Gardi 1974 – III 20238

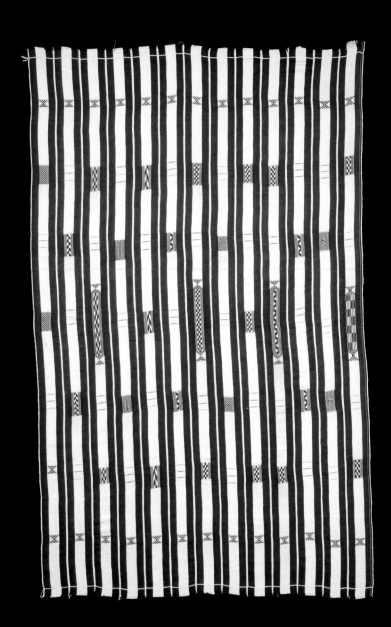

110 – LARGE COTTON CLOTH. MANINKA/KOYARA? CÔTE D'IVOIRE.
Purchased in Mankono. Blue and white warp stripes. Mainly blue weft float patterns.
Red warp stripe down one length. At both ends twined white threads and white fringes
decorate the borders

253×160 cm. 13 strips, each 12 cm wide – collected by Boser/Gardi 1974 – III 20584

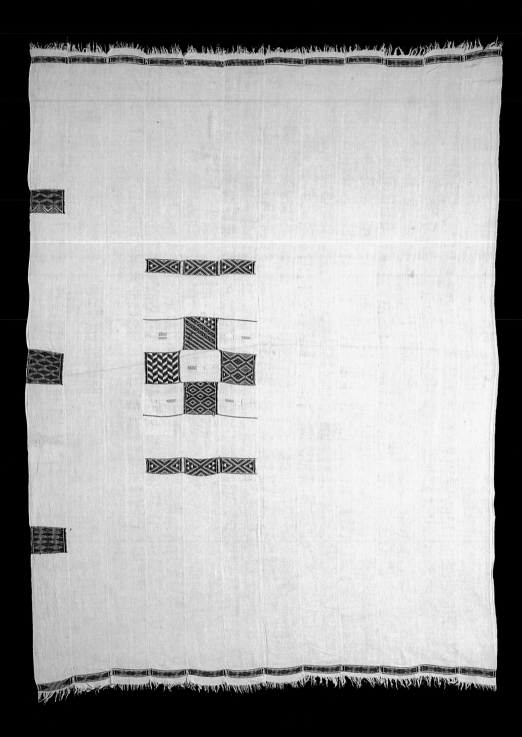

111 – 'PAGNE' *SO FU*. GURO. CÔTE D'IVOIRE.
Dark blue motifs on a light background. Border *pèè*. Produced and purchased in Blefla

206×159 cm. 12 strips, each 13 cm wide – collected by Boser/Gardi 1974 – III 20555

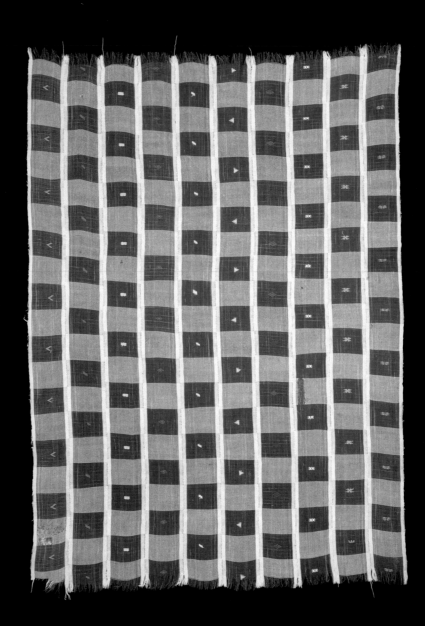

112 – 'PAGNE' *KPALO*. GURO. CÔTE D'IVOIRE.
The ground pattern consists of chequers. The dark-coloured chequers contain smaller motifs.
Within each strip the colour of the motifs is the same. Produced and purchased in Gouitafla

161×120 cm. 10 strips, each 12 cm wide – collected by Boser/Gardi 1974 – III 20566

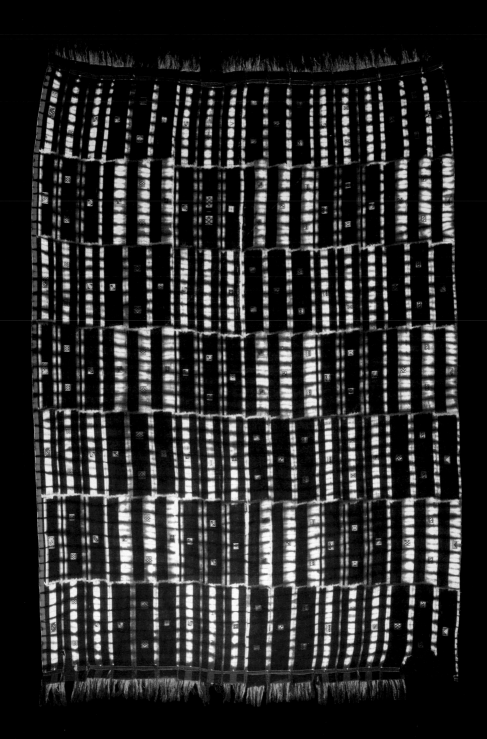

113 – MAN'S WRAP CLOTH. BAULE? DYULA? CÔTE D'IVOIRE.
Ikat with fine weft float patterns. Fold resist dyeing with indigo. Here the reverse
of the cloth is shown. Purchased in Mankono

243 × 150 cm. 18 strips, each 9 cm wide – collected by Boser/Gardi 1974 – III 20582

114 – 'PAGNE' *FANI SIRI*. DYULA. CÔTE D'IVOIRE.
Blue and white warp stripes with evenly arranged weft float patterns. Red warp stripe down one length.
The finished cloth was coloured by way of fold resist and tie-dyeing. Produced and purchased in Kong

150 × 116 cm. 14 strips, each 8.5 cm wide – collected by Boser/Gardi 1974 – III 20581

ZAZA – MIXING PATTERNS

Kerstin Bauer

Zaza or *nzassa* ('mixing patterns') is a term used for describing textiles and garments displaying a mixture of patterns. The origin of this term which is also used outside Côte d'Ivoire is not clear. Old photographs from West Africa taken at the end of the 19th century show that the technique of combining differently patterned strips or pieces of cloth to create a large-sized textile or an item of dress was already then common practice.

The hand-woven *zaza* textiles of the Dyula and Baule are ornate cloths displaying rectangular blocks with changing patterns and regularly alternating ikat patterns. Usually Duyla and Baule *zaza* cloths are decorated with colourful weft float patterns and have a red warp stripe down the length of one side, which looks like a seam when worn. Pattern compositions like this, where the cloth consists of a number of strips sewn together and with the pattern blocks extending over three or four strips require great skill on the part of the man dyeing the ikat skeins as well as on the part of the weaver.

The first *zaza* textiles with ikat and the typical colourful pattern blocks to appear in the Baule region date back to the early 1950s. [97] It is here in the central part of Côte d'Ivoire that this new type of cloth was created as a blend between Baule and Dyula textile traditions but it is difficult to say whether it was first produced by Baule or by Dyula craftsmen. In all probability, the dyeing of the ikat skeins – a highly complex process – was carried out by Dyula specialists who were famous for their skill as dyers. Dyula craftsmen began moving to the economically flourishing central part of the old French colony Côte d'Ivoire after the Baule region had been finally pacified (after 1916); here they started dyeing yarn and cloth for Baule weavers. It appears that the Baule themselves did not apply the ikat technique much before 1960, so early ikat cloths from the Baule region were most likely manufactured by Dyula craftsmen. At the same time, however, information gathered from interviews with the producers indicates that the design of the *zaza* cloths with their large, alternating pattern blocks was developed by Baule weavers. Thus, *zaza* textiles really appear to be the result of a collaboration between textile workers from two different ethnic groups. However, what we know for sure is that Dyula craftsmen who had been living and working in the Baule region as migrant workers returned to their home area – the once famous textile centre Kong in northern Côte d'Ivoire – in the course of the 1950s and 1960s, taking the new type of cloth with them. In Kong, the *zaza* design was incorporated into local production, which led to the creation of new styles, for example, *zaza* cloths displaying traditional Dyula patterns. In the course of time, these new cloths spread from Kong to other areas by means of trade and migrant Duyla craftsmen. Today, *zaza* cloths are not only manufactured in Côte d'Ivoire but also in Burkina Faso. Production is still in the hands of Dyula and Baule dyers and weavers; however they no longer work to stockpile, only to order. *Zaza* cloths are regarded as expensive and valuable textiles and are only worn for special occasions. Among the Dyula they are used in ritual contexts, for example, as wedding cloths; among the Baule they are worn on festive days and for official events.

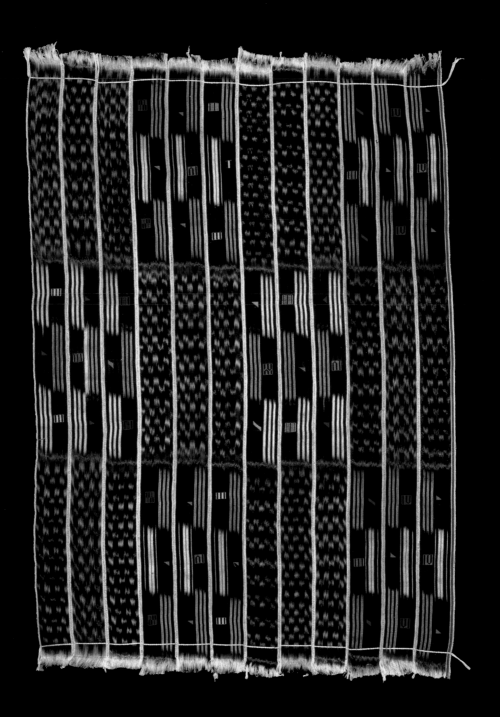

115 – 'PAGNE' *ZAZA*. BAULE. CÔTE D'IVOIRE.
Ikat, weft float patterns: red warp stripe down one length

154 × 116 cm. 12 strips, each 10 cm wide – collected by
André Aeschlimann 1958 – 62 – III 16752

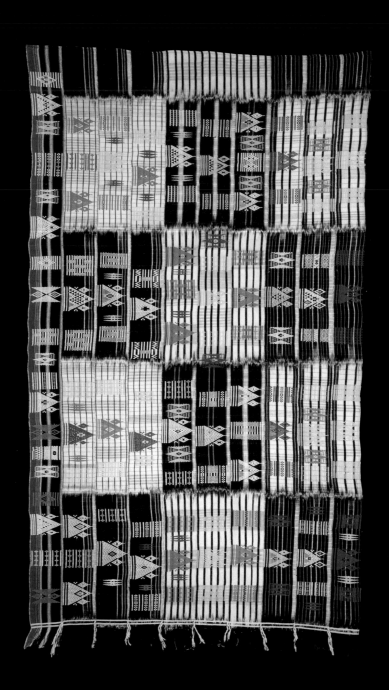

116 – 'PAGNE' *ZAZA*. BAULE. CÔTE D'IVOIRE. AROUND 1970.
Purchased from the master weaver and dyer Babou Traoré (see fig. 142) in Kong. Produced by
him in 1970. Ikat. Red warp stripe down one length. The cloth combines old, typical Dyula
cloth patterns. The cloth was produced for the marriage of one of the weaver's daughters – however,
the marriage never took place. No further information was given

166 × 100 cm. 10 strips, each 10 cm wide – collected by Boser/Gardi 1974 – III 20239 b

117 – 'PAGNE' *ZAZA*. DYULA. BURKINA FASO.
Ikat, weft float patterns (*misiri*, 'mosque'). Red warp stripe down one length.
Produced and purchased in Bobo Dioulasso

166 × 112 cm. 12 strips, each 9.5 cm wide – collected by Boser/Gardi 1974 – III 20236

SURUKU KAWA – THE 'SPOTTED HYENA'

Kerstin Bauer

The ikat cloths that are produced nowadays by craftsmen in Côte d'Ivoire and Burkina Faso originated from the Dyula. *Suruku kawa*, 'spotted hyena', is verifiably the oldest known pattern, going back to pre-colonial days. In fact, in many areas *suruku kawa* has become the generic term for ikat – especially when the basic pattern resembles a chequerboard.

The *suruku kawa* pattern is a warp ikat. It consists of blue and white squares covering the entire width of the strip. The colour of the squares in the weft switches from blue to white, and when the strips are joined in alternating sequence they produce a chequerboard pattern. A combination of *suruku kawa* and blue-striped strips are also quite frequent.

The *suruku kawa* ikat cloths are produced today by Dyula craftsmen in Côte d'Ivoire and Burkina Faso and by a few weavers among neighbouring groups. Their place of origin is definitely the town of Kong, the famous old textile and trading centre in northern Côte d'Ivoire. Beyond doubt, Kong also constituted the former centre of ikat dyeing in this part of West Africa. The highly differentiated idiomatic references in the Kong version of the Dyula language provide evidence that the *suruku kawa* cloth was first designed there and was only adopted in other regions at a later stage. The term *kawa* ('stains', 'contrasts') from the Kong variant of Dyula provides a first clue in this respect. The idiom also appears in the name *malaka kawa* ('stains on the dyer'), serving as reference to the age-old profession of dyeing in Duyla society. But even Dyula-speaking weavers are occasionally unfamiliar with the term *kawa*. Due to this lexical hiatus the term *kawa* experienced a consonant shift in some areas (for example in Bobo-Dioulasso, Burkina Faso) and became *kaba*, leading,

at the same time, to a semantic distortion of the term *suruku kawa* which was transformed to *suruku kaba* which means literally 'hyena's maize'.

In the past, *suruku kawa* textiles were worn by women as 'pagnes', while men had shirts made of this design. Today they are mainly used in ritual-ceremonial contexts, as wedding cloths or for festive purposes, but in everyday life they are becoming increasingly rare. In earlier days, a young Dyula woman received a *suruku kawa* 'pagne' when she got married. Today the wedding cloths (*konyoya fani*) have been replaced by more popular cloth types such as *zaza* (see fig. 117) or *dame*, a simplified version of *suruku kawa* decorated with small rectangular patterns that do not extend over the entire width of the cloth, and with the weft in plain white.

Until today the *suruku kawa* pattern is closely associated with the town of Kong. Local textile craftsmen are versed in numerous variations of *suruku kawa*, many of them displaying quite elaborate patterns (*suruku kawa kamini, suruku kawa matchuatigi*). Through trade and the migration of Dyula craftsmen the design has spread to all parts of the Dyula settlement area. In some regions weavers from other ethnic groups began copying the design, but kept to the Dyula name *suruku kawa*.

118 – 'PAGNE' *SURUKU KAWA*. DYULA. CÔTE D'IVOIRE.
The 'pagne' consists of four different strips: 1 – five dark-blue strips with red stripes in the middle and weft
float patterns; 2 – five ikat strips with blue and white squares (*suruku kawa kamini*); 3 – two strips of
ikat of the type *zaza* on which smaller chequer patterns (*dame*) alternate with yellow and orange weft floats;
4 – a single strip of ikat (*suruku kawa macuatigi*) on the far right. Produced and purchased in Kong

152 × 132 cm. 13 strips, each 10 cm wide – collected by Boser/Gardi 1974 – III 20237

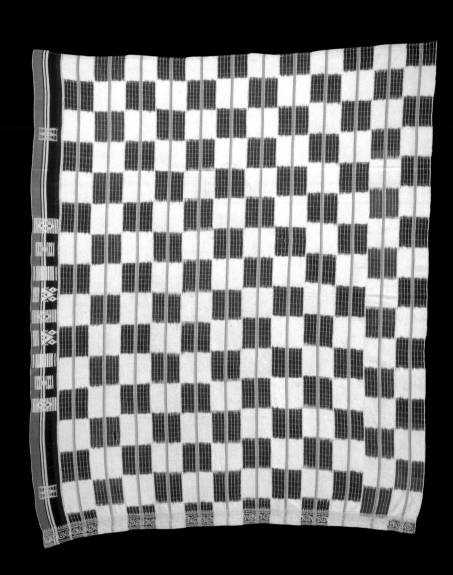

119 – 'PAGNE' *SURUKU KAWA*. DYULA. CÔTE D'IVOIRE.
Typical Dyula ikat. Red warp stripe down one length. At both ends twined white threads
and white fringes decorate the borders. Produced and purchased in Kong

151×120/127 cm. 13 strips, each approx. 10 cm wide – collected by Boser/Gardi 1974 – III 20233

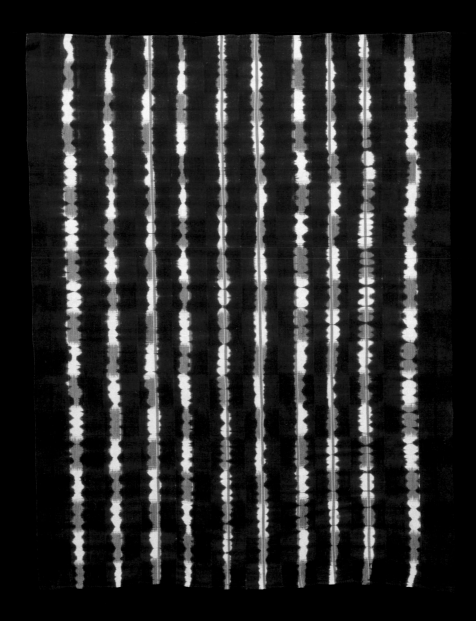

120 – 'PAGNE' *SURUKU KAWA KAMINI*. DYULA. CÔTE D'IVOIRE.
The ground pattern consists of an ikat chequerboard displaying white and blue-and-white
stripes (*suruku kawa kamini*), each with a red line down the middle. The woven cloth
was coloured by way of indigo fold resist and tie-dyeing. Produced and purchased in Kong

158×120 cm. 12 strips, each approx. 10 cm wide – collected by Boser/Gardi 1974 – III 20257

— 121 —

PREMPEH II. KUMASI. GHANA.
This official photograph of the Asantehene (king) Sir Nana Osei Tutu Agyeman Prempeh II, taken in 1933,
was signed and dated by the Asantehene himself (28/2/1940). He wears full Asante regalia including an elaborate *kente*
with a great variety of different weft designs.

GHANA

A Textile to Wear: *Kente* Cloth in Ghana
Malika Kraamer

Kente is one of the best-known hand-woven textiles from southern Ghana and Togo, widely used both locally and abroad, especially in the United States (Ross 1998). At many civic, personal and ceremonial occasions, it is used by large numbers of people. *Kente* is worn by wrapping the cloth around the body; men use one large cloth, women often two smaller ones. This practice has changed little over the time.[98] Festivals are the main events at which to see people wearing *kente* cloth (see fig. 122). Some festivals have been around for centuries; others are newly invented, like the *kente* cloth festivals in Bonwire and Agotime (two of the main weaving centres in southern Ghana). These textiles, made out of narrow strips sewn together and wrapped around the body, are often very colourful. They are always eye-catching, especially in motion, for example in the procession of chiefs, queen mothers and other court officials to a festival ground. Since the second half of the 20th century, *kente* also figures prominently in the worlds of politics, fashion and design (see Ross 1998; Kraamer 1996).

The weaving of *kente* is clearly a continuously changing tradition, with many types of textiles being produced at any one time. As Picton says "one can write with ease and justification about a textile tradition, in the sense of practice handed on, thus configuring the narrative within temporal and social contexts that imply process and entail at least the possibilities of development." (Picton 1995: 11) *Kente* is such a practice, handed on for centuries and constantly evolving as weavers incorporate, adapt and further develop elements of the *kente* and other textile traditions. Weavers also experiment constantly with leftover materials, both restricted and stimulated by the harsh economic conditions they work in (Kraamer 2005a: 257–279). This has resulted in an astonishing diversity of *kente*, of which some types have found their way to museum collections. Often these collections consist of 20th-century holdings and are divided between Asante and Ewe textiles as weavers predominantly come from these backgrounds.[99] We will see, however, that the interrelationships between the different weaving centres are historically ongoing. The Museum der Kulturen Basel is one of the few museums that also has some 19th-century cloths, including the oldest extant *kente* (see fig. 128), and its holdings will form the thread through this article.

WEAVING AND TRADING *KENTE*
Kofi Agbemehia is an artist-weaver with a great reputation in the coastal Ewe region for weaving *asidanuvo* 'hand-picked creative textile', with designs woven on one side of the cloth that almost seem to be embroidered (see fig. 123).[100] He has been weaving since childhood and belonged to the first group of weavers to make this new type of textile, invented in the 1930s. Like Kofi, most weavers were men, but this gender division has gradually diminished since the mid-20th century (as in Nigeria).

When I met him at the end of the 1990s to discuss Ewe cloth, he was in his eighties and still wove almost every day. He mainly worked for others, receiving a fixed amount for every strip woven. He hardly ever managed to be self-employed, even though this is the ambition of most weavers, as it would allow them to make a profit on cloths woven on commission or for the market in Agbozume, and therefore achieve a better income (personal communication 1999 and 2000).

His typical work pattern is as follows. In the morning he takes the warp with the finished strips rolled up and hangs it in his loom, fastens the heddle strings between his toes, takes the necessary shuttles and starts to weave (see fig. 126). A day spent weaving is physically demanding and requires concentration, especially when he weaves a complicated design, such as a butterfly. He hardly ever makes mistakes, even though the design is face down. Sometimes he experiments on a leftover piece of warp to create alterations to existing designs, experiment with colour schemes or design a completely new motif. He carefully measures the placement of the patterns. He needs to know the overall layout of the cloth beforehand, as it is only after completion that the length of woven warp is cut into strips which are sewn together edge to edge to form a textile. [101]

The Ewe coast where Kofi Agbemehia lives and works is one of the three main *kente* weaving centres. The second, Agotime, is situated in the middle of the Ewe region while the third centre encloses several villages around Kumasi, including Bonwire, in the Asante region. *Kente* is also produced in workshops in Ghanaian and Togolese cities, especially Accra, Lomé, Kumasi and Kpalimé (see map 'Expedition', front cover flap).

One reason for change in these textiles lies in the mobility of both cloth and weavers. Weavers, especially from the Ewe coast, have a long history of migration along the coast, as many are also fishermen. The largest retail market for *kente*, now in Agbozume, also on the Ewe coast, [102] can be traced back to at least the late 19th century; and cloth from other weaving centres have also been traded around. The market in Agbozume is held every four days and is mainly controlled by first- and later-generation Zarma traders from Niger. They mediate between local weavers and traders from all over West Africa. [103] Innovations and stylistic changes are often inspired by weavers looking at other textiles rather than through direct contact between weavers from different textile traditions. Weavers are able to analyze cloth samples, as they are visually trained people with strong numerical skills. One example of innovation typical for Yoruba and Ewe textiles came about in the 1990s, when many coastal Ewe weavers travelled back and forth to Lagos (see p. 180).

TEXTILES IN THE 18TH AND 19TH CENTURIES

We know little about the way people in the former Gold Coast (present-day Ghana) dressed before the 16th century, and written, archaeological, or other sources, including examples of cloth pre-dating the 19th century are scarce. Until the 16th century, the most common outfit was probably bark-cloth in the south, and leaves and skins in the north. The use of cotton became more common in the 17th and 18th centuries. These textiles, plain or with warp- or weft stripes created with dyed yarns, were probably reserved for elite groups in society at first but gradually developed into the everyday dress of common people.

From at least the 17th century onwards, dress for the economic and political elites became more elaborate as more complicated techniques and the use of red materials (especially silk) unravelled from European cloth exchanged for slaves and gold, opened up new design possibilities (Rømer 2000 [1760]: 36; Bowdich 1966 [1819]: 35; Isert 1992 [1788]:

92). In terms of materials, red silk was especially used in the Asante region where the rise of the Asante Empire in the 17th century stimulated the weaving of more expensive textiles for the king and the aristocracy (Rattray 1927: 234; Johnson 1979: 60–63, 78–82). Weavers stood under royal patronage and control, but restrictions dwindled with the exile of the Asante king in 1897 and the rise of new economic elites. [104] In the Ewe-speaking region, there was no single, large royal court. At least since the 16th century, this region consisted of a large number of 'states', sometimes comprising just a few villages. Weavers mainly explored design possibilities in cotton. Partly due to the lack of restrictions on what to produce for whom, and the existence of separate weaving centres, the variety of textiles woven has been greater here than in the Asante region. [105] However, in the 19th century many design characteristics were shared between the different weaving centres.

In all weaving centres in southern Ghana, except Agotime, textiles have been woven in such a way that the warp is predominantly visible (warp-faced textiles). In Agotime, textiles have long been made in which only the weft is visible (weft-faced textiles). Locally, these *titriku* cloths are considered the oldest type (see fig. 138). These textiles – *titriku* means 'thick cloth' – have seldom found their way to museum collections. They are, however, of importance to the stylistic development of both Asante and Ewe textiles. Most 19th-century *kente*, including textiles in the Museum der Kulturen, are difficult if not impossible to identify as being the specific product of either an Ewe or an Asante weaving centre, as the exact stylistic developments and the interrelationships between these centres have not yet been fully established, and because the common trade in textiles means the place of collection is insufficient evidence on which to attribute a textile to a specific weaving centre. Two particular features of many 19th and 20th-century *kente* include the alternation of warp-faced and weft-faced plain weave areas in one length of strip and the use of motifs woven with an extra weft. The weaving of such alternations (creating visual block effects in textiles) and the making of different kinds of designs is done with two different pairs of heddles, one also used to make warp-faced plain weave textiles, the other to make weft-faced plain weave textiles. This feature of *kente* was well established by the mid-19th century at the latest, and most likely began in Agotime in the Ewe region (Kraamer 2006a).

The oldest *kente* in the Museum der Kulturen Basel was given by the king of Akropong to the Basel missionary Andreas Riis in 1840 (see fig. 128). The cloth has areas of three red weft blocks. Their lining up in alternate strips results in an elongated chessboard pattern that resembles Ewe and Asante textiles with alternating weft-faced and warp-faced blocks, but this cloth, like another 19th-century textile on display, is woven with just one pair of heddles. The latter cloth (see fig. 129) was acquired in Abetifi by the missionary Gottlob Dilger in 1886. Both textiles could have been woven by either Ewe or Asante weavers. Although Abetifi is considerably closer to the Asante than to the Ewe region, which would favour an Asante attribution, the photograph of a Basel missionary taken in Abetifi shows an Asante and an Ewe loom standing next to each other (see fig. 125). This image is also suggestive of the long tradition of migrating weavers. The oldest existing textile displaying weft-faced and warp-faced areas was collected before 1888 in Kumasi, and was therefore thought to be woven in the Asante region (Ross 1998: 154; see fig. 130). However, some of the weft-faced blocks are made of plied yarns of two colours, a distinctive feature of Ewe textiles. A second old cotton textile in the collection could be attributed for the same reason to an Ewe weaving centre (see fig. 131). This male cloth was collected before 1911 at an unrecorded place on the Gold Coast.

DESIGNING AND DEVELOPING *KENTE* IN THE 20TH CENTURY

It seems clear that Asante and Ewe weavers have been mutually inspired by each other's textile traditions (and by those of other weaving centres) over the last few centuries. Ewe weavers, both in Agotime and on the coast, continued to work mainly in cotton until the first half of the 20th century. In the high-prestige textile sector, they explored the weaving of all kinds of figurative and non-figurative motifs (see fig. 132), a tradition that goes back to at least the mid-19th century. These textiles are often in more subdued colour-combinations than Asante cloths. In the 1930s and 1940s, the most impressive variety of motifs in one textile was produced in Agotime. Ativoe Te from Agotime-Afegame recalls, for instance, how they were in constant competition with each other to come up with new designs (personal communication, April 1999). In most museum collections, it is this type of cloth that most frequently represents Ewe textiles.

Another 19th and early-20th-century kind of Ewe textile shows the placing of motifs without framing weft-blocks (see fig. 137). These textiles have been collected from different parts of the Ewe-speaking region, including the Peki region and several places in Togo. Ewe weavers also developed weaving with two sets of warps (see fig. 136). The weaving of this form of cloth seems very complicated but it is often the first kind that apprentices learn to weave after mastering plain weave textiles. As textiles woven with two sets of warps, like plain weave cloth, are much quicker to produce, and therefore affordable for larger groups of people, they have been produced in large quantities. The coastal weavers in particular are pre-eminent in constantly creating new warp-patterned textiles. They are able to create the illusion of all shades of colour through an intricate combination of different colour weft- and warp-threads, including the experimentation with plied yarn and supplementary warps, and, since the 1980s, lurex (a shiny synthetic material). In the 20th century, new types of textiles were developed in different Ewe weaving centres, such as the aforementioned *asidanuvor* (see fig. 123) and *Nigerian weave* (see p. 180) and also *worgagba* (see p. 178).

In the 18th or 19th century, Asante weavers developed the weaving of all kinds of non-figurative motifs. They also gradually increased their use of silk and rayon (the replacement of silk). At the end of the 19th century much of their finest weaving was done entirely in silk and consisted of an abundance of different motifs in contrasting colours. In the 20th century the combination of cotton and rayon (see fig. 133), or rayon alone, became the norm. Changes in the second half of the 20th century include new formats to place the designs together, a much denser use of weft-float patterns and a decrease in the number of patterns in one cloth.

In the mid-20th century *kente* acquired the status of national dress. Nationalists before independence in 1957, and the political elite afterwards, used *kente* as part of a mental decolonization campaign, with a connotation, amongst others, of the cultural richness of Ghana. The first president, Dr Kwame Nkrumah, used *kente* as produced in the Asante region in his politics of national identity building. His example was widely followed by many Ghanaians, which caused a shift in production in the Ewe-speaking region. First in Agotime, and much later also on the coast, weavers started to weave these shiny rayon textiles; later this type of textile became dominant at many Ewe events, including festivals. Since then, Ewe and Asante weavers have continued to develop this particular style, constantly coming up with new designs. One weaver working in this tradition, Yaw Agidi from Agotime-Akpokofe, is known for his creative skills. In 1999 he designed a new cloth which he called *Virgin Mary*, in which he combines two weft-float patterns (see fig. 127). One design he had

122 — Procession to the festival ground at a festival organized to promote literacy in Agotime

Photo M. Kraamer 2000 (Batume, Togo)

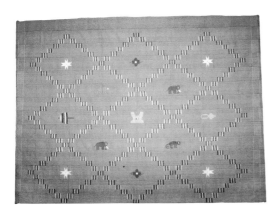

123 — Rayon textile (*asidanuvor*) probably woven by Kofi Agbemehia for Bobbo Ahiagble in the 1990s. This cloth was on exhibition at the opening of Bobbo's Ewe Kete School.

Photo M. Kraamer 1999 (Hatsukofe, Ghana)

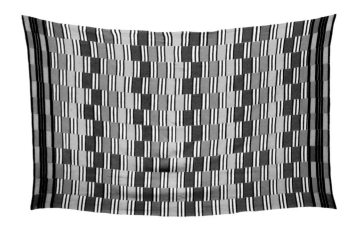

124 — *Titriku*, 'thick cloth' (weft-faced plain weave cloth) woven by Adze Ameko of Agotime in 1962 to celebrate the birth of his firstborn

Photo M. Kraamer 1999 (Agotime-Amuzukofe, Togo)

created for use in another combination, the second pattern he developed together with his apprentice, Wisdom Gidiga. Gidiga had designed a new pattern based on a familiar domestic object – a lattice used for roasting food. He discussed the design with Gidiga and together they developed it in a new pattern, changing the shape and the colour combinations (which were inspired by a pottery fragment). Agidi guided Gidiga in the process of weaving by turning the rhombus shape, for instance, into a six-angle shape. They called this design *The Ten Commandments* because it needs ten shuttles to weave, and the entire cloth *Virgin Mary* 'because it is hard to do' (personal communication Gidiga, August 2000).

CHANGING TRADITIONS

Changes in the formal qualities of *kente* cloth take place all the time. Individual weavers react to new visual inputs, adapt them to their inherited aesthetic and technological reference, and in so doing change the framework. Weavers survive in difficult economic circumstances. They constantly seek to satisfy their customers' demands but they are themselves the cause of change, as customers have high expectations but lack specificity in their demands. Weavers decide, for instance, what to produce or how to execute a commission, which materials to buy, where to live, when and how to change their career, and where to go to gain new customers. All these elements account for the large variety and continuous changes in *kente* cloth production.

125 — The weaver on the left is Jonathan Ata; he was a senior church council member in Abetifi. The loom on the left is an Asante type, the loom on the right an Ewe type

Photo Fritz Ramseyer, missionary, before 1895 – F(III) 586

126 — Kofi Agbemehia weaving *asidanuvor* on his loom at home

Photo M. Kraamer 2000 (Kpedzakofe, Ghana)

127 — *Virgin Mary*, a design created in 1999

Photo M. Kraamer 2000 (Agotime-Akpokofe, Togo)

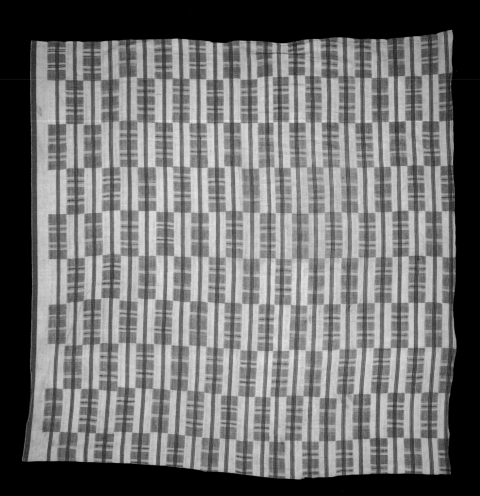

128 – MEN'S CLOTH *KENTE* (*ADANUVOR* IN EWE, *NSADUASO* IN TWI).
EWE OR ASANTE. GHANA. 1840.
The King of Akropong (Ghana) gave this cotton textile decorated with
an elongated chequer board pattern to the Basel missionary Andreas Riis
in 1840 as a gift. It is the oldest known *kente* cloth in the world

145×145 cm. 24 strips, each 6 cm wide – coll. by the missionary Andreas Riis 1840.
Basler Mission Collection in the MKB – III 23334

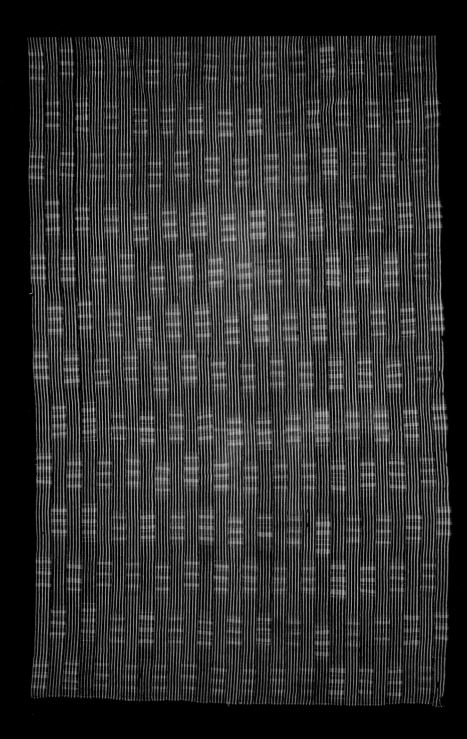

129 – MEN'S CLOTH *KENTE* (*VEDO, VUTSE,* AND *VUTSATSA* IN EWE,
AHWEPAN IN TWI). EWE OR ASANTE. GHANA. 1886.
The King of Abetifi gave this cotton cloth to the missionary Dilger as a fare-
well gift. In technique and overall patterning it resembles the 1840 cloth
from Ghana shown in fig. 128. It was probably woven in an Asante workshop,
as Abetifi is much closer to the Asante than to the Ewe region

284 × 166 cm. 28 strips, each 6 cm wide – coll. by the missionary Gottlob Dilger 1886.
Basler Mission Collection in the MKB – III 23335

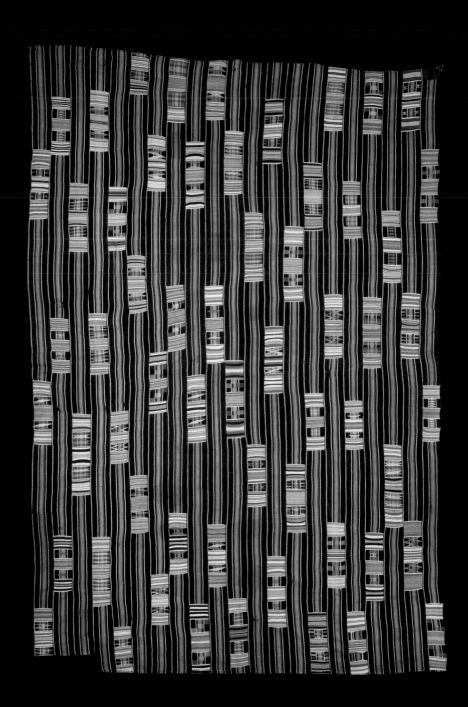

130 – MEN'S CLOTH *KENTE* (*NTSRIM*, *ATITRALA-ADANUVOR* AND *AKPEDO* IN EWE, *TOPREKO* IN TWI). EWE OR ASANTE. GHANA. BEFORE 1888.
This cotton cloth is the oldest example showing the typical way that Asante and Ewe weavers alternate weft blocks with warp sections in their expensive cloths. Its provenance (Kumasi) suggests that it was woven by Asante weavers, the use of plied yarn, however, suggests that it was produced by Ewe weavers

264 × 176 cm. 21 strips, each approx. 8.4 cm wide – Basler Mission Collection in the MKB 1888 – III 23336

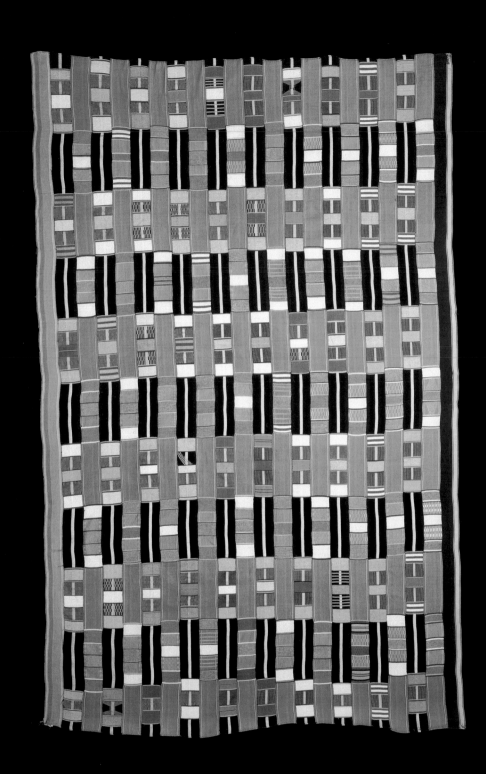

131 – MEN'S CLOTH *KENTE* (*ADANUVOR*). EWE. SOUTHERN GHANA. BEFORE 1911.
An old example of a cotton textile using plied yarn (*gbesike* or *kabaliworwor*) of two colours for many of the weft blocks (*ampa* or *novi*). Two strips with different warp patterns are alternated. The two outer strips (*torbla* or *torblabla*) have a different patterning

284×182 cm. 21 strips, each approx. 8.5 cm wide – coll. by the missionary Kirchner 1911. Basler Mission Collection in the MKB – III 23333

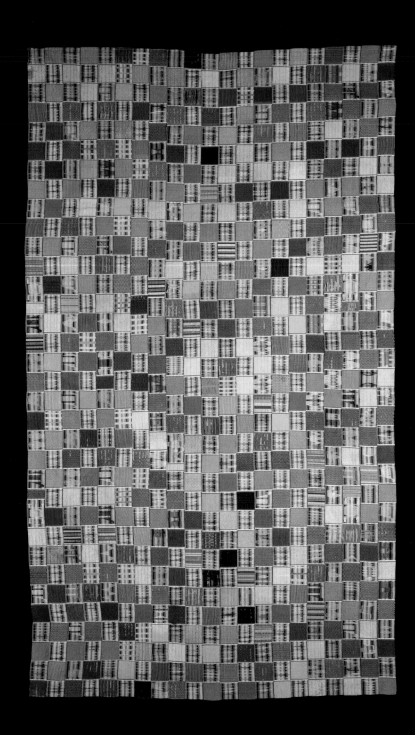

132 – MEN'S CLOTH *KENTE* (*ADANUVOR, NOVIVOR, ATIKPEMEVOR* AND *AKPEDO*). EWE. GHANA. BEFORE 1991.
As for most textiles, this early or mid 20th-century rayon and cotton cloth is referred to by several generic names. *Adanuvor*, 'creative textile', refers to the high quality of the cloth and the imaginative skill of the weaver, *novivor*, 'textile woven with *novi* heddles', to the weaving equipment, and *atikpemevor*, 'short measure stick cloth', to the arrangement of patterns on the cloth. This very expensive textile is only used on special official or ceremonial occasions. The cloth is from Adidome

330 × 195 cm. 21 strips, each 9.2 cm wide – acquired through Mama Mekano, Accra, in 1991 – III 25946

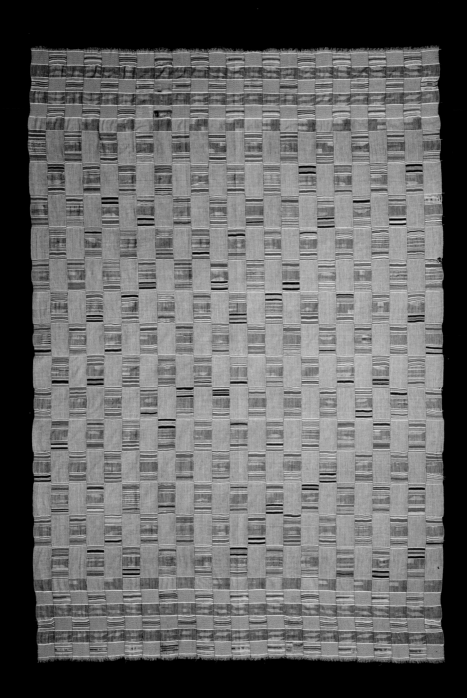

133 – MEN'S CLOTH *KENTE* (*TOPREKO*, *ASAMBO* AND *ASAM TAKRA*). ASANTE. GHANA.
This elaborate cotton and rayon *kente* has many different non-figurative patterns between the weft blocks. The weaver used his measure stick carefully, neatly matching the blocks of adjoining strips. Most weavers use a bamboo stick divided into three equal parts. The pattern of the warp stripes and the cloths as such displaying this pattern are often called guinea fowl (*asam takra*) or breast (*asambo*). Cloth names are flexible and change over time and space

295 × 205 cm. 23 strips, each approx. 9 cm wide – collected by Anton Stalder, acquired in 1996 – III 26850

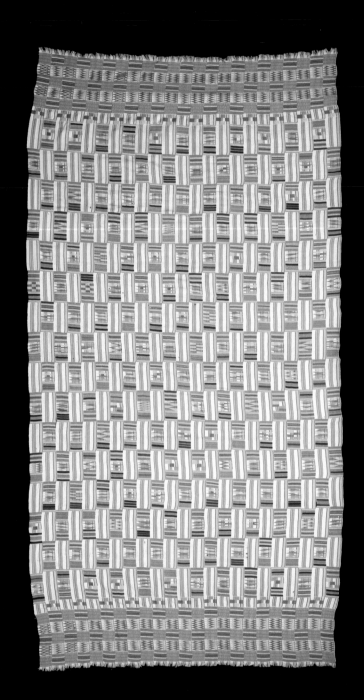

134 – MEN'S CLOTH *KENTE (TOPREKO, TOKU AKRA NTOMA)*. **ASANTE. GHANA. BEFORE 1996.**
The arrangement of this cloth with one warp design (*toku*), areas of weft designs alternating neatly with plain weave in and across the strips, a border and a limited number of weft designs just about fits the ideal of many 20th-century Asante rayon cloths. This cloth is often called *Toku akra ntoma* 'Toku's soul cloth'; Toku was a queen mother and warrior who was defeated in battle in the early 18th century

318 × 170 cm. 23 strips, each 7 cm wide – coll. by Anton Stalder, acquired in 1996 – III 26852

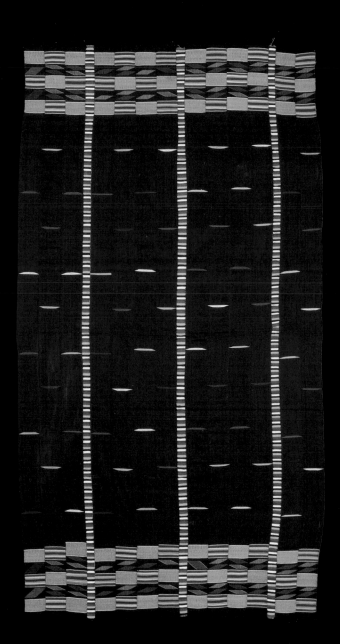

135 – WOMEN'S CLOTH *KENTE*. PROBABLY ASANTE. PURCHASED IN ACCRA.
GHANA. BEFORE 1992.
The multicoloured stitching joining several strips together in this cotton cloth is a
common feature of Asante hand-stamped *adinkra* mourning cloths. It is unusual to see
it in combination with common features of *kente*

215×120 cm. 13 strips, each 8.5 cm wide – coll. and donated by Meinhard & Gisela Schuster 1992 – III 26530

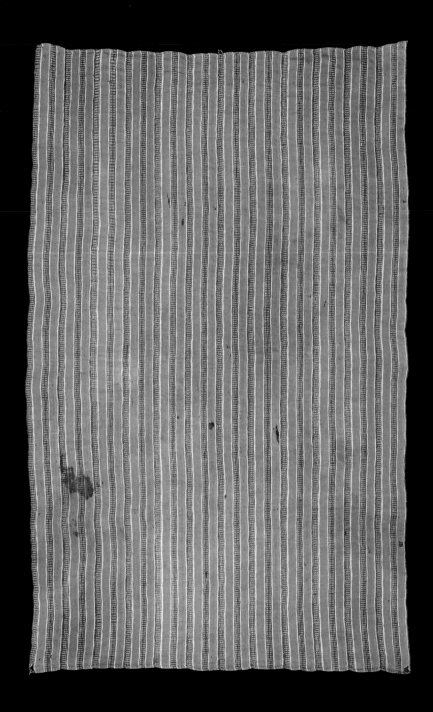

136 – WOMEN'S CLOTH *KENTE* (*KEDEDZIVOR* OR *KPEVIVOR*). EWE. GHANA. BEFORE 1910.
This cotton cloth is one of the earliest existing examples of a textile woven with two sets
of warp. This technique is still employed in many Ewe cloths. The use of industrially woven red cotton
indicates the longstanding tradition of incorporating yarn from other parts of the world into
Ewe (and Asante) textile traditions

164 × 101 cm. 12 strips, each 8.5 cm wide – Basler Mission Collection in the MKB – III 26485

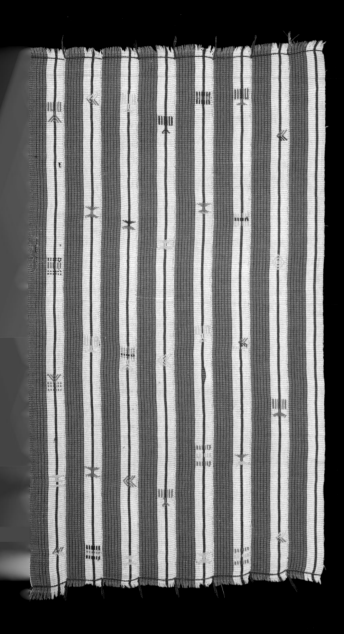

137 — WOMEN'S CLOTH, *KENTE (ADANUVOR)*. EWE.
COLLECTED IN LOMÉ, TOGO. BEFORE 1990.
These cotton textiles with figurative motifs that are not
framed by weft blocks have been woven since at least the 19th
century. The weaver deliberately placed the designs not
exactly in line with each other over different strips, sometimes
using four and sometimes five motifs within a single strip

52 × 75 cm. 8 strips, each of approx. 8–10 cm wide – acquired through
David Mensah, Dakar, in 1990 – III 25950

138 — SINGLE STRIP *KENTE (TITRIKU)*. EWE. SOUTHERN
GHANA. BEFORE 1900.
In the Agotime region (eastern Ghana/southern Togo) this
type of cotton cloth is considered the oldest kind. The
generic term *titriku* refers to the thickness of the cloth. It is
the only cloth that is prescribed at certain events, such
as *vidzikpedodo*. This thanksgiving ceremony after delivery
of the firstborn child is only held very rarely today

115 × 7 cm – collected by the missionary Widmann 1900. Basler
Mission Collection in the MKB – III 26499

WORGAGBA AND *ATAKPAMEVOR*

Malika Kraamer

Ewe textiles are characterized by a bewildering diversity. New types of textiles are added, whilst older types are changed and sometimes abandoned. A new cloth developed in the 1980s (see fig. 139) gives us insight into how changes in textile traditions often take place and how they get distributed.

In the 1970s, Kwevi Kanyi from Agotime moved to Atakpamé in central Togo and founded a weaving workshop. He contracted weavers from different Ewe weaving centres in Togo and Ghana, including Agotime and the coastal region. The workshop did well, and in the 1980s he received a large order for 'Ghana-style' *kente*, in the common Asante-derived style of rayon textiles with non-figurative motifs in contrasting colours. Since the 1960s, this type of textile had been produced and further developed in most Asante and Ewe weaving centres.

The large order had to be produced in short time, shorter than normally feasible for such cloths. Kwevi and some of his weavers found a solution to reduce production time by transforming an already familiar technique. This technique, developed in the 1930s in the coastal Ewe region to make figurative motifs visible mainly on one side of the cloth, stimulated the production of many different cloths. In Atakpamé, the modified technique was now used to make a cloth of which one side is more or less covered with extra wefts to make designs that resemble the rayon non-figurative textiles. The weavers of Kanyi used cotton for the ground weave, and rayon for the supplementary patterning. The resulting textile was much appreciated and new orders followed.

Due to the political turmoil in Togo at the beginning of the 1990s, the mainly Ghanaian weavers scattered to the different weaving centres in eastern Ghana and took with them this new way of weaving. In the coastal area, these textiles became known as *worgagba*, 'bowl full of corn', making a comparison between the time to weave this cloth and the time required to fill a bowl full of corn. *Worgagba* has been very popular and entire villages have moved to its production. They have mainly been produced for the Agbozume textile market, the market that attracts traders from the Asante region, Togo, Côte d'Ivoire and other West African countries to buy *kente* in bulk. In Agotime, the new textiles were simply called *Atakpamevor*, 'cloth from Atakpamé'. They have been less popular, as they are often perceived as a mere imitation, and weavers, who mainly work on commission, have predominantly been asked to weave the more expensive rayon textiles with motifs on both sides of the cloth.

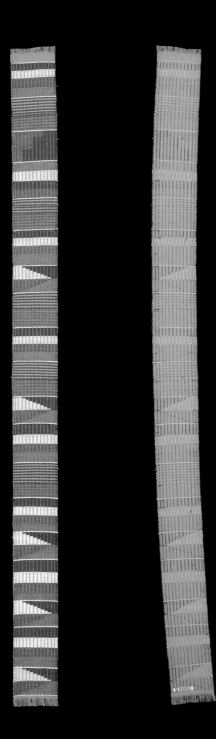

139 – SINGLE STRIP *KENTE* (*WORGAGBA* OR *ATAKPAMEVOR*). EWE. GHANA. BEFORE 1992.
Front and reverse. Textiles woven with an orange ground weave covered on one side with rayon
patterning were invented in the 1980s in Atakpamé, Togo. This style of weaving spread quickly to
other Ewe weaving centres where it was further developed. In the coastal area the cloth became
an especially popular item for the West African export market

162 × 11.5 cm – collected and donated by Meinhard & Gisela Schuster 1992 – III 26528

SUPER-Q, ASO KENTE AND NIGERIAN WEAVE

Malika Kraamer

180 New visual and technological innovations are highly appreciated in the fashion scene of coastal West Africa. They are sometimes informed by entrepreneurial patrons, migrating weavers, and adaptations from other textile traditions. The story of *Super-Q* and *Nigerian weave* is an exciting example that dramatically transformed the appearance of Yoruba hand-woven cloth and added a new type of cloth to Ewe textiles in a remarkably short period.

In the early 1990s, a Lagos cloth trader started to import hand-woven narrow strips from Dakar, selling it as a new type of *aso oke* (the local name for Yoruba hand-woven cloth), which she called *Super-Q*. In Dakar she met some Ewe weavers attempting to market their cloth in Senegal and invited them to establish a workshop in her compound in Gbagada, Lagos. Other traders followed her example, encouraging young coastal Ewe weavers to move to Lagos. By the mid-1990s several hundred Ewe weavers had moved to Nigeria, often setting up their own workshops.

Ewe weavers kept the wider web of 14 centimetres of the Senegalese samples, and in response to the Yoruba elite taste, extended the use of lurex, used a mix of cotton and synthetic material (locally called *mirai*), employed a thicker weft to create a ribbed effect and used the Yoruba metal beater instead of the Ewe wooden one to give a smoother finish to the cloth. Sometimes they also incorporated warp floats already common in the Volta Region, but not seen in *aso oke* before.

The popularity of *Super-Q* meant that individuals and traders placed orders with Yoruba weavers, who rapidly absorbed the new features and extended the range of designs. At first the Ghanaian origins of this new style were known only to a few elite cloth traders but by the end of the 1990s the new type of cloth became also known as *aso Ghana, Ghanaian style* or *kente*. In the fashion-conscious Nigerian market for *aso oke* the new wider strips entirely displaced the 10-centimetre wide strips that had been the norm throughout the 20th century. Ewe and Yoruba weavers rarely adopted features of each other's cloth traditions through physical contact, but carefully studied cloth samples brought to them by customers. Ewe weavers, facing more and more hardship in Nigeria as competition from local weavers increased, returned to Ghana and reworked the new kinds of cloth to make it more suitable for the Ghanaian market. They called the textiles *Nigerian weave*. The main change was to reduce the thickness of the weft and use less lurex – but still far more than common in Ghana until then – to make the cloth more flexible and lighter. They also added a new technique, the use of openwork, to their repertoire. Openwork has been an old feature of *aso oke*. One of the most radical inventions that Ewe weavers in Lagos took back to Ghana was the introduction of one or more supplementary single heddles to make weft float designs. This made quicker weaving of existing designs possible, and opened a completely new range of design possibilities. This new type of textile quickly became part and parcel of what Ewe weavers make and are locally supposed to make. This sense of tradition was also facilitated by the process of naming these textiles. By 2003 weavers who never had been to Nigeria had also created designs in this new style and incorporated more features of other Ewe textiles. It was now common to give individual Ewe names to particular designs. Innovation therefore lay at the core of coastal West African textile traditions. The incorporation of foreign elements is common, but the processes of localization, such as seen in the way cloth acquired new names, may obscure mutual influences. It has been an old feature of many of these textile traditions.

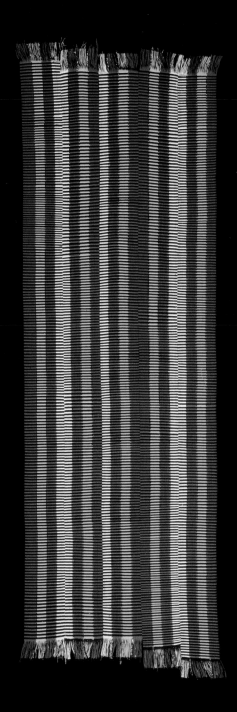

140 — MODERN INNOVATION *SUPER* Q.
This is a Yoruba women's shawl, woven around 1995, that illustrates the impact of Ghanaian and Senegalese textiles and weavers on *aso oke* designs during that period. New was the supplementary floating warp along with wider strips. It was collected in November 2007 at the Jankara market, Lagos.

Collected and donated by Duncan Clarke 2008 - III 27545

141 – THE MASTER WEAVER MOHAMMADOU ALI FOFANA DIT MAYGA.
The *kerka* in the background was woven by him around 1950 on the occasion
of his second marriage. Most of the patterns are new creations. He provided the
following information concerning his life story: he was born around 1912.
His mother was a *maabo* Bocoum from Sareyamou. Her brother taught him to
weave. By 1940 he was a famous weaver, which is the reason why he was re-
cruited by the Frenchman Caseneuve who was attempting to introduce Euro-
pean-sized strips, new patterns and weaving with the aid of four heddles.
So Mohammadou travelled to Bamako to learn these new European techniques.
He spent two years in Niafounké (around 1945) in the house of the 'chef de
canton' Hammadun Babakar Gaata. He manufactured an *arkilla jenngo* with 30
strips for Gaata's daughter. Since he was versed in the patterns from Lake
Faguibine as well as in those of Niafounké he was able to blend them and create
a new overall design. When he had finished the work he spread the word,
challenging all *maabuube* to come and see his blanket, and to try to top it. The
maabuube of Soumpi, Kassoum and Niafounké came but none of them was
able to produce a blanket of the same quality and beauty. The 'chef de canton'
was so pleased with Mohammadou that he gave him an additional cow for
each set of ten woven strips (i.e. three cows). Following this, he was invited by
the village chief of M'Bouna to weave a *kerka*, for which he again received
three cows.

Photo B. Gardi January 1980 – 45/1-2

142 – BABOU TRAORÉ,
MASTER WEAVER FROM KONG, CÔTE D'IVOIRE.
Born around 1898. His father and grandfather had
been weavers too. He produced the 'pagne' shown in fig.116

Photo B. Gardi 1.10.1974 – (F)III 12495

143 – MRS NANA AL HAJJ SHEHU,
MASTER WEAVER FROM KUTIGI, NIGERIA.
She (sitting on the far left) wove the shawl shown in fig. 98

Photo R. Boser-Sarivaxévanis 2.4.1974 – (F)III 11408

144 – AL HAJJ SULE,
MASTER WEAVER FROM BIDA, NIGERIA.
He produced the shawl shown in fig. 97

Photo B. Gardi 1.4.1974 – (F)III 8064

NOTES

INTRODUCTION

[1] The project proposal was titled 'Recherche ethnologique dans l'Ouest africain sur l'artisanat des textiles tissés et teints' and filed under the number 1.7220.72. The approved grant amounted to CHF 132,000. In her proposal Renée Boser-Sarivaxévanis described the project as follows: "Recherche fondamentale dans l'Ouest africain sur la technologie, la typologie et la terminologie de l'artisanat des textiles traditionnels tissés et teints, situés sur l'axe primaire de leur apparition et de leur diffusion en Afrique Noire.

La recherche dans le domaine des textiles artisanaux de l'A.O. se trouve encore à ses débuts. Tandis que quelques ouvrages ont été consacrés aux régions côtières de cette partie du continent africain, la zone soudanienne – qui a vu la naissance et la diffusion du tissage et da la teinture – a été profondément ignorée.

Faisant suite aux ouvrages du requérant réalisés *in vitro* (première esquisse de l'histoire culturelle des tissus tissés et teints de l'Ouest africain), le présent projet de recherche se propose de recueillir les documents originaux indispensables qui permettraient de procéder à une synthèse de cet aspect de l'histoire culturelle de l'Afrique Occidentale."

[2] In November 1983 she published an article in Swissair Gazette (the in-flight magazine of Swissair) with a print run of 300,000 copies. The booklet served as the accompanying brochure to her exhibition in the Museum der Kulturen Basel.
Boser-Sarivaxévanis originally planned to publish her work in three volumes: 1. History and Distribution of Looms in West Africa. – 2. History and Distribution of Indigo-dyeing. – 3. The Textiles of West Africa. The first two volumes were to include material from the Near East. The 'Boser Legacy' at the Museum der Kulturen contains next to the records of our journey from 1973 to 1975 files with examples of looms from all parts of the world and a documentation on indigo-dyeing. On her life-history: Renée Boser-Sarivaxévanis (16 November 1921 to 21 April 2005) was born and grew up in Athens. Her father worked as a French teacher, her mother was a member of the old Bancal family from St. Louis, Senegal. Through marriage she became a Swiss citizen. Together with her husband and her two children she spent several years in Senegal and Nigeria. In 1958 she commenced her studies in anthropology under Alfred Bühler at the University of Basel. In 1972 she published her PhD thesis *Les Tissus de l'Afrique Occidentale*. She was curator at the Museum der Kulturen from 1967 to 1984. During the last years of life, Renée suffered from Alzheimer's. Renée was a very strong personality and made a lasting impression on the people who got to know her. She loved to talk, and she talked a lot, not least because she enjoyed testing her ideas and theories in discourse.

[3] Towards the end of the 19th century, the Iklé family had branch offices in Paris, New York, Berlin, Vienna, and, of course, St. Gallen. The Iklé Frères headquarters was in Hamburg. One of their specialities was 'St. Galler' lace and embroidery. Fritz Iklé-Huber was very interested in 'primary technologies', that is, technologies where fabrics were produced without the use of technical equipment such as a loom. The collection established by the father Léopold Iklé found its way into the St. Gallen textile museum around 1900 where it formed the main part of the museum collection. Later, the large majority of the 1,100 items in total was left to Alfred and Kristin Bühler-Oppenheim who donated the collection to the Basel museum in 1947.

[4] The 'Textile Collection Fritz Iklé-Huber' carried the significant sub-title 'Foundations of a Systematic Classification of all Textile Technologies'. Years later, his work was systematically revised and extended by Annemarie Seiler-Baldinger (1973 and 1991).

[5] Alfred Bühler (1900–1981), curator from 1938 on; director of the Museum der Kulturen from 1950–1964 and 1965–1967 (at the time called Museum of Ethnography and Swiss Museum of Folk Studies Basel); from 1959 to 1970 first full-time professor of anthropology at the University of Basel; married to Kristin Oppenheim (1915–1984).

[6] These included the textile collections in Basel, Bern, Zurich, Berlin, Paris (Musée de l'Homme) and London (Museum of Mankind).

[7] Originally, Brigitte Menzel (1930–1998) had a fourth volume in mind, which, however, never materialized. It was planned as a scientific back-up volume to the three earlier, more descriptive volumes. The Deutsche Textilmuseum Krefeld organized a special exhibition in honour of Menzel in 2007. In the accompanying catalogue Vera Bendt paid tribute to her achievements as a scholar. Menzel's scientific estate is held at the Rijksmuseum voor Volkenkunde, Leiden.

BOTTOM TELLS THE STORY OF CLOTH

[8] The double-heddle loom is used by professional male weavers throughout West Africa, though since the 1970s in both Nigeria and Ghana women have entered this art. The vertical loom, worked mainly by women in Nigeria for domestic use, is technically less efficient.

[9] By 'modernity' I mean the conditions that define a given place and time. I do not regard the word 'modern' as defining a specific era. The modern world is always where one is at. Modernity, the conditions of that world, is thus always shifting; and it is always local. It is, however, useful to distinguish between modernity and 'modernism', which, for the present, remains a term that describes developments in the visual and other arts since the mid-19th century. Modernist developments in Europe were, of course, conveyed to Africa through the medium of educational systems set up during the colonial period and since maintained; but these developments have been informed by concerns and forms local to West Africa.

[10] Two obvious examples of this are the evolution of a sense of national dress in Nigeria, a process that began in the late 19th century when some Lagos intellectuals repatriated from Sierra Leone took up wearing the wide-sleeved gown; and the mid-20th-century encouragement in Ghana given by Nkrumah to wearing *kente* cloth.

[11] As the Dutch re-colonized Indonesia in the second quarter of the 19th century, the local wax batik process was seen as a technique capable of adaptation to a mass-production technology that would benefit colonial enterprise. By the 1890s a duplex roller system was developed that printed hot resin on both faces of the cloth in the manner of the wax used in Indonesia (hence the term 'wax print'). The resin resisted the indigo, and once cleaned off, one or two other colours could be added. However, the Dutch textile manufacturers encountered intractable problems in handling the resin: it cracked, allowing a random veining to appear, and then it was not easy to clean off, making for a spotted effect in the additional colours. What emerged were textiles with clear-cut designs on a variegated ground, which Indonesians did not like; and yet, when Dutch merchants, probably in Elmina (the precise details remain unknown), tried these fabrics on their customers they proved to be extremely popular (Picton 1995; 2004b).

INDIGO

[12] According to Seefelder 1982; Heller 1989; Petrossian & Roussel 2000.

[13] The distribution or prevalence of *Indigofera* is actually more complicated than described here. Thus, the Indian *Indigofera tinctoria* is said also to grow wild in West Africa, while African *Indigofera arrecta* was exported to Asia as far back as the 19th century where it was marketed as 'Java blue' (Petrossian/Roussel 2000: 17–18).

[14] Terms like *bulu-bulu* stem from the English 'blue'. The Hausa dyers in Kano distinguish between five shades of indigo: *baki* (blue-black); *nati* (navy-blue); *shudi* (blue); *farin shudi* (light blue); *farar gira* (very light blue).

[15] The common Hausa term for indigo is *baba*, but the people also have different terms, for example, *shuni* for concentrated indigo in powder form which is used to produce the metallic sheen on turbans and cloths. In Yoruba, the term *elu* covers the colour indigo, an indigo bath, the indigo plant, as well as a ball of dried indigo.

IYA ALARU, THE MOTHER OF ASH

[16] Long-used dye sites are usually surrounded by mounds of ash collected from exhausted dye baths. During our journey of 1973/75 we never had time to watch how a new dye bath is prepared.

[17] Old tin cans were used for the purpose, each one holding four gallons (4.5 litres to the gallon).

[18] On these kilns, see also Boser-Sarivaxévanis 1981. We saw intact kilns in Ede, Ilorin, Iseyin, Somorika, Owo and Oyo, disused ones in nearly all Yoruba towns and villages. Not all the kilns were built in the same way. Some had no intermediate floor so that, each time, a filter made out of old pottery shards had to be constructed. The kilns were usually large and solid clay constructions with thick walls measuring up to 20 centimetres at the top. On some occasions we saw ash balls being heated in large pots instead of a kiln. Some women insisted on using water from an exhausted indigo bath, others used normal water; some examined each fired ash ball closely, sorting out the bad (i.e. the differently-coloured) ones.

THE RESEARCH EXPEDITION 1973–1975

[19] The questionnaire was structured as follows: information on weaver – information on techniques: raw materials; seeding cotton; cropping the sheep; warping; spinning yarn; forming skeins – double-heddle loom – vertical loom – general textile terms – colours – indigo-dyeing.

[20] At the time, Ekpo Eyo was director, assisted by Emmanuel Arinze (1945–2005) who later himself became director of the Federal Department of Antiquities.

[21] We are speaking of *Tabernaemontana pachysiphon*, a milkwood plant (after R. W. Keay, C. F. A. Onochie and D. P. Stanfield. 1964. *Nigerian Trees*, Vol. II: 385–287. Ibadan, Federal Department of Forest Research). Its fruit – the size of oranges, growing in pairs – and leaves are shown in Boser 1975, fig. 14. One tree we were shown in Ubulu Uku was nearly eight metres in height and 30 centimetres in diameter. Basden (1921: 180–181) mentions *ufa* cloth, stating: "It is highly prized and very strong, but its price is prohibitive to any well-to-do folk." It is possible that there are other trees whose barks are also utilized. Further north, in Igara, we were told that the fibres came from Okene; in Okene they said they came from Kaaba. The latter information is probably correct.

Before leaving Nigeria for the north we handed over 46 textiles to the Federal Department of Antiquities in Lagos for its collection.

[22] Alfred Bühler conducted research on this topic for years. His monumental work on the subject was published in 1972, the same year that Boser and Menzel published their seminal research. At practically the same time, Urs Ramseyer and Peter Horner of the Museum der Kulturen released their famous film on ikat in Bali, Indonesia.

[23] She must have been 65 years old at the time. Born in Owo, she later moved to Ondo with her husband, an Egba-Yoruba man from Abeokuta. In Ondo she learnt the art of tying off ikat, which cost her an apprenticeship fee of £5. Later, in Abeokuta, she taught young women weavers. When her husband died she returned to Owo.

[24] The terms were transferred to index cards later in Basel. In her report to the Swiss National Science Foundation, Boser-Sarivaxévanis mentions the figure of 10,000 index cards containing terms in 34 African languages. In many cases tape recordings were made.

[25] May all the people who so generously helped us in Nigeria 35 years ago accept my apologies for only being mentioned in a footnote.

Rulers and dignitaries: Akenzua II, *Oba* of Benin; Ekhoayato Omoregie, the *Ihaza* of Benin, and his family; Ejiebo, the *Oliha* of Benin; the family of Chief Oshodi, Benin; Eghobamien, the *Obadagbonyi* of Benin; the *Ineh* of Benin; Ogieva Emokpao, the *Ewekaguosadoba* of Benin. – Oba Adetoyese Laoye II, *Timi* of Ede. – Edward Ofulue II, *Obi* of Ubulu Uku – Mallam

Sanni Omonori, *Ohinoyi* of the Ebira – Mallam Ali Obaje C.B.E., *Atah* of Idah – The *Imah* of Somorika; the *Orangun* of Illa. – Chief Longe, the *Areegbeomo Timi* of Ede. – Al Hajj Mallam Tifin, the *Sarkin Kudu* of Bida.

Federal Department of Antiquities: Ekpo Eyo, Emmanuel Arinze, Brian Stafford (Lagos); Richard York (Jos), Brian Edwards (Enugu).

Universities and national museums: Boniface Aganyi; Robert Armstrong; Jean Borgatti; Michael Crowder; Donald Hartle; David Heathcote; Carl Hoffmann; Phil Jaggar; Danny Lindersay; Donald Morrison; Judith Perani; Robin Poynor; Thurstan Shaw; Janet Stanley; Roslyn Walker; Robert Wren.

As well as in Benin City: I. O. Ibude; Osemwegie Ebohon; Tony Uwaifo. – E. A. Ikem (Ubulu Uku); R. P. M. Maguire (Igara).

[26] Originally bronze armlets were wrapped in the cloths, which is probably why some textile fragments survived. The fragments were excavated at a site called Igbo Isaiah on 6 January 1960.

Our notes contain measurements (in cm) for the following ten fragments. The first figure refers to the assumed warp: BS.1: 10.6×7.7 / BS.2: 8.5×14.5 / BS.3: 8.4×11 / BS.4: 8×17 / BS.5: 13×8.8 / BS.6: 13.4×6.5 / BS.7: 6.5×4 / BS.8: missing / BS.9: 11.2×7.6 / BS.10: 27×25.

For the purpose of analysis we took with us very small material samples. In the Museum der Kulturen they are inventoried under III 21073–21081.

[27] In Niger my thanks goes to: Niamey: Musée national, Director Albert Ferral. – Centre national de recherche et de sciences humaines; Centre régional de la documentation pour la tradition orale: Issaaka Dankoussou; Altinine Agarias; Abubakar Mahamane. – Centre pédagogique : Ousman Bâ, Soumana Hassan. – Service alphabétique : Seini Harouna. – Gérard Fourage. – Dosso: Abdou Aouta, *Djermakoye*; Baro Insa; Zibo Sandi.

[28] In Burkina Faso my thanks goes to: Ouagadougou: Centre Voltaïque de la Recherche Scientifique. – Musée National. – Jim Rosselini (Archives sonores du CVRS). – Boussouma: Ammah Diko, commandant du Canton; Théodore Ouédraogo, chef du Canton. – Kaya: Daniel Ouédraogo.

[29] In Côte d'Ivoire my thanks goes to: Abidjan: Centre des Sciences Humaines. – Musée du CSH. – Niangoran-Bouah (University). – Philip Ravenhill, Judith Timiyan, Jean Devisse, Jean Polet. – Korhogo: Bernard Dudot ; Mamadou Konaté.

[30] In Mali my thanks goes to:
Bamako: Institut des Sciences Humaines: Kléna Sanogo; Mamadou Sarr, Almami Malicki Yattara, Ibrahim Guindo, Mamadou Diarra. – Musée National: Yaya Coulibaly. – Archives Nationales: Moussa Niakaté. – Youssouf Tata Cissé. – Ségou: Moulaye Demba Kida. – Mopti: Tiémoko Coulibaly, Moulaye Kanté, Arsiké Coulibaly. – Nioro du Sahel: Amadou Abdoulaye Bâ. – Kayes: Oumar Bâ, Ibrahim Bâ.

[31] In Senegal my thanks goes to:
Dakar: I.F.A.N.: Amar Samb, Director. – Musée de l'I.F.A.N.: Bodiel Thiam, Curator. – Université, Centre de Linguistique Appliquée: Jean Doneux, Abdoul Aziz Diaw, Mamadou Guèye. – Le village artisanal de Soumbédioune. – St.-Louis: Musée Adanson. Insa Coilibaly. – Diourbel: Cheick Touré.

[32] The five expeditions were headed by Moussa Konaté (National Museum of Mali) and Rachel Hofmann (UCLA). Multiple samples of the same textile were purchased so that they could be shared between Bamako and Los Angeles.

[33] Here I should like to thank the directorate of the Swiss Agency for Development and Cooperation (SDC), the Syngenta Foundation for Sustainable Development (Basel) and Dr. Hartmann P. Koechlin (Basel), former honorary consul of Republic of Mali. For further information, see the annual report for 2003 of the Museum der Kulturen Basel.

MUNNYUURE

[34] *Munnyuure* blankets are often manufactured with the aid of pattern heddles. In Pinia, three such heddles were used. When passing the warp threads through the heddles mistakes can occur with the result that the same slips also appear in the repeat. Such flaws are also found on Tellem textiles, providing evidence that pattern heddles must have been in use already hundreds of years ago.

[35] On the *arkilla kerka* marriage blankets (fig. 67) we have the same correlation between the number of strips and patterns, in this case six. I suspect that such correlations exist on other textiles as well, for example, on the marriage blankets called *arkilla jenngo*; here the number is seven (fig. 70).

[36] I must confess, this is something I never quite understood. In a country where bartering is part of every sale or purchase, you have a product into which more than a hundred hours of work have gone, but the price is not negotiable! Six years later, in 1985, nothing had changed – except that the CFA had replaced the Franc Malien (FM) – and the blanket still cost the same amount: CFA 10,000, that is CHF 56.

[37] In 1979, Ismail Ali Silla, the village chief of Pinia gave me the names of eight places where the people came from to buy *uldebe* blankets: Sanga, Kani-Kombole, Dourou, Ningari, Bandiagara, Ilili, Ibi and Yaba.

[38] This information comes from Heidrun Mezger, Cologne, and my friend Arian Blom, the brother of Huib Bloom who runs the website www.Dogon-Lobi.ch. Both are experts on the Dogon country.

[39] Field photographs showing *uldebe* blankets are quite common (see e.g. Griaule 1938: fig. 44; pls. I A; VI B, C; XII A, B). After Griaule died in Paris, the people in Sanga staged a funerary ceremony for him, using a dummy wearing French leather boots and wrapped in an *uldebe* blanket (see Life Magazine 3, December 1956). – Nadine Wanono published a remarkable photograph in Bedaux & van der Waals 2003: 106. It shows the newly enthroned, highest religious authority of the Dogon – the *hogon* of the Arou clan. Draped around his neck like a gigantic snake is an *uldebe* blanket. He himself is sitting on an unfurled, red [!] *uldebe* blanket on the ground (on the meaning of the colour red, see Brust & Schmid 2007).

[40] I am grateful to Dr Salia Malé, Musée National du Mali, Bamako, for this information.

[41] Danish National Museum in Copenhagen, Gd. 13 and Gd. 14. They were collected by the governor of the last Danish possessions in Africa, Eduard Carstensen, between 1844 and 1851.

REFLECTIONS ON THE HISTORY OF WEST AFRICAN LOOMS

[42] Picton and Mack were well aware of this fact, and they cautioned against drawing hasty conclusions (1989: 8), stating that pointing out technical analogies alone was rather pointless. One way of disclosing historical interrelationships, they maintained, was by way of comparative work on textile terminology (1989: 21).

[43] We are dealing here with highly complex historical questions which, possibly, can never be fully answered. Boser-Sarivaxévanis loved to talk and enjoyed testing her theories on me in discourse. On our long journey through West Africa I became her 'guinea-pig' as it were. Some of the statements which I render here in her name actually grew from the discussions we had underway. She had red Leroi-Gourhan (1943) very closely and, as a student, had held many discussions with Alfred Bühler. Although she admired Leroi-Gourhan's scientific approach in general, she was very critical of his views on textiles.

[44] See notes 21 and 26; also Shaw 1977.

[45] Rita Bolland 1991 published a book on the Tellem textile complex. Next to that she issued several scholarly articles together with Rogier M. A. Bedaux.

[46] The invention of the loom and weaving respectively probably go back further in time. See Lamb 2005: 1–6 for a summary of the facts and views on the subject.

[47] I do not intend to go into weaving and textile techniques in detail here. The purpose of this paragraph is to underline the prime significance of heddles in weaving. For a comprehensive review of textile techniques, see Seiler-Baldinger (1991: German; 1994: English).

[48] Lamb 2005 has a chapter on this type of loom including rich comparative data. Unfortunately her text on this loom from the southern fringe of the Sahara contains some erroneous statements, for example, on wool weaving in Mali.

[49] Photographs of this loom in Northern Cameroon, namely from the Koma (village: Bimlérou) and the Dowayo (Poli), were issued by René Gardi in several publications, last in Gardi 1995. As regards the unknown vegetable fibre, he spoke of 'nettle fibres'. – Lamb (1980: 141–145) published pictures from the Mumuye on the upper Benue River in Nigeria, as well as from Poli (2005: figs. 69–71). – Unfortunately Picton (1992: 18–19) follows Lamb here and classifies this loom as a category of its own. In line with Boser's arguments, I believe his categories 2 and 5 constitute one single category.

[50] Lamb 2005 has a chapter on this loom including a lot of comparative data.

[51] In German, often the term 'Schmalbandweberei' (narrow-strip weaving) is used, which, actually, makes very little sense since every type of loom is capable of producing 'narrow strips'. However, in German the term has become established.

[52] Boser-Sarivaxévanis not only assumed, but also wrote in her final report to the Swiss National Science Foundation (1982) that this loom had been invented in China during the Han Dynasty (400 BC – 200 AD). She described the double-heddle loom as found in West Africa – and in the Himalayas up to this day – as an adaptation to a nomadic way of life. The warp-weighted loom is unknown in Africa. Boser-Sarivaxévanis mentions that this loom was used in Iceland well into the 19th century – a unique technological success story.

[53] This too is one of Boser-Sarivaxévanis' lines of argument, actually a very convincing one! Why this hybrid type only developed in this specific area but nowhere else begs an explanation.

[54] The early French sources on the topic of domestic wool sheep (Monteil 1903; Pierre and Monteil 1905) describe how the Fulani bred sheep, mention that the animals needed ample water and that they were more prone to disease than other breeds of sheep. Why in the whole of sub-Saharan Africa is the wool sheep only to be found in Mali? Did its ancestors originally come from the Maghreb, or from the Middle East, or are we, less likely, dealing with a breed of its own? What would a DNA analysis tell us? Ryder (1983: 559) traces the Macina wool sheep back to North Africa, but his data on Africa are rather poor in general.

[55] Personal communication Christiane Seydou, 10 January 1992.

[56] Boser-Sarvaxévanis published this example very early on (see 1972: 138). She writes: "Or, d'après Wipszycka (1965) les termes de κάσσον et κασσοποιοì (kasson et kassopoioi) apparaissent très souvent sur les papyrus et des ostraca ptolémaïques datant du IIe siècle avant notre ère." There follows a quote from Wipszycka: « Le terme signifie un manteau de grosse étoffe. Hesychius (...) écrit 'kasson – vêtement épais et manteau grossier'. Les conclusions que nous pouvons tirer de ces données sont assez évidentes. Ces artisans étaient donc des fabricants de gros manteaux de laine de très mauvaise qualité. »

[57] Various authors have pointed out the aesthetic analogies between wool weaving in Mali and the Berber weaving tradition of North Africa. However, the comparisons were not based on an analysis of kaasa blankets but of arkilla wedding blankets instead. The latter have tapestry weave. A comparative analysis of the techniques applied has not been attempted up to this day. With regard to wool weaving such analogies actually do exist, but the same could be said of textiles from the Hindu Kush ...

[58] The wordlists published here are based on data collected during research in 1973/75, complemented with a few terms from the literature. The records are kept in the files of the 'Boser Legacy' at the Museum der Kulturen. I published an abridged version of the lists in Gardi (2003: 20–22).

[59] The Asante people, famous for their kente cloths, are an exception here, in the sense that asa not only refers to the heddle, but to the loom as a whole. As a word stem, asa also features in the terms for cotton and cotton yarn (asawa) and for certain types of fabric (asaaba, asabi). See Menzel (1973, III) for further examples, and also Picton (1992: 40–41) for reflections on adwinasa and asasia.

[60] The two-and-a-half-page letter by the theologian Prof. Dr. E. Jenni is kept in the 'Boser Legacy' in the archives of the Museum der Kulturen. The letter runs as follows:
Basel 1 July 1982
Dear Mrs Boser
In answer to your question as to the origins of the word nīr – 'yoke' or 'loom heddle' – I can confirm that the term (together with the object) originated in the Middle East, although, I must confess, I understand little of looms and weaving. I have drawn my knowledge mainly from the following sources, which, I believe, are known to you as well:
Gustaf Dalman, Arbeit und Sitte in Palästina, Vol. V, Webstuhl, Spinnen, Weben, Kleidung, 1937: pp. 94–144 (with figures), and Kurt Galling, Biblisches Reallexikon, 1977: pp. 360–361 (+ Lit.). (Dalman describes the situation in the Old Testament, in Jewish culture – containing the passage in Maimonides mentioned by you – and in later Syria-Palestine with the Hebr. and Arab. terms).
The term is first documented for Akkadian, i.e. the Semitic language of the Babylonians and Assyrians, in the third millennium BC; from there it found its way into Sumerian spoken in the Ur III-period, (I. J. Gelb 1957, Glossary of Old Akkadian, 1957: p. 193). The records for nīrum / nīru (word stem nīr-, -um or -u in the later ages, is the nominative ending) have now been collected in the recently published volume N/2 by A. L. Oppenheim et al., The Assyrian Dictionary, Vol. II, N, Part II, 1980: pp. 260–264: nīru 1.) yoke, cross-piece; 2.) (in figurative use) dominion, rule; 3.) part of a door, of a loom; 4.) ... However, as a term for a part of the loom, nīru does not appear in the normal texts, but only once in a word list next to other terms describing components of the loom. Furthermore, the noun nīr appears in the various dialects of Aramaic (Syrian, Jewish-Aramaic, Mandaic, etc.), all of them dating from the first millennium AD. According to H. Zimmern, Akkadische Fremdwörter als Beweis für babylonischen Kultureinfluss, 1917: p. 42, the Aramaic nīra (word stem nīr + article –a) was adopted as a loanword from the Akkadian niru, the same as it moved later from Aramaic to Arabic. S. A. Kaufmann, The Akkadian Influences on Aramaic, 1974: p. 77, holds a different view; she sees in nīr- simply a word that is common to both related language branches; the biblical-Hebraic term manor, describing a component of the loom, would support this view (ma- as a prefix for tools, -nor from the same stem as nīr).
In any case, in Aramaic there is evidence that the term was used for 'yoke' as well as for 'crossbeam of the loom'. For example, C. Brockelmann, Lexicon Syriacum, 1928: p. 428: nīrā 1.) jugum, 2.) jugum textoris, 3.) ... (1st millennium AD, Upper Mesopotamia) for Syrian, and M. Jastrow, Dictionary of the Targumim, the Talmud Babli and Yerushalmi, and the Midrashic Literature, 1903: II, p. 909: Middle Hebraic nīr 'crossbeam of the loom', 'the crossrod under the cross-beam (liciatorium) to which the ends of the leashes are fastened', then in a figurative sense (usually in the plural) 'the leashes or thrums to which the threads of the warp are fastened', also 'the warp'. Furthermore in Aramaic, nīrā 'the cross-rod' (liciatorium). It shows that the term also moved from Aramaic to Middle-Hebraic.
But what is more important for your research is the fact that, according to all leading specialists, the word nīr was adopted into Arabic as a loan word from Aramaic, in both senses of the term, i.e. 'yoke' and 'crossbeam of the loom'. See also: S. Fraenkel, Die aramäischen Fremdwörter im Arabischen, 1886: pp. 94 and 131. The standard dictionary by H. Wehr, Arabisches Wörterbuch für die Schriftsprache der Gegenwart, 1953: p. 901 only notes the term nīr in the sense of 'yoke', but see also the dialect dictionaries: L. Bauer, Wörterbuch der arabischen Umgangssprache, 1957: 167a, 355a; and A. Barthélemy, Dictionnaire Arabe-Français. Dialectes de Syrie, 1935: p. 858: c 1.) joug pour atteler les boeufs de labour, 2.) lisse ou lice (du métier de tisserand).
In Old-Ethiopic, the southernmost of the Semitic languages, there are two separate words for 'yoke' and 'loom crossbeam/heddle'. In Tigre, one of the languages that succeeded Old-Ethiopic, the loanword nirat for 'heddle' was again incorporated (E. Littmann – M.Höfer, Wörterbuch der Tigre-Sprache, 1962: p.324). I do not know the present situation in Amharic. So much for the Semitic languages. Thus, we see that the term was taken over in Arabic from Aramaic, and then transferred to the various African languages. I am not familiar with the situation in Ancient Egyptian, Berber and Cushitic. However, I discovered that the word (in both senses of the term) was taken over in Swahili (a Bantu language) from Arabic: Ch. Sacleux, Dictionnaire Swahili-Français, II, 1941: p.685. I hope I have been of service to you and remain with kind regards
E. Jenni.

OLDEST ARCHAEOLOGICAL EVIDENCE OF WEAVING IN WEST AFRICA

[61] Among other places, spindle whorls were discovered in an archaeological context in Koumbi Saleh and Tegdaoust in Mauretania; in Tekrour, Senegal; in Niani, Guinea; in the Niger Inland Delta in Mali;

189

especially also in Killi and in El Oualadji, in Galia and Doupwil, in Djenné-Djeno, in Dia and in Akumbu – all of them excavation sites in Mali (Schmidt & Bedaux 2005).

MALI

[62] See Meyerowitz 1949: 123, figs. 13, 15; Kyerematen 1965: 7, 20, 63; Lamb 1975: 89; Féau 1989: 189; Ross 1998: 2.8, 6.7, 6.8.

[63] The observation is based on the analysis of 20 blankets. Old blankets contained between 92 and 104 warp threads per strip measuring on average 21 to 22 centimetres. Blankets in 1990 only had 48 to 64 warp threads per strip of the same width.

[64] Millet stems are called *sokomba* in Fulfulde, the hibiscus flower *polle*. Both dyes were cooked; potash was not added. The yarns for *sakkalaare* blankets were preferably dyed with *polle*. Red yarns dyed with *sokomba* were used for *kaasa* and *arkilla kerka* blankets.

[65] These final work steps were often completed by traders at the market, a fact that Imperato (1973), the author of an otherwise very good article, failed to understand. He thought that the Fulani he met in the market in Mopti were mending old *kaasa* blankets.

[66] My fieldnotes show at least 15 names (Gardi 1985: 196).

[67] It is no longer known where the first *sakkalaare* blankets were made. *Sakkalaare* blankets contain small almond-shaped patterns in tapestry weave, like the Hausa blankets called *sakala*. The blankets produced by Fulani weavers in the Liptako area in Burkina Faso (made of wool *and* cotton) are also called *sakala*. *Sakkalaare* blankets are a modern blend of three types of blanket: *kaasa* (Fulani: pure wool), *sakala* (Hausa: pure cotton) and *sakala* (Fulani of Dori: cotton and wool). Possibly the first *sakkalaare* blankets were made in Dori.

[68] In Arabic *al killat*. Around 1980, women were selling off *arkilla kerka* blankets by the hundreds. They wanted modern beds with metal frames and nylon mosquito nets. In 1985 I wrote in my fieldnotes: "Dozens of *kerka*, *munnga* and *jenngo*, hundreds of *kaasa* for sale at the Marché rose in Bamako."

[69] In the early 1980s, Fulani women were never involved in indigo-dyeing; this was done by Maraka or Soninke women, which, once again, shows how technology is intricately interwoven with the social sphere.

[70] Yellow dye was produced from the leaves of the *ngalama* tree (*Anogeissus leiocarpus*), brown from the bark of the *npekuba* tree (*Lannea microcarpa*).

[71] A small series of very neat 'pagnes' from the National Museum in Mali is shown in Gardi 2003a.

[72] Information provided by Kolado Cissé, November 2008, Basel.

[73] Mage (1868: 275) writes that the village of Sansanding hat to pay the King of Ségou 1,000 *dampe* blankets a year in punishment, each blanket valuing between 4,000 and 8,000 cowries. At the time, an oxen cost between 5,000 and 6,000 cowries (Mage 1868: 440).

KAASA BLANKETS

[74] I wish to thank Christiane Seydou and Almaamy Maliki Yattara for their help on the linguistic terms.

[75] *Kaasa* blankets in museums verifiably collected before the First World War are rare. Most of them were collected in Ghana. In Mali there must have such an abundance of *kaasa* blankets that European collectors did not deem them worthy of collection. The oldest *kaasa* I am aware of in a museum was accessioned by the Historisches Museum Bern in 1903 (Goldk. 99). The oldest photograph of a *kaasa* blanket I know of dates from 1893/94 and was taken in Djenné. It is in the photo album of Albert Rousseau held in the Ruth and Peter Herzog Collection, Basel (Gardi 1995: 059).

ARKILLA KERKA

[76] Whether the *sigaretti* strip is a new invention or not is difficult to say. I received differing answers to this question: in 1982 I was told in N'Gouma that it was a practice that had been introduced from the Fittuga area (the region of Saraféré, across from Niafounké), which is why it was called *fittugawol* in the Guimballa region. Often it was not manufactured by the weaver, but by his apprentice. According to another source this strip can also be called *bippol*, like the concluding strips that are decorated differently.

[77] This finding is based on the analysis of five *kerka*. The quantity of yarn varies considerably (between 11,000 and 27,000 metres); accordingly the quality varies too.

ARKILLA KUNTA

[78] Sawani is located on an island in the middle of the Niger River, 20 kilometres north of Tillabéry in the Republic of Niger. In June 1974 we stayed there for four hours. Next to the *arkilla kunta* published here, we purchased two further blankets (III 20455, 20456). We were offered a fourth one which

we did not buy. The blankets were no longer in use. One *kunta* was being used as a rain cover for the grass roof of a house (fig. 22).

[79] According to Olivier de Sardan 1969: 64–70 and 107–109. Sardan is the only author I know of who ever saw, and wrote about, the *arkilla kunta*. He uses the Songhay term *kunta arkila*. The few published *arkilla kunta* all seem to have been purchased in Ghana (Menzel 1973: A 45; Sieber 1972: 190). Most of them are classified as *arkilla kerka*.

ARKILLA JENNGO

[80] The number of strips on *jenngo* blankets may vary. But irrespective of whether a simple *jenngo* features 12, 14 or 16 strips, the outer two, four or even six strips are always without patterns in tapestry weave. They are decorated with chequers only.

[81] In 1957, the 'Cantons' introduced by the French in the colonial era were abolished, together with the corresponding 'Chefferies'. The Gaata family trace their origins back to the nomadic Tuareg; they settled in Niafounké around 1850. Their Tuareg background finds expression in their *arkilla jenngo*.

'COUVERTURES PERSONNAGES'

[82] In Fulfulde *gwòòtal* means as much as 'unique'. 'Bambara' refers to the place name Bambara Maoudé. This means that the man was from the Guimballa region and ranked, already then, as an exceptional weaver.

[83] Already very early on in his career Kwame Nkrumah wore *kente* cloths during public appearances with intention. We may assume that in 1960 the people of Mopti had already heard of these cloths, but had never seen them being worn in Mali. Many Malians had travelled to Ghana as traders. Photographs in the daily newspapers were black-and-white only.

[84] He was from the village of Komogo in the Arrondissement de Saraféré in the western Guimballa region.

[85] Kolado Cissé received this information from Ousman Saré, a grandson of the first weaver, Ousman Baba Dramé better known as Gwòòtal Bambara. Ousman Saré lives in Kagnimé, a village between Douentza and Bambara Maoudé.

NIGERIA

[86] Ethnic identities in Africa are complex and continually evolving. Mainly as a result of political contestation of resources in colonial and post-colonial states, many previously independent but culturally related peoples have coalesced since the late 19th century. Thus some 20–30 million people now identify themselves as Yoruba (on the basis of factors such as linguistic similarity, shared ancestral myths, religious heritage) and make up the bulk of the population of southwestern Nigeria, with smaller numbers living in neighbouring Togo and Benin.

[87] On the basis of my fieldwork in the 1990s I would estimate that there are in excess of 25,000 active *aso oke* weavers in Nigeria. The first women to weave *aso oke* began to do so in the 1960s in Shaki, a remote northern Yoruba town near the Benin border where migration reduced the available supply of male labour. See Clarke 1997: 174–215.

[88] Today they are woven using black machine-spun thread rather than indigo-dyed local cotton.

[89] For a recent overview of Akwete weaving see Lisa Aronson 2001.

[90] Ebira was previously spelled Igbirra, see John Picton 1980.

A TALE OF TWO SISTERS

[91] For a more complete discussion of the title system, the ceremony, and the symbolism of associated painted and carved images, see Jean Borgatti 1989: 175–195.

[92] For a discussion of Okpella's masking traditions, and specifically the masks commemorating women, see Jean Borgatti, 'Okpella Masking Traditions', *African Arts* 9, 4, 1976: 24–33; and 'Dead Mothers of Okpella', *African Arts* 12, 4, 1979: 48–57.

[93] The Okpella speak an Edo language, like the people of Benin, and are one of numerous small Edo-speaking ethnicities who trace their origins to Benin, having migrated north between the 12th and the 18th centuries, according to their orthodox histories. Their boundaries reflect the northernmost reaches of the Benin Empire at its height. Cultural practices throughout Edo North suggest a more complex ethnic background for most of these people.

[94] Formal interviews took place with Achetu Obamina on 2, 16, and 23 November 2002. There was in addition a video recorded interview of November 2003 and a video recorded family gathering and singing (May 2003).

CÔTE D'IVOIRE

[95] For the famous red-patterned cloths from Kong see Bauer 2001 and 2007b

[96] Samory Touré, a Muslim Manding, and his forces fought against French colonial expansion at the end of the 19th century.

ZAZA – MIXING PATTERNS

[97] Men's cloth, collected by D.W. Ritz, 1953 (MKB: (F)III 4480); photos by Urs Rahm, Sakassou, 1957.

GHANA

[98] Some changes have taken place in the use of wrappers by women. The use of a second wrapper to cover the breast, rather than just to carry a child or protect against the evening cold, became more common in the 19th century under missionary influence (Meyer 1997). This is also the time that the female outfit called *kaba* developed, a blouse with matching skirt in printed, batik or tie-dyed materials. At the end of 20th century, some women also made a *kaba* out of *kente*, though most people still feel the material is too valuable to cut.

[99] *Kente* is often divided into Asante and Ewe textiles, but these terms are not unproblematic. Art traditions do not coincide neatly with ethnic and linguistic groups (Vansina 1984: 29–33; Kasfir 1984: 163–193). Furthermore, the development of ethnic identities has its histories and changes over time. Ewe identity only developed in the early 20th century, as widely discussed in the literature (e.g. Amenumey 1989; Nugent 1991; Meyer 2002; Kraamer 2005a). The ethnic labelling of art and people is always somewhat arbitrary and may overlook the strong interrelationships between different textile traditions.

[100] In the Ewe region, weavers make a difference between ordinary weavers and artist-weavers. The latter have either high skills to produce the most complicated existing designs, or are also able to come out with new designs (Kraamer 2005a: 222).

[101] A men's cloth, worn in a toga-like manner, measures approximately two by four metres or 20 to 28 strips; a female wrapper, worn around the hips, approximately 1.20 metres by 1.50 metres, or 10 to 14 strips (see fig. 122).

[102] Keta, on the coast, has historically been the largest retail market for *kente*, but this market moved to Agbozume on the upper part of the Keta lagoon in the 1960s.

[103] One cloth in the Museum der Kulturen, Basel was bought from David Mensah (see fig. 137). He is an Ewe speaker from Lomé who acquires his *kente* from Lomé for his gallery in Dakar, Senegal. Many traders who bring cloth to Lomé buy them from the Agbozume market, but cloth is also directly bought from owners in the Ewe-speaking region.

[104] Royal patronage has, however, not dwindled completely. Even today, nominated weavers in Bonwire and Adanwomase, two of the better-known weaving places, still produce for the royal court.

[105] Some weaving centres lost prominence, such as Peki in the west of the Ewe region, at the end of the 19th century; others developed, like Kpalimé with the migration of many coastal Ewe weavers to this Togolese city

Spelling of place names according to Carte Michelin No. 153

Departure from Basel	**17.10.1973**

Lagos	**10.11. – 22.11.1973**
Benin City	24.11. – 05.12.
Ubulu Uku, Ogwashi Uku	06.12. – 08.12.
Enugu	09.12. – 11.12.
Aku, Ohebe	12.12. – 14.12.
Enugu	14.12. – 16.12.
Nsukka, Ibagwa	17.12. – 19.12.
Idah	19.12. – 26.12.
Auchi, Iguoba, Yeluwa, Okpella	26.12. – 27.12.
Igara, Somorika, Ososo	**28.12. – 10.01.1974**
Okene	11.01. – 15.01.
Benin City	16.01. – 24.01.
Ogwashi Uku, Ubulu Uku	25.01. – 29.01.
Lagos	31.01. – 10.02.
Abeokuta	11.02. – 14.02.
Ibadan	15.02. – 26.02.
Oshogbo	27.02. – 28.02.
Ede	01.03. – 06.03.
Ikirun, Illa, Esie, Oro	07.03.
Akure, Owo	08.03. – 14.03.
Ife	15.03.
Ilorin	16.03. – 18.03.
Iseyin, Oyo	19.03. – 22.03.
Ilorin	23.03. – 26.03.
Bida	28.03. – 08.04.
Kaduna	10.04. – 16.04.
Jos	18.04. – 24.04.
Zaria, Baganda	26.04. – 28.04.
Kano	29.04. – 14.05.
Katsina	15.05. – 18.05.
Jibiya, Maradi	**19.05.1974**

Madaoua, Dosso	**20.05.1974**
Niamey	22.05. – 05.06.
Dosso	06.06. – 09.06.
Niamey	10.06. – 11.06.
Filingué, Bonkoukou	12.06. – 14.06.
Niamey	15.06. – 17.06.
Tillabéry, Sawani	18.06. – 20.06.
Niamey	21.06. – 26.06.
Tera, Dori	**27.06.1974**

Ouagadougou	**28.06. – 08.07.1974**
Dori	09.07. – 12.07.
Dori, Yalogo, Dori	13.07.
Ouagadougou	14.07. – 18.07.
Kaya, Boussouma	19.07. – 21.07.
Zinaré, Sawana	22.07.
Ouagadougou	23.07. – 27.07.
Bobo Dioulasso	28.07. – 09.08.
Journey to Abidjan	**10.08. – 11.08.1974**

Abidjan	**12.08. – 30.08.1974**
Bouaflé	31.08. – 06.09.
Yamoussoukro	07.09. – 10.09.
Bouaké	11.09. – 17.09.
Béoumi	18.09.
Mankono	19.09. – 20.09.
Korhogo	21.09. – 27.09.
Kong	**28.09. – 30.09.1974**

Korhogo, Sikasso, Bamako	**01.10. – 13.10.1974**
Ségou	14.10. – 18.10.
San	19.10. – 22.10.
Mopti	23.10. – 26.10.
Journey by boat to Akka	27.10.
Akka, Férobé, Ambiri Abe	28.10. – 29.10.
Niafounké	30.10. – 05.11.
Attara	06.11.
Youvarou	07.11. – 09.11.
Akka	10.11.
Travel day	11.11.
Mopti	12.11. – 18.11.
Bamako–Bern (Bernhard Gardi)	**19.11. – 25.11.1974**

Boser-Sarivaxévanis with Ibrahim Guindo:

Mopti, Sévaré; Fatoma	**18.11. – 21.11.1974**
Sangha	22.11. – 24.11.
Bandiagara	25.11.
Djenné	26.11.
Bamako	27.11. – 06.12.
Bamako, Kélé, Kirina, Kangaba	07.12. – 08.12.
Bamako	10.12. – 15.12.
Journey to Mourdiah	16.12.
Goumbou	17.12.
Nara	18.12.
Nioro	20.12. – 23.12.
Journey to Nioro–Kayes	24.12.
Kayes, Médine, Maréna	25.12. – 31.12.
Tambacounda	**01.01. – 02.01.1975**
Kaolack, Mbour	03.01. – 04.01.
Dakar	05.01. – 11.01.
St.-Louis	13.01. – 17.01.
Matam	18.19. – 19.01.
St.-Louis, Gandiol	20.01. – 26.01.
Thiès	26.01.
Djourbel	27.01. – 29.01.
Dakar, Gorée, Rufisque, Mbour	**01.02. – 26.02.1975**

Return to Basel, end of expedition	**27.02.1975**

Adire: general term for indigo resist-dyed cloths. For example, *adire eleko:* batik based on cassava pulp. This women's art of dyeing is very common in Abeokuta. Yoruba, Nigeria.

Alaari: from the 18th century onwards, European schappe silk/silk waste was sold to North Africa, especially to Tripoli, where it was dyed magenta and traded to northern Nigeria. Hausa, Nigeria.

Arkilla: very large blankets, often used as curtains. Fulani and Songhay, Mali. The term comes from Arabic and means 'mosquito net'.

Aso iro: cloths produced by women in Nigeria. Yoruba.

Aso oke: cloths produced by men in Nigeria. Yoruba.

Baba: Indigo. Hausa, Nigeria.

Bazin: damask manufactured on a Jacquard loom. The term 'bazin' comes from the Italian 'bombasin', a compound of the terms 'bambagia' (cotton) and the Latin 'bombyx (silk). One also finds the spelling 'basin'.

Biccirgal: motif on a woollen *kaasa* blanket.

Bolooti: industrially spun yarn. Malian malapropism of the French 'la pelote' (ball of yarn).

Elu: Indigo. Yoruba, Nigeria.

Fancy: printed cotton cloth. Cheaper quality than 'Wax'.

Fulfulde: language of the Fulani.

Gara: indigo. The term is common in the entire western part of West Africa, reaching from Mauritania over Mali and Guinea to Senegambia. Mande languages.

Ghana: the old Ghana Empire rose in the 4th century AD and declined again in the course of the 11th century. The empire's main centres lay in what is today Mauritania.

Griot: historian, genealogical specialist, musician, artist and mediator. The origin of the term is not clear. Probably it is a French malapropism of a Wolof word.

Harness: heddles, beater, pulley, treadles and breast-beam – the movable parts which the male weavers take into the house after finishing work in the evening.

Heddle: loop or some other device to lift the warp threads in order to create a shed or counter-shed.

Ikat: Indonesian term for to 'tie off', 'wrap around'. Warp yarn is tied off before weaving, and dyed. The tied-off areas retain their natural light colour. As cotton is absorbent, the colour boundaries tend to be blurred.

Kaasa: general term for textiles containing wool. Fulani, Mali. Specifically a type of woollen blanket.

Kente: Colourful cloths made by the Asante and Ewe in Ghana and Togo

Koso: Cotton blanket of the Bamana, Mali. Probably derived from the Fulfulde term *kaasa*.

Maabo, pl. *maabuube:* Fulani weavers, Mali. In the literature they are occasionally defined as a 'caste'.

Macina: geographical term, used today for the entire Niger Inland Delta. To the Fulani the term Macina designates the area around Ténénkou. Mali.

Malle, pl. *malleebe:* Among Songhay speakers, *malle* is a title of honour which translates as 'master weaver'. Among the Fulani, *malle* refers to a weaver who was not born a *maabo. Malleebe* principally accept the *maabuube* weavers as belonging to a higher social class.

Mande: large language family in West Africa.

Manding: certain languages in Mali including Bamanan, Maninka and Bozo; part of the Mande language family.

Munnyuure (Fulfulde, Mali): Cotton blanket with rich weft patterns. Corresponds to the Bamanan *koso kalan* and the Dogon *uldebe.*

Pagne: from the Portuguese word 'panaria' (Carreira 1968). Used in Francophone countries of West Africa for women's wrap cloth.

Fulani: ethnic group, their settlement area reaches from the Atlantic Ocean to the Nile. Other names used include Peul, Ful or Fulbe.

Primary technique: the textile is created with the aid of a single continuous thread which is worked into meshes at definite and repeated intervals, as against weaving where two separate sets of yarn – warp and weft – are interlaced.

Raffia (also raphia): leave fibres of the raffia palm (*Raphia vinifera*). The processed fibres are suitable for weaving, but not for spinning.

Schappe silk: also called florette silk; silk waste yarn, from the middle section of the cocoon.

Sword: instrument applied by women weaving on a vertical loom to open the shed and beat in the weft.

Warp: set of yarn threads held in tension, crossed by and interlaced with the weft.

Wax: expensive version of printed cloths. Produced in Europe.

Weft: also called woof. Weft threads are interlaced at right angles with the warp threads.

Weft float patterns: designs created by having supplementary weft threads pass over several warp threads, as against plain weave which is based on a one over/one under structure. If they are worked across the whole width of the strip they are called continuous, if only over a section discontinuous.

Wrapper: woman's wrap cloth, term used in Nigerian English. The French counterpart is 'pagne'.

REFERENCES

[A] **Abiodun, Rowland; Beier, Ulli and John Pemberton III.** 2004. *Cloth Only Wears to Shreds. Yoruba Textiles and Photographs from the Beier Collection.* Ed. by John Pemberton III. Amherst, Massachusetts: Mead Art Museum, Amherst College.

Adams, John. 1823. *Remarks on the Country Extending from Cape Palmas to the River Congo.* London: Whittacker.

Adler, Peter and Nicholas Barnard. 1992. *African Majesty: The Textile Art of the Ashanti and Ewe.* New York: Thames and Hudson.

Akinwumi, Tunde M. 1990. *The Commemorative Phenomenon of Textile Use Among the Yoruba: A Survey of Significance and Form.* Unpublished PhD thesis, University of Ibadan.

Allman, Jean. 2004. ‹Let Your Fashion Be in Line with Our Ghanaian Costume›: Nation, Gender, and the Politics of Clothing in Nkrumah's Ghana. In: Jean Allman (ed.). *Fashioning Africa. Power and the Politics of Dress.* Bloomington and Indianapolis: Indiana University Press.

Aronson, Lisa. 1982. Popo Weaving: The Dynamics of Trade in Southeastern Nigeria. *African Arts* 15, 3: 43–47, 90–91.

Aronson, Lisa. 1992a. The Language of West African Textiles. *African Arts* 25, 3: 36–40, 100.

Aronson, Lisa. 1992b. Ijebu Yoruba Aso Olona. A Contextual and Historical Overview. *African Arts* 25, 3: 52–63, 101.

Aronson, Lisa. 2001. We Weave it: Akwete Weavers, their Patrons, and Innovation in a Global Economy. In: Susan J. Torntore (ed.). *Cloth is the Center of the World: Nigerian Textiles, Global Perspectives.* University of Minnesota.

[B] **Balandier, Georges.** 1968. *Daily Life in the Kingdom of the Kongo. From the Sixteenth to the Eighteenth Century.* London: Allen and Unwin.

Balfour-Paul, Jenny. 1998. *Indigo.* London: The British Museum Press.

Barber, E. J. W. 1991. *Prehistoric Textiles, the Development of Cloth in the Neolithic and Bronze Ages.* Princeton: Princeton University Press.

Barth, Heinrich. 1857–1859. *Travels and Discoveries in North and Central Africa.* London: Frank Cass, 1965 edition.

Basden, George Thomas. 1921. *Among the Ibos of Nigeria: An Account of the Curious and Interesting Habits, Customs and Beliefs.* London: Seeley and Service.

Bauer, Kerstin, 2001: *African Styles – Kleidung und Textilien aus Afrika. Die Sammlung des Iwalewa-Hauses.* Köln: Rüdiger Köppe.

Bauer, Kerstin, 2007a: *Kleidung und Kleidungspraktiken im Norden der Côte d'Ivoire. Geschichte und Dynamiken des Wandels vom Ende des 19. Jahrhunderts bis zur Gegenwart.* Münster: LIT.

Bauer, Kerstin, 2007b: Zwischen Expansion, Transformation und Tradition. Die rot gemusterten Textilien aus Kong, Côte d'Ivoire. In: Anna Schmid and Alexander Brust (eds): *Rot. Wenn Farbe zur Täterin wird.* Museum der Kulturen Basel: Christoph Merian Verlag. 122–126.

Bedaux, Rogier M. A. 1993. Les plus anciens textiles retrouvés par les archéologues. *Vallées du Niger,* édité par Jean Devisse. Paris: Réunion des Musées Nationaux. 456–463.

Bedaux, Rogier M. A. and Rita Bolland. 1980. Tellem, reconnaissance archéologique d'une culture de l'Ouest africain au moyen âge: Les textiles. *Journal des Africanistes* 50, 1, 1980: 9–23

Bedaux, Rogier M. A. and Rita Bolland. 1980–1981. Medieval Textiles from the Tellem Caves in Central Mali. *Textile Museum Journal* 19/20: 65–74.

Bedaux, Rogier M. A. and Rita Bolland. 1989. Vêtements féminins médiévaux du Mali: Les cache-sexe en fibres Tellem. In: Beate Engelbrecht and Bernhard Gardi (eds). Man Does Not Go Naked. Textilien und Handwerk aus afrikanischen und anderen Ländern. *Basler Beiträge zur Ethnologie* 30. Basel. 15–34.

Bedaux, Rogier M. A. et al. 1978. Recherches archéologiques dans le Delta intérieur du Niger. *Palaeohistoria* 20: 91–220.

Bedaux, Rogier M. A.; Polet, J.; Sanogo, K. and A. Schmidt (eds). 2005. Recherches archéologiques à Dia dans le Delta intérieur du Niger (Mali): Bilan des saisons de fouilles 1998–2003. *Mededelingen van het Rijksmuseum voor Volkenkunde 33.* Leiden: CNWS Publications.

Ben-Amos Girshik, Paula. 2007. Gürtelanhänger egbele. In: Barbara Plankensteiner (ed.). *Benin. Könige und Rituale.* Snoeck Publ. Fig. 128, p. 358.

Bendt, Vera. 2007. *Afrikanische Textilien. Aus der Sammlung des Deutschen Textilmuseums Krefeld. In Memoriam Brigitte Menzel.* Krefeld: Deutsches Textilmuseum.

Binger, Louis-Gustave, 1889/90: Transactions, objets de commerce, monnaie des contrées entre le Niger et la Côte d'Or. *Bulletin de la Société de Géographie Commerciale* 12. Paris. 77–90.

Bolland, Rita. 1991. Tellem Textiles: Archaeological Finds from Burial Caves in Mali's Bandiagara Cliffs. *Mededelingen Rijksmuseum voor Volkenkunde 27.* Amsterdam, Leiden and Bamako: Koninklijk Instituut voor de Tropen; Rijksmuseum voor Volkenkunde; Institut des Sciences Humaines and Musée National du Mali.

Bolland, Rita. 1992. Clothing from Burial Caves in Mali, 11th–18th Century. In: *History, Design, and Craft in West African Strip-Woven Cloth.* Papers Presented at a Symposium Organized by the National Museum of African Art, Smithsonian Institution, February 18–19, 1988. 53–81.

Borgatti, Jean. 1976. Okpella Masking Traditions. *African Arts* 9, 4: 24–33.

Borgatti, Jean. 1979. Dead Mothers of Okpella. *African Arts* 12, 4: 48–57.

Borgatti, Jean. 1983. *Cloth as Metaphor: Nigerian Textiles from the Museum of Cultural History, UCLA.* Monograph Series 20. Los Angeles.

Borgatti, Jean. 1989. Atsu Atsogwa: Art and Morality among the Northern Edo of Okpella, Nigeria. In: Beate Engelbrecht and Bernhard Gardi (eds). Man Does Not Go Naked. Textilien und Handwerk aus afrikanischen und anderen Ländern. *Basler Beiträge zur Ethnologie* 30. Basel. 175–195.

Boser-Sarivaxévanis, Renée. 1969. Aperçus sur la teinture à l'indigo en Afrique Occidentale. *Verhandlungen der Naturforschenden Gesellschaft in Basel,* 80, 1: 151–208.

Boser-Sarivaxévanis, Renée. 1972. Les tissus de l'Afrique Occidentale. Méthode de classification et catalogue raisonné des étoffes tissées de l'Afrique de l'Ouest établis à partir de données techniques et historiques. *Basler Beiträge zur Ethnologie* 13. Basel.

Boser-Sarivaxévanis, Renée. 1972. *Textilhandwerk in West-Afrika. Weberei und Färberei.* Führer durch das Museum für Völkerkunde Basel.

Boser-Sarivaxévanis, Renée. 1975. Recherche sur l'histoire des textiles traditionnels tissés et teints de l'Afrique Occidentale. *Verhandlungen der Naturforschenden Gesellschaft in Basel 86, 1–2:* 301–341.

Boser-Sarivaxévanis, Renée. 1980. Review of: John Picton and John Mack. 1979. *African Textiles.* London: British Museum Publications. In: *Textile History* 11. 213–216.

194

Boser-Sarivaxévanis, Renée. 1981. Iya alaru, Mutter der Asche. In: Noa Zanolli (ed.). *Handwerk, eine Sprache im Dialog Süd-Nord*. Sonceboz: OS 3. 28–31.

Boser-Sarivaxévanis, Renée. 1983. African Textiles. Ariadne's Thread Through a West African Textile Labyrinth. Zurich: *Swissair Gazette*, November edition.

Boser-Sarivaxévanis, Renée. 1986. *The Dawn of West African Loom-Woven Textile Arts*. Paper presented at the 7th Triennial Symposium of African Art, 2–6 April, UCLA, Museum of Cultural History, Los Angeles.

Bowdich, Thomas E. 1966 [1819]. *Mission from Cape Coast Castle to Ashantee*. London: Frank Cass.

Bühler, Alfred. 1972. *Ikat, Batik, Plangi*. 3 Vols. Basel: Pharos-Verlag.

Bühler-Oppenheim, Alfred and Kristin. 1948. Die Textilsammlung Fritz Iklé-Huber im Museum für Völkerkunde und Schweizerischen Museum für Volkskunde Basel. Grundlage zur Systematik der gesamten textilen Techniken. *Denkschriften der Schweizerischen Naturforschenden Gesellschaft*. Zurich: Gebrüder Fretz.

[C] Campell, Robert. 1861. *A Pilgrimage to my Motherland; An Account of a Journey among the Egbas and Yorubas of Central Africa in 1859–60*. New York: Thomas Hamilton.

Cardon, Dominique. 2007. *Natural Dyes. Sources, Tradition, Technology and Science*. London: Archetype.

Carreira, António. 1968. *Panaria Cabo-Verdiano-Guineense. Aspectos históricos e sócio-económicos*. Junta de Investigações do Ultramar. Museu de Etnologia do Ultramar. Lisboa.

Clarke, Duncan. 1997. *Aso Oke: the Evolving Tradition of Hand-woven Textile Design among the Yoruba of South-Western Nigeria*. PhD., University of London (School of Oriental and African Studies), London.

Clarke, William. H. 1972. *Travels and Explorations in Yorubaland (1854–1858)* Ibadan: Ibadan University Press.

Clouzot, Henri. 1930. *Tissus Nègres*. Librairies des Arts Décoratifs. Paris: A. Calavas.

Cole, Herbert M. and Doran H. Ross. 1977. *The Arts of Ghana*. Los Angeles: University of California.

[D] Dolz, Silvia. 2005. Textilien aus Westafrika im Museum für Völkerkunde Dresden. *Abhandlungen und Berichte der Staatlichen Ethnographischen Sammlungen Sachsen*. Berlin: Verlag für Wissenschaft und Bildung.

Duponchel, Pauline. 1987. *Le tissage du coton à San, République du Mali. L'homme, l'outil, la production*. Mémoire de maîtrise, sous la direction de José Garanger et Louis Perrois. Université de Paris I, Panthéon, Sorbonne. UFR d'Histoire de l'Art et d'Archéologie (photocopy).

[E] Easmon, M.C.F. 1924. *Sierra Leone Country Cloths*. British Empire Exhibition, Sierra Leone Section. London: Waterlow & Sons.

[F] Falgayrettes-Leveau, Christiane (ed.). 1995. *Au fil de la parole*. Paris: Editions Dapper.

Féau, Etienne (ed.). 1989. *Corps sculptés, corps parés, corps masqués. Chefs-d'œuvre de Côte d'Ivoire*. Paris: Galeries Nationales du Grand Palais.

Fianu, Docea A.G. 2007. *Ghana's Kente and Adinkra: History and Socio-cultural Significance in a Contemporary Global Economy*. Accra: Black Mask.

[G] Gardi, Bernhard. 1985. Ein Markt wie Mopti. Handwerkerkasten und traditionelle Techniken in Mali. *Basler Beiträge zur Ethnologie* 25. Basel.

Gardi, Bernhard. 2000. *Boubou – c'est chic. Gewänder aus Mali und anderen Ländern Westafrikas / Le boubou – c'est chic: Les boubous du Mali et d'autres pays de l'Afrique de l'Ouest*. Basel: Museum der Kulturen Basel. Christoph Merian Verlag.

Gardi, Bernhard. 2003a. *Textiles du Mali d'après les collections du Musée National du Mali*. Bamako.

Gardi, Bernhard. 2003b. Textiles Dogon. In: Rogier M.A. Bedaux and Diderik van der Waals (eds). *Regards sur les Dogon du Mali*. Rijksmuseum voor Volkenkunde, Leiden. Gand: Editions Snoeck. 176–181.

Gardi, Bernhard and Christiane Seydou. 1989. Arkilla kerka. La tenture de mariage chez les Peuls du Mali. In: Beate Engelbrecht and Bernhard Gardi (eds). Man Does Not Go Naked. Textilien und Handwerk aus afrikanischen und anderen Ländern. *Basler Beiträge zur Ethnologie* 30. Basel. 83–106.

Gardi, Bernhard; Maas, Pierre and Geert Mommersteeg. 1995. *Djenné il y a cent ans*. Amsterdam, Basel, Bamako: Koninkljik Instituut voor de Tropen; Museum für Völkerkunde; Musée National du Mali.

Gardi, René. 1995. *Momente des Alltags. Fotodokumente aus Nordkamerun 1950–1985 (Tschadsee, Mandara, Alantika)*. Bernhard Gardi (ed.). Contributions by Christraud Geary, René Gardi, Bernhard Gardi. Basel: Museum für Völkerkunde Basel.

Genevière, J. 1950. Les Kountas et leurs activités commerciales. *Bulletin de l'IFAN* XII, 4.

Geurts, Kathryn Linn. 2002. *Culture and the Senses: Bodily Ways of Knowing in an African Community*. Los Angeles and London: University of California Press.

Gilfoy, Peggy Stoltz. 1987. *Patterns of Life. West African Strip-Weaving Traditions*. Washington, D.C.: National Museum of African Art, Smithsonian Institution Press.

Golvin, Lucien. 1950. *Les arts populaires en Algérie. Tome I: Les techniques de tissages*. Alger: Publication du Gouvernement Général de l'Algérie.

Goody, Esther. 1982. Daboya weavers: Relations of Production, Dependence and Reciprocity. In: Esther Goody (ed.). *From Craft to Industry: The Ethnography of Proto-industry cloth Production*. Cambridge: Cambridge University Press.

Goody, Esther and Jack Goody. 1996. The Naked and the Clothed. In: J. Hunwick and N. Lawler (eds). *The Cloth of Many Colored Silks. Papers on History and Society, Ghanaian and Islamic, in Honor of Ivor Wilks*. Evanston, Ill.: Northwestern University Press.

Griaule, Marcel. 1938. *Masques Dogons*. Paris: Institut d'Ethnologie.

Griaule, Marcel. 1948. *Dieu d'eau. Entretiens avec Ogotemmêli*. Paris: Les éditions du Chêne.

Gumpert, Lynn (ed.). 2008. *The Poetics of Cloth: African Textiles / Recent Art*. New York: Grey Art Gallery, New York University.

[H] Heller, Eva. 1989. *Wie Farben wirken. Farbpsychologie. Farbsymbolik. Kreative Farbgestaltung*. Reinbek bei Hamburg: Rowohlt.

Heuzey, A.J. 1936: *Rapport sur l'artisanat indigène. Gouvernement Général de l'AOF, Colonie de la Côte d'Ivoire, Service de l'enseignement*.

Heuzey, J.A. 1941. Note sur le tissage au Soudan. *Bulletin de l'IFAN* III, 1–4: 145–150.

[I] Imperato, James Pascal. 1973. Wool Blankets of the Peul of Mali. *African Arts* 6, 3: 40–47, 84.

Imperato, James Pascal. 1974. Bamana and Maninka Covers and Blankets. *African Arts* 7, 3: 56–67.

Imperato, James Pascal. 1976. Kereka Blankets of the Peul. *African Arts* 9, 4: 56–59.

Imperato, James Pascal. 1979. Blankets and Covers from the Niger Bend. *African Arts* 12, 4: 38–43.

195

Isaacson, Allen and Richard Roberts (eds). 1995. *Cotton, Colonialism, and Social History in Sub-Saharan Africa*. Social History of Africa Series. Portsmouth, NH, London: Heinemann, James Currey.

Isert, Paul E. 1992 [1788]. *Letters on West Africa and the Slave Trade*. Oxford: Oxford University Press.

[J] Johnson, Marion. 1979. Ashanti Craft Organization. *African Arts* 13, 1: 60–63, 78–82.

Jones, Adam. 1994. A Collection of African Art in Seventeenth-Century Germany: Christoph Weickman's Kunst- und Naturkammer. *African Arts* 27, 2: 28–43, 92–94.

[K] Klein, Aviva. 1974. Tesig-Bandweberei mit Gold- und Silberfaden in San'a. *Baessler Archiv, Neue Folge*, XXII, 2: 225–246.

Konaré, Alpha Oumar and Adam Ba. 1983. *Grandes dates du Mali*. Bamako: Editions-Imprimeries du Mali.

Kraamer, Malika. 1996. *Kleurrijke Veranderingen. De Dynamiek van de Kentekunstwereld in Ghana*. MA thesis, Erasmus Universiteit Rotterdam, Rotterdam.

Kraamer, Malika. 2005a. *Colourful Changes: Two Hundred Years of Social and Design History in the Hand-woven Textiles of the Ewe-speaking Regions of Ghana and Togo (1800–2000)*. PhD thesis, University of London (School of Oriental and African Studies), London.

Kraamer, Malika. 2005b. Visual Arts of the Ewe in Togo and Benin. In: B. Lawrence (ed.). *A Handbook of Eweland*. Volume III: *The Ewes of Togo and Benin*. Accra: Woeli Publishing Services.

Kraamer, Malika. 2006a. Ghanaian Interweaving in the 19th Century: A New Perspective on Ewe and Asante Textile History. *African Arts* 39, 4: 36–53, 93–94.

Kraamer, Malika. 2006b. Origin Disputed. The Making, Use, and Evaluation of Ghanaian Textiles. *Afrique: Arts & Archéologie* 4: 53–76.

Kriger, Colleen E. 2006. *Cloth in West African History*. Lanham: AltaMira Press.

Kuhn, Dieter. 1977. Die Webstühle des Tzu-jen i-chih aus der Yüan-Zeit. *Sinologica Coloniensia* 5. Wiesbaden, Franz Steiner.

Kyerematen, A.A.Y. 1965. *Panoply of Ghana*. 2nd ed. London, Accra: Longmans.

[L] LaGamma, Alisa and Christine Giuntini. 2008. *The Essential Art of African Textiles: Design Without End*. New York: Metropolitan Museum of Art.

Lamb, Venice. 1975. *West African Weaving*. London: Duckworth.

Lamb, Venice and Judy Holmes. 1980. *Nigerian Weaving*. Hertingfordbury: Roxford Books.

Lamb, Venice and Alastair. 1984. *Sierra Leone Weaving*. Hertingfordbury: Roxford Books.

Lamb, Venice. 2005. *Looms Past and Present. Around the Mediterranean and Elsewhere*. Hertingfordbury: Roxford Books.

Leroi-Gourhan, André. 1943. *Evolution et technique. L'homme et la matière. Sciences d'aujourd'hui*. Paris: Albin Michel.

Levtzion, Nehemia. 1973. *Ancient Ghana and Mali*. London: Methuen.

Lombard, Maurice. 1978. *Etudes d'économie médiévale, Vol. 3: Les textiles dans le monde Musulman du VIIe au XIIe siècle*. Paris, La Haye, New York: Mouton.

[M] Mage, Eugène. 1868. *Voyage dans le Soudan Occidental (Sénégambie-Niger), 1863–1866*. Paris: Librairie de L. Hachette.

Magnin, André (ed.). 1997. *Seydou Keïta*. Zurich-Berlin-New York: Scalo.

Mauny, Raymond. 1961. Tableau géographique de l'Ouest africain au Moyen Age, d'après les sources écrites, la tradition et l'archéologie. *Mémoires de l'IFAN* 61. Dakar: IFAN.

McIntosh, Susan K. (ed.). 1995. Excavations at Jenné-Jeno, Hambarketolo, and Kaniana (Inland Niger Delta, Mali), the 1981 Season. *University of California Monographs in Anthropology* 20. Berkeley, Los Angeles and London: University of California Press.

McLeod, Malcom D. 1981. *The Asante*. London: British Museum Publications.

Malé, Salia. 2003. Textiles contemporains du Mali: utiles à porter, beaux à regarder. In: Bernhard Gardi (ed.). *Textiles du Mali d'après les collections du Musée National du Mali*. 106–115 (Malé's contribution is wrongly attributed to B. Gardi).

Meillassoux, Claude (ed.). 1971. *The Development of Indigenous Trade and Markets in West Africa*. London and Oxford: Oxford University Press.

Meillassoux, Claude. 1973. Etat et conditions des esclaves à Gumbu (Mali). *Journal of African History* 14: 429–452.

Menzel, Brigitte. 1972, 1973. *Textilien aus Westafrika*. Veröffentlichungen des Museums für Völkerkunde Berlin. Neue Folge 26. 3 Vols. Berlin.

Meyer, Birgit. 1997. Christian Mind and Worldly Matters. *Journal of Material Culture* 2, 3: 311–337.

Meyerowitz, Eva L.R. 1949. *The Sacred State of the Akan*. London: Faber and Faber.

Monteil, Charles. 1903. *Monographie de Djenné, cercle et ville*. Tulle: Jean Mazeyrie.

Monteil, Charles. 1927. Le coton chez les noirs. *Bulletin du comité d'études historiques et scientifiques de l'A.O.F.* Paris.

Monteil, Charles. 1971. *Djenné: une cité soudanasie. Métropole du Delta central du Niger*. Paris: Editions Anthropos. Institut international africain.

Murray, Shawn S. 2005. Recherches archéo-botaniques. In: Rogier M.A. Bedaux et al. (eds). Recherches archéologiques à Dia dans le Delta intérieur du Niger (Mali): Bilan des saisons de fouilles 1998–2003. *Mededelingen van het Rijksmuseum voor Volkenkunde* 33. Leiden: CNWS Publications. 386–400.

[N] Nadel, Siegfried F. 1946. *A Black Byzantium. The Kingdom of Nupe in Nigeria*. Oxford: International African Institute.

[O] Olivier de Sardan, Jean-Pierre. 1969. *Système des relations économiques et sociales chez les Wogo (Niger)*. Paris: Institut d'ethnologie, Musée de l'Homme.

Olivier de Sardan, Jean-Pierre. 1978. *Métiers manuels: division du travail et classifications sociales. Systèmes de signes*. Textes réunis en hommage à Germaine Dieterlen. Paris: Hermann. 393–412.

Olivier de Sardan, Jean-Pierre. 1982. *Concepts et conceptions songhay-zarma*. Paris: Nubia.

Oppenheim, Kristin. 1942. Die primären textilen Techniken der Neukaledonier und Loyalty-Insulaner. *Internationales Archiv für Ethnographie* 41 (Supplement)

[P] Perani, Judith. 1977. *Nupe Crafts: The Dynamics of Change in Nineteenth and Twentieth Century Weaving and Brass Working*. Unpublished PhD thesis, University of Indiana.

Petrossian, Karen and Bernard Roussel (eds). 2000. *Afrique bleue. Les routes de l'indigo*. Musée du tapis et des arts textiles de Clermont-Ferrand. Aix-en-Provence: Edisud.

Picton, John. 1980. Women's Weaving: the Manufacture and Use of Textiles Among the Igbirra People of Nigeria. In: Dale Idiens and K.G. Ponting (eds). *Textiles of Africa*. Bath: The Pasold Research Fund.

196

Picton, John. 1992. Tradition, Technology, and Lurex. Some Comments on Textile History and Design in West Africa. In: *History, Design, and Craft in West African Strip-Woven Cloth*. Papers Presented at a Symposium Organized by the National Museum of African Art, Smithsonian Institution, February 18–19, 1988. 13–52.

Picton, John. 1995. Technology, Tradition and Lurex: The Art of Textiles in Africa. In: J. Picton (ed.). *The Art of African Textiles. Technology, Tradition and Lurex*. London: Barbican Art Gallery, Lund Humphries Publications.

Picton, John. 2004a. On Marking and Masking in the Art of Bruce Onobrakpeya. In: P. Foss (ed.). *Where Gods and Mortals Meet: Continuity and Renewal in Urhobo Art*. New York: Museum of African Art. 131–133.

Picton, John. 2004b. What to Wear in West Africa: Textile Design, Dress and Self-Representation. In: Carol Tulloch (ed.). *Black Style*. London: V&A Publications.

Picton, John. 2008. Seeing and Wearing: Textiles in West Africa [a revised version of 2004b with some additional material]. In: Lynn Gumpert (ed.). *The Poetics of Cloth: African Textiles / Recent Art*. New York: Grey Art Gallery, New York University. 11–31.

Picton, John and John Mack. 1979. *African Textiles*. London: British Museum Publications.

Picton, John and John Mack. 1980. When is the Heddle of a Fixed Heddle Fixed? Response to Renée Boser-Sarivaxévanis's Review. 1980. In: *Textile History* 11: 216–217.

Picton, John and John Mack. 1989. *African Textiles*. 2nd edition. London: British Museum Publications.

Pierre, C. and Charles Monteil. 1905. *L'élevage au Soudan*. Paris: Challamel.

Plankensteiner, Barbara (ed.). 2007. *Benin. Könige und Rituale. Höfische Kunst aus Nigeria*. Wien: Ausstellungskataloge des Museums für Völkerkunde.

Prod'hom, Chantal. 2003. *Photographies et textiles contemporains*. mudac, Musée de design et d'arts appliqués contemporains. Lausanne.

[R] Renne, Elisha P. 1992. Aso Ipo, Red Cloth from Bunu. *African Arts* 25, 3: 64–69, 102.

Renne, Elisha P. 1995. *Cloth That Does Not Die. The Meaning of Cloth in Bunu Social Life*. Seattle: University of Washington Press.

Rattray, Robert S. 1927. *Religion and Art in Ashanti*. Oxford: The Clarendon Press.

Robert-Chaleix, D. 1983. Fusaïoles décorées du site de Tegdaoust. In: D. Jean Devisse and S. Robert (eds). *Tegdaoust III: Recherches sur Audaghost. Campagnes 1960–1965, enquêtes générales*. Mémoire 25, Institut Mauritanien de la Recherche Scientifique. Paris: Recherche sur les Civilisations. 447–513.

Roberts, Richard. 1980. Long Distance Trade and Production: Sinsani in the 19th Century. *Journal of African History* 21: 169–188.

Rømer, Ludewig F. 2000 [1760]. *A Reliable Account of the Coast of Guinea*. Oxford: Oxford University Press.

Ross, Doran H. 1998. *Wrapped in Pride. Ghanaian Kente and African American Identity*. Los Angeles: UCLA Fowler Museum of Cultural History.

Ryder, Michael L. 1983. *Sheep and Man*. London: Duckworth.

[S] Saint Léon, Pascal-Martin (ed.). 1998. *Anthologie de la photographie africaine et de l'océan Indien*. Paris: Revue Noire.

Schmid, Anna und Alexander Brust (eds). 2007. *Rot. Wenn Farbe zur Täterin wird*. Museum der Kulturen Basel. Basel: Christoph Merian Verlag.

Schmidt, Annette and Rogier M. A. Bedaux. 2005. Fusaïoles. In: Rogier M. A. Bedaux et al. (eds) Recherches archéologiques à Dia dans le Delta intérieur du Niger (Mali): Bilan des saisons de fouilles 1998–2003. *Mededelingen van het Rijksmuseum voor Volkenkunde* 33. Leiden: CNWS Publications. 282–287.

Seefelder, Matthias. 1982. *Indigo in Kultur, Wissenschaft und Technik*. Vortrag vor der Akademie der Wissenschaften und der Literatur zu Mainz am 8.11.1980. Ludwigshafen: BASF Aktiengesellschaft.

Seiler-Baldinger, Annemarie. 1973. Systematik der Textilen Techniken. *Basler Beiträge zur Ethnologie* 14. Basel: Pharos-Verlag.

Seiler-Baldinger, Annemarie. 1991. Systematik der Textilen Techniken. New edition. *Basler Beiträge zur Ethnologie* 32. Basel: Wepf.

Seiler-Baldinger, Annemarie. 1994. *Textiles. A Classification of Techniques*. Bathurst: Crawford House.

Seydou, Christiane. 1998. *Dictionnaire pluridialectal des racines verbales du peul. Peul – français – anglais*. Paris: Karthala – Agence de la Francophonie (ACCT).

Shaw, Thurstan. 1977. *Unearthing Igbo-Ukwu. Archaeological Discoveries in Eastern Nigeria*. Ibadan: Oxford University Press. Reprint 1979.

Shea, Philip. 1975. *The Development of an Export Orientated Dyed Cloth Industry in Kano Emirate in the Nineteenth Century*. Unpublished PhD thesis, University of Wisconsin.

Sieber, Roy. 1972. *African Textiles and Decorative Arts*. New York: The Museum of Modern Art.

Spring, Christopher and Julie Hudson. 1995. *North African Textiles*. London: The British Museum Press.

Sumberg, Barbara. 2001: *A History of Cloth. Production and Use in the Gouro Region of Côte d'Ivoire*. Minnesota: University of Minnesota.

[T] Tauxier, Louis. 1924: *Nègres Gouro et Gagou: Centre de la Côte d'Ivoire*. Paris: Geuthner.

Torntore, Susan J. (ed.). 2002. *Cloth is the Center of the World: Nigerian Textiles, Global Perspectives*. Minnesota: University of Minnesota.

Traoré, Aminata Dramane. 1999. *Mille tisserands en quête de futur*. Bamako: EDIM.

[W] Wendl, Tobias and Heike Behrend. 1998. *Snap Me One*. München: Prestel.

Wipszycka, Ewa. 1965. L'industrie textile dans l'Egypte romaine. *Archivum Filologiczne pod redakcja Kazimierka Kumanieckiego i Bronislawa Bilińskiego* IX. Wroclaw, Warszawa, Krakow.

Kerstin Bauer (born 1969) is a senior lecturer at the Institute of Social Anthropology of the University of Basel. She has been conducting research in Côte d'Ivoire and Burkina Faso since 1994. She received her PhD degree from the University of Basel in 2005 based on her thesis on clothing and clothing practices in northern Côte d'Ivoire. She is currently doing research on transformation processes in (post-)conflict societies.

Rogier M. A. Bedaux (born 1943) retired curator of the African Department at the Rijksmuseum voor Volkenkunde Leiden (1989–2006) and professor for material culture at the University of Leiden (1997–2007). He has conducted research in Mali since 1971 including archaeological research on the Tellem caves in the Dogon cliffs and excavations and archaeological surveys in the Inner Niger Delta. In Djenné he was occupied with the preservation and restoration of traditional houses (1997–2005). He has fought fervently against illegal excavations and art trafficking for years and is engaged in long-term collaboration with the Musée National du Mali, the Institut des Sciences Humaines, Bamako and the Mission Culturelle in Djenné.

Jean M. Borgatti (born 1945) whose concentration on modern art history at Wellesley College in the middle 1960s stimulated an interest in non-Western art. She pursued this interest at UCLA where she acquired a PhD in art history with a research focus on Africa. In Nigeria, she has worked among the northern Edo, most significantly among the Okpella, where her studies over a 30-year period have ranged from reconstructing the history of local festivals to survey research on aesthetic preference. She has also become known for her work on portraiture – beyond likeness – in an African and world context.

Kolado Ahmadou Modibo Cissé (born 1949) is a Fulani from Sindégué Ouro Boulo, a village at the eastern end of Lake Debo. Originally he worked as an embroiderer on the market in Mopti. Through his friendship with Bernhard Gardi he became a cloth dealer. He has been selling cloths in his boutique in the Maison des Artisans in Bamako since 1999. In November 2008 he inspected all the woollen textiles held in the Museum der Kulturen Basel. Textiles acquired with the help of his services are held by museums in Bamako, Basel, Bern, Zurich, Geneva, Krefeld, London and Los Angeles.

Duncan Clarke (born 1962) has degrees from Oxford and London Universities. In 1999 he completed his PhD on Yoruba *aso oke* weaving at the School of Oriental and African Studies, London University. He has published several books and articles on African textiles and related fields. He is now a textile dealer and researcher based in London.

Bernhard Gardi (born 1946) is curator of the Africa Department at the Museum der Kulturen Basel. In 1973–1974 he accompanied the former curator Renée Boser-Sarivaxévanis as her assistant on a research and collecting expedition through various countries of West Africa. Later he conducted own research in Mali with a focus on social stratification and material culture.

Malika Kraamer (born 1969) is curator of World Cultures at New Walk Museum and Art Gallery in Leicester, Great-Britain, focusing on Africa, East Europe and South Asia. She did research on Asante and Ewe weaving in Ghana and Togo as well as in many museums in Europe and the USA. In 2005 she completed her PhD on Ewe *kente* cloth at the School of Oriental and African Studies, University of London. She has worked in several museums, published in the field of African textiles and taught African art in the Netherlands and Great Britain.

John Picton (born 1938) is Emeritus Professor of African Art at the School of Oriental and African Studies, University of London, where he was teaching and writing from 1979 to 2003. He was previously employed by the British Museum (1970–1979), and by the Department of Antiquities of the Federal Government of Nigeria (1961–1970). His research and publication interests include Yoruba and Edo (Benin) sculpture; masquerade; textile history; the Niger-Benue confluence region of Nigeria with particular reference to Ebira and Akoko-Edo; and developments in sub-Saharan visual practice since the mid-19th century. He was presented with an ACASA (the Arts Council of the African Studies Association) Leadership Award at its Triennial Symposium, Virgin Islands, May 2001, and was awarded an Honorary Fellowship of the Pan-African Circle of Artists at its 4th Biennale in Lagos, October 2002.

Annette Schmidt (born 1967) succeeded Rogier M. A. Bedaux as curator of the African Department at the Rijksmuseum voor Volkenkunde Leiden. She participated in archaeological research in the Inner Niger Delta, Mali, from 1990 onwards, and she has also been part of several projects concerned with the restoration and preservation of mud brick architecture in Djenné (since 2003) and among the Dogon (2004–2008). She is engaged in long-term collaboration with the Musée National du Mali, the Institut des Sciences Humaines, Bamako and the Mission Culturelle in Djenné.

145 – Mrs Janet Adedeke weaving at her loom (Owo, Nigeria).

Photo B. Gardi 12.3.1974 – (F)III 7935

IMPRINT

Publication accompanying the exhibition
'Woven Beauty – The Art of West African Textiles'
August 28, 2009 – May 16, 2010

(→**Museum der Kulturen. Basel.**)

Bibliographic information published by
Die Deutsche Bibliothek: Die Deutsche Bibliothek lists this
publication in the Deutsche Nationalbibliografie;
detailed bibliographic data is available in the Internet at
http://dnb.ddb.de

ISBN 978-3-85616-484-3

Ein Unternehmen der Christoph Merian Stiftung

© 2009 Christoph Merian Verlag

Editorial reading Museum der Kulturen Basel: Nigel Stephenson, Basel

Translations: Nigel Stephenson, Basel

Textile photos: Markus Gruber/MKB,
with exception of figs. 65, 85, 116, 128–130 (Peter Horner/MKB)
and figs. 67, 69, 70, 72 (Jürg Bernhardt, Bern)

Drawings fig. 27: Peter Meyes/MKB (shuttles) and
Christine Schäublin/MKB (beaters)

Maps: Neeser & Müller and Bernhard Gardi

Graphic design: Neeser & Müller, Basel; Collaboration: Ramon Classen

Lithography: Andreas Muster, Basel

Printed by: Offsetdruckerei Karl Grammlich, Pliezhausen

Bindings: IDUPA, Owen/Teck

Typefaces: FF Scala, Neutraface

Paper: Luxo Samtoffset 150 g/m², Invercote 280 g/m²

www.mkb.ch
www.merianverlag.ch

**Werenfels-Fonds in support of
the Museum der Kulturen Basel**